Reclaiming the Sacred: The Bible in Gay and Lesbian Culture

"The Sink of Solitude," Beresford Egan's cartoon of Radclyffe Hall's biblical earnestness. (pages 176 and 195)

Raymond-Jean Frontain, PhD
Editor

Reclaiming the Sacred: The Bible in Gay and Lesbian Culture

Pre-publication
REVIEWS,
COMMENTARIES,
EVALUATIONS . . .

"**T**his finely wrought, sharply focused, daring and always dignified gathering of essays, each important in its own right, constitutes an essay in criticism, the topics of which include transgressive maneuvers and subversive gestures, narrative inversions, as well as encodings, and revisionary emplotments. Through such strategies, these essays, in their complex interrogations, show a culture still wrangling over what the Bible says, as well as over rival claims concerning its presumptive morality. But more important still, these essays suggest how a text, hitherto used to confirm orthodoxies, may now, in acts of reappropriation, be deployed against those same orthodoxies. Texts that have been used to reinforce are here turned against homophobia and, in the process, are now used both to explore and legitimate homoerotic yearnings and to reclaim the sacred for gay and lesbian experience. Described variously as an epistomological anchor, an intertext, a source book for a homoerotic poetics, the Bible is shown in essay after essay not to be an oppressive text but rather a text with some oppressive traditions, hence to be a more sympathetic and humane book in its attitudes toward homosexuality than usually thought and a challenge equally to the straight and gay moral imagination. Impressive in their range, which runs from Milton to Thom Gunn, from seventeenth-century sodomite discourse in Venice to Pre-Raphaelite painting in nineteenth-century England, these essays are a triumph in their intellectual agility and grasp."

Joseph Wittreich, PhD
Distinguished Professor of English, The Graduate School, The City University of New York

❝**T**his edition is an impressive collection of ten outstanding essays on gay spirituality in literature and culture. Gregory Bredbeck's study of E. M. Forster's "The Life to Come" propels the reader to further investigate human sexuality in the Bible and the Vedic scriptures. Armando Maggi and Raymond-Jean Frontain's analysis of the satiric-transgressive uses of the Bible are overwhelmingly insightful. Ellis Hansen's essay on Oscar Wilde offers a refreshing look on the theme of biblical sensuality and subversive identity. Gayle M. Seymour's unique study of Pre-Raphaelite painter Simeon Solomon underscores the strong relationship between art and sexual identity. The essays are often theoretically vigorous, sometimes morally challenging, but always splendidly argued. Indeed, this edition is a significant contribution to the advancement of studies on queer sanctity."

Rafael Robert Delfin, PhD
Editor & Publisher, INK Literary Review

Reclaiming the Sacred: The Bible in Gay and Lesbian Culture

Raymond-Jean Frontain, PhD
Editor

Reclaiming the Sacred: The Bible in Gay and Lesbian Culture, edited by Raymond-Jean Frontain, was simultaneously issued by The Haworth Press, Inc., under the same title, as a special issue of *Journal of Homosexuality,* Volume 33, Numbers 3/4 1997, John P. De Cecco, Editor.

Harrington Park Press
An Imprint of
The Haworth Press, Inc.
New York • London

ISBN 1-56023-097-5

Published by

Harrington Park Press, 10 Alice Street, Binghamton, NY 13904-1580 USA

Harrington Park Press is an Imprint of the Haworth Press, Inc., 10 Alice Street, Binghamton, NY 13904-1580 USA

Reclaiming the Sacred: The Bible in Gay and Lesbian Culture has also been published as *Journal of Homosexuality*, Volume 33, Numbers 3/4 1997.

The development, preparation, and publication of this work has been undertaken with great care. However, the publisher, employees, editors, and agents of The Haworth Press and all imprints of The Haworth Press, Inc., including The Haworth Medical Press and Pharmaceutical Products Press, are not responsible for any errors contained herein or for consequences that may ensue from use of materials or information contained in this work. Opinions expressed by the author(s) are not necessarily those of The Haworth Press, Inc.

Cover design by Marylouise E. Doyle

Library of Congress Cataloging-in-Publication Data

Reclaiming the sacred : the Bible in Gay and lesbian culture / Raymond-Jean Frontain, editor.
    p. cm.
    Includes bibliographical references and index.
    ISBN 1-56023-097-5 (alk. paper)
    1. Gays' writings, English–History and criticism. 2. Homosexuality and literature–Great Britain. 3. Christianity and literature–Great Britain. 4. English literature–History and criticism. 5. Holy, The, in literature. 6. Religion and literature. 7. Lesbians in literature. 8. Gay men in literature. 9. Bible–In literature. I. Frontain, Raymond-Jean.
PR120.G39R43 1997
820.9'920664–dc21

                                                      97-25341
                                                        CIP

INDEXING & ABSTRACTING

Contributions to this publication are selectively indexed or abstracted in print, electronic, online, or CD-ROM version(s) of the reference tools and information services listed below. This list is current as of the copyright date of this publication. See the end of this section for additional notes.

- *Abstracts in Anthropology*, Baywood Publishing Company, 26 Austin Avenue, P.O. Box 337, Amityville, NY 11701

- *Abstracts of Research in Pastoral Care & Counseling*, Loyola College, 7135 Minstrel Way, Suite 101, Columbia, MD 21045

- *Academic Abstracts/CD-ROM*, EBSCO Publishing Editorial Department, P.O. Box 590, Ipswich, MA 01938-0590

- *Academic Search: database of 2,000 selected academic serials, updated monthly*, EBSCO publishing, 83 Pine Street, Peabody, MA 01960

- *Alternative Press Index*, Alternative Press Center, Inc., P.O. Box 33109, Baltimore, MD 21218-0401

- *Applied Social Sciences Index & Abstracts (ASSIA) (Online: ASSI via Data-Star) (CD Rom: ASSIA Plus)*, Bowker-Saur Limited, Maypole House, Maypole Road, East Grinstead, West Sussex RH19 1HH England

- *Book Review Index,* Gale Research, Inc., P.O. Box 2867, Detroit, MI 48231

- *Cambridge Scientific Abstracts*, 7200 Wisconsin Avenue #601, Bethesda, MD 20814

- *CNPIEC Reference Guide: Chinese National Directory of Foreign Periodicals*, P.O. Box 88, Beijing, People's Republic of China

- *Criminal Justice Abstracts*, Willow Tree Press, 15 Washington Street, 4th Floor, Newark NJ 07102

(continued)

- *Criminology, Penology and Police Science Abstracts*, Kugler Publications, P.O. Box 11188, 1001 GD-Amsterdam, The Netherlands

- *Current Contents/Clinical Medicine/Life Sciences (CC: CM/LS) (weekly Table of Contents Service), and* Social Science Citation Index. *Articles also searchable through* Social SciSearch, *ISI's online database and in ISI's* Research Alert *current awareness service*, Institute for Scientific Information, 3501 Market Street, Philadelphia, PA 19104-3302

- *Digest of Neurology and Psychiatry*, The Institute of Living, 400 Washington Street, Hartford, CT 06106

- *Excerpta Medica/Secondary Publishing Division*, Elsevier Science, Inc., Secondary Publishing Division, 655 Avenue of the Americas, New York, NY 10010

- *Expanded Academic Index*, Information Access Company, 362 Lakeside Drive, Forest City, CA 94404

- *Family Studies Database (online and CD/ROM)*, National Information Services Corporation, 306 East Baltimore Pike, 2nd Floor, Media, PA 19063

- *Family Violence & Sexual Assault Bulletin*, Family Violence & Sexual Assault Institute, 1121 East South East Loop #323, Suite 130, Tyler, TX 75701

- *Higher Education Abstracts,* Claremont Graduate School, 231 East Tenth Street, Claremont, CA 91711

- *HOMODOK/"Relevant" Bibliographic database, Documentation Centre for Gay & Lesbian Studies, University of Amsterdam (selective printed abstracts in "Homologie" and bibliographic computer databases covering cultural, historical, social and political aspects of gay & lesbian topics*, c/o HOMODOK-ILGA Archive, O.Z. Acterburgwal 185, NL-1012 DK Amsterdam, The Netherlands

- *IBZ International Bibliography of Periodical Literature*, Zeller Verlag GmbH & Co., P.O.B. 1949, d-49009 Osnabruck, Germany

(continued)

- *Index Medicus*, National Library of Medicine, 8600 Rockville Pike, Bethesda, MD 20894

- *Index to Periodical Articles Related to Law*, University of Texas, 727 East 26th Street, Austin, TX 78705

- *INTERNET ACCESS (& additional networks) Bulletin Board for Libraries ("BUBL"), coverage of information resources on INTERNET, JANET, and other networks.*
  - JANET X.29: UK.AC.BATH.BUBL or 00006012101300
  - TELNET: BUBL.BATH.AC.UK or 138.38.32.45 login 'bubl'
  - Gopher: BUBL.BATH.AC.UK (138.32.32.45). Port 7070
  - World Wide Web: http: / / www.bubl.bath.ac.uk./BUBL/ home.html
  - NISSWAIS: telnetniss.ac.uk (for the NISS gateway)
  The Andersonian Library, Curran Building, 101 St. James Road, Glasgow G4 ONS, Scotland

- *Leeds Medical Information,* University of Leeds, Leeds LS2 9JT, United Kingdom

- *MasterFILE: updated database from EBSCO Publishing*, 83 Pine Street, Peabody, MA 01960

- *Mental Health Abstracts (online through DIALOG)*, IFI/Plenum Data Company, 3202 Kirkwood Highway, Wilmington, DE 19808

- *MLA International Bibliography,* Modern Language Association of America, 10 Astor Place, New York, NY 10003

- *PASCAL, c/o Institute de l'information Scientifique et Technique. Cross-disciplinary electronic database covering the fields of science, technology & medicine. Also available on CD-ROM, and can generate customized retrospective searches.* INIST/CNRS-Service Gestion des Documents Primaires, 2, allée du Parc de Brabois, F-54514 Vandoeuvre-les-Nancy, Cedex, France [http//www.inist.fr]

- *Periodical Abstracts, Research I (general and basic reference indexing and abstracting data-base from University Micro-films International (UMI), 300 North Zeeb Road, P.O. Box 1346, Ann Arbor, MI 48106-1346)*, UMI Data Courier, P.O. Box 32770, Louisville, KY 40232-2770

(continued)

- *Periodical Abstracts, Research II (broad coverage indexing and abstracting data-base from University Microfilms International (UMI), 300 North Zeeb Road, P.O. Box 1346, Ann Arbor, MI 48106-1346)*, UMI Data Courier, P.O. Box 32770, Louisville, KY 40232-2770

- *PsychNet*, PsychNet Inc., P.O. Box 369, Georgetown, CO 80444

- *Public Affairs Information Bulletin (PAIS)*, Public Affairs Information Service, Inc., 521 West 43rd Street, New York, NY 10036-4396

- *Religion Index One: Periodicals, the Index to Book Reviews in Religion, Religion Indexes: RIO/RIT/IBRR 1975– on CD-ROM*, American Theological Library Association, 820 Church Street, 3rd Floor, Evanston, IL 60201
  - E-mail: atla@atla.com
  - WWW: http://atla.library.vanderbilt.edu/atla/home.html

- *Sage Family Studies Abstracts (SFSA)*, Sage Publications, Inc., 2455 Teller Road, Newbury Park, CA 91320

- *Social Planning/Policy & Development Abstracts (SOPODA)*, Sociological Abstracts, Inc., P.O. Box 22206, San Diego, CA 92192-0206

- *Social Science Source: Coverage of 400 journals in the social sciences area; updated monthly*, EBSCO Publishing, 83 Pine Street, P. O. Box 2250, Peabody, MA 01960

- *Social Sciences Index (from Volume 1 & continuing)*, The H.W. Wilson Company, 950 University Avenue, Bronx, NY 10452

- *Social Work Abstracts*, National Association of Social Workers, 750 First Street NW, 8th Floor, Washington, DC 20002

- *Sociological Abstracts (SA)*, Sociological Abstracts, Inc., P.O. Box 22206, San Diego, CA 92192-0206

- *Studies on Women Abstracts*, Carfax Publishing Company, P.O. Box 25, Abingdon, Oxfordshire OX14 3UE, United Kingdom

- *Violence and Abuse Abstracts: A Review of Current Literature on Interpersonal Violence (VAA)*, Sage Publications, Inc. 2455 Teller Road, Newbury Park, CA 91320

Book reviews are selectively excerpted by the Guide to Professional Literature of the Journal of Academic Librarianship.

SPECIAL BIBLIOGRAPHIC NOTES

related to special journal issues (separates)
and indexing/abstracting

❏ indexing/abstracting services in this list will also cover material in any "separate" that is co-published simultaneously with Haworth's special thematic journal issue or DocuSerial. Indexing/abstracting usually covers material at the article/chapter level.

❏ monographic co-editions are intended for either non-subscribers or libraries which intend to purchase a second copy for their circulating collections.

❏ monographic co-editions are reported to all jobbers/wholesalers/approval plans. The source journal is listed as the "series" to assist the prevention of duplicate purchasing in the same manner utilized for books-in-series.

❏ to facilitate user/access services all indexing/abstracting services are encouraged to utilize the co-indexing entry note indicated at the bottom of the first page of each article/chapter/contribution.

❏ this is intended to assist a library user of any reference tool (whether print, electronic, online, or CD-ROM) to locate the monographic version if the library has purchased this version but not a subscription to the source journal.

❏ individual articles/chapters in any Haworth publication are also available through the Haworth Document Delivery Services (HDDS).

ABOUT THE EDITOR

Raymond-Jean Frontain, PhD, is Associate Professor of English and Interdisciplinary Studies at the University of Central Arkansas in Conway, where he teaches courses in the Bible as literature, gay and lesbian literary traditions, and the Bible and gender construction. He is the editor of three collections of essays on biblically related literary traditions: *The David Myth in Western Literature* (Purdue University Press, 1980), *Poetic Prophecy in Western Literature* (Fairleigh Dickinson University Press, 1984), and *Old Testament Women in Western Literature* (UCA Press, 1991). His articles on the appropriation of biblical motifs in English Renaissance texts and on homoerotic appropriations of the biblical story of David have appeared in numerous scholarly journals.

CONTENTS

ALL HARRINGTON PARK PRESS BOOKS
ARE PRINTED ON CERTIFIED
ACID-FREE PAPER

Introduction:
Reclaiming the Sacred:
The Bible in Gay and Lesbian Culture

Criticism has only recently begun to attend to what David Bergman calls "the genealogy of transformation that occurs as successive generations of gay writers work through each others' material, transfiguring a homophobic trope into a somewhat celebratory one" (22). Such a process, notes Bergman, "is dialectical, the product of the interaction between the dominant society and the gay subculture. The end result is *not* a pure gay discourse (no such thing can exist) but a discourse made more sympathetic to the lives of gay men" and women (22).

The essays that follow are interested generally in how Bergman's observations apply in two distinct but obviously interconnected ways to the Bible, perhaps the dominant text in Western culture and the one most often cited as authorizing antihomosexual feeling. They are interested, first, in how gay writers transfigure biblical tropes to undermine what is traditionally used for homophobic purposes, such as the story of Sodom and Gomorrah in Genesis or Paul's New Testament imprecations. And they are interested, second, in how biblical texts that admit or even invite the possibility of a homoerotic reading have been co-opted by orthodox tradition, and how they can be reappropriated by gay writers and artists–most obviously the same-sex relationships of David and Jonathan, of Ruth and Naomi, and of Jesus and John the Beloved Disciple, the details of whose narratives suggest powerful emotional bonds the implications of which centuries of religiously conservative readers have attempted to control, and which advocates of same-sex love have cited, explicitly or implicitly, as biblically sanctioned models for their own relationships.

[Haworth co-indexing entry note]: "Introduction: Reclaiming the Sacred: The Bible in Gay and Lesbian Culture." Frontain, Raymond-Jean. Co-published simultaneously in *Journal of Homosexuality* (The Haworth Press, Inc.) Vol. 33, No. 3/4, 1997, pp. 1-23; and: *Reclaiming the Sacred: The Bible in Gay and Lesbian Culture* (ed: Raymond-Jean Frontain) Harrington Park Press, an imprint of The Haworth Press, Inc., 1997, pp. 1-23. Single or multiple copies of this article are available for a fee from The Haworth Document Delivery Service [1-800-342-9678, 9:00 a.m. - 5:00 p.m. (EST). E-mail address: getinfo@haworth.com].

1

But perhaps it is more productive to speak of two impulses: the transgressive, which challenges the authority of the Bible in order to resist oppression by those who read the Bible in an ideologically narrow way; and the appropriative, which finds in the Bible's tropes and figures both the basis of a gay and lesbian spirituality, and the means of dignifying and possibly even sacralizing gay and lesbian existence.

SATIRIC CONTROVERSION: THE TRANSGRESSIVE IMPULSE

Insofar as debate concerning the authority of the Bible plays a critical role in the battle between the heterosexual majority and a gay/lesbian minority over the construction of social values, the Bible becomes–fairly or unfairly–an obstacle to gay and lesbian self-definition. And as long as strident voices from among the straight majority justify discrimination by insisting that gay and lesbian experience is *not* dignified by the Bible, there is a danger that gay and lesbian readers become angry with the Bible itself, rather than with fundamentalist ideologues who commandeer it for political purposes.[1] When the Bible is used to support discriminatory ideology, the gay and lesbian struggle for dignity inevitably involves one in a struggle with the Bible.

One strategy of defense developed by gay and lesbian writers is to challenge outright the Bible's preemptive authority. In Jeanette Winterson's *Oranges Are Not the Only Fruit* (1985), for example, the authority of the Bible is effectively undermined by the foolishness and gullibility of the characters who believe most fervently in it. Young Jeanette's adoptive mother is convinced that her daughter has been chosen by the Lord to fulfill her own frustrated desire to become a missionary. Satirizing the elect's interpretation–or misinterpretation–of signs (the "fizz" that Jeanette's mother felt in youth for a seductive Frenchman, for example, proved to be, not love, but an ulcer), the novel reveals how the seemingly most faithful members of the congregation are exploiting the church for personal financial gain; exposes Jeanette's mother as a spiritual "whore" (134); and discovers Jeanette to be filled with a spirit not recognized by the "holy" and "called" to a very different ministry than the one for which her mother prepared her.

Winterson analyzes the seductive assurance of fundamentalism when, years after leaving the pulpit from which she preached to acclaim as a teenaged evangelist, Jeanette draws upon the tension in ancient Israel between two divinely appointed groups to explain how, if she had stayed in the church,

> I could have been a priest instead of a prophet. The priest has a book with the words set out. Old words, known words, words of power. Words that are always on the surface. Words for every occasion. The words work. They do what they're supposed to do; comfort and discipline. (161)

The priestly mission offered her depends upon her acceptance of pre-scribed tradition; the priest is not allowed a voice of her own, but is expected to ventriloquize the words scripted for her, whether from the Bible or from another authoritative source. The priest's is a useful mission in that she can glibly comfort others, offering assurance of an unambiva-lent scheme of divine judgment of human actions. And reassurance that, however miserable they are in this life, they will be glorified in the next–and that however powerless and socially marginalized they feel now, their voice will sound in heaven–is all that some people look for. But, Winter-son shrewdly observes, the words that comfort are also words that "disci-pline" and constrain, keeping people in line by dictating their values and controlling their actions, stunting both their emotional and spiritual devel-opment. The church reduces the priest to a prison warden and the Bible to a dictatorial source of behavioral do's and don't's.

By asserting her sexual difference, Jeanette becomes a prophet instead. "The prophet has no book. The prophet is a voice that cries in the wilder-ness, full of sounds that do not always set into meaning. The prophets cry out because they are troubled by demons" (161). The prophet's is not a comfortable existence emotionally, socially, or even spiritually; the demon of difference will never let her rest, never let her feel comfortable with the status quo; it will drive her to question and challenge in a way that the pious will always judge blasphemous. But as a prophet, Jeanette creates her own book–an alternate scripture as it were. The chapters of *Oranges* are named for the first eight books of the Bible, the action narrated in each chapter providing an ironic commentary upon the biblical text insofar as it juxtaposes how a lesbian experiences and understands the world with how the evangelical orthodox try to force people to regard it. As a prophet, Jeanette discovers her name and power in the novel's final chapter, one appropriately named for Ruth, the Bible's most lesbian-sympathetic text.

It is important to note that, even while challenging one group's self-jus-tifying interpretation of the Bible, Winterson makes no attempt to erase the Bible's authority. The compassion of dotty Elsie, Jeanette's friend and comforter, is the standard by which Winterson herself seems to judge all of her characters; she is as willing to allow the "holy" their Bible as she is determined to assert the value of her own. To paraphrase the novel's concluding line, she encourages the reader to follow whatever "light" is available, as long as it is a "kindly" one.

Gore Vidal's *Live from Golgotha: The Gospel According to Gore Vidal* (1992), by contrast, deals with the oppressive weight of the Bible by going on the offensive, exposing to ridicule both inconsistencies within the Bible itself, and the enormous gap between biblical teaching and daily Christian practice. He does this in three ways. First, he exploits for satiric effect the uncertain process by which the New Testament texts were transmitted and canonized,[2] revealing that the man whom witnesses saw crucified was Judas Iscariot, not Jesus of Nazareth–and a very fat, effeminate, lisping Judas at that. The narrator, Timothy, hears Paul's actual description of his famous encounter with Jesus on the road to Damascus, and records what he acknowledges is the "unedited" version:

> Wide as He was tall, Jesus waddled toward me. . . . That face. Those luminous eyes hidden somewhere in all that golden fat. The ineffable smile like the first slice from a honeydew melon. Oh, delight! He held up a hand, a tiny starfish cunningly fashioned of lard. He spoke, His voice so high, so shrill that only the odd canine ever got the whole message, hence the need for interpretation and self-consciousness–in short, mega-fiction [sic]. . . . "Why," shrilled the Son of the One God, "dost thou persecuteth me-th?" (32)

"Naturally," the narrator admits, "we do not teach the real cause for the Crucifixion but only the cover story. In actual life, Jesus was indeed the Jewish king, who had threatened the rule of Rome as well as that of the Temple rabbinate, whose bank controlled the monetary policy not only of the Middle East but that of Greece and Egypt as well" (119). Indeed, the history of biblical Christianity is revealed to have been a battle between Jesus' "full-employment supply-side" economic policies and the Temple bank's commitment to anti-inflationary, high interest rates (118). James, the brother of Jesus, conspires with other knowledgeable witnesses, remaining silent about the truth, in order to promote a fiscal ideology linked to messianic zionism.

Second, Vidal underscores Paul's hijacking of Christianity by having Timothy repeatedly assert that Paul is the religion's true founder, not Jesus. "The Jesus story was never much of anything until Saint cooked up the vision-on-the-road-to-Damascus number and then we pulled the whole story together," Timothy boasts (173), praising Paul for creating a marketable image of Jesus and for distracting believers' attention from the vexing problem of Jesus' thus-far-unfulfilled promise of imminent return. The novel's "real" Jesus, in fact, is furious when his message of social reform and fanatical zionism is supplanted by Paul's fantasy about crucifixion, resurrection, and world dominion (164); indeed, as Timothy comes to realize, "the actual Jesus" "is a formidable enemy of the church that we have based upon his teachings" (191-92). But, the novel emphasizes, Paul was not the last to hijack Christ by teasing from Jesus' words support for one's own idiosyncratic beliefs: patristic theologians promoted a trinitarian god that even late first-century Christians would have found thoroughly alien (124); and later "visionaries" and media personalities like Mary Baker Eddy, Marianne Williamson, Helen Schucman, Selma Suydam, and Jerry Falwell prosper by altering the Bible to support their own ideology. The novel's oftentimes confusing plot concerns, at bottom, a wrangling over who will control what the Bible says.

Vidal is particularly brutal in showing how the mass media participates in this process: Paul is a vaudeville performer who distracts the attention of the masses by tap-dancing and juggling while preaching; the Crusades and Lourdes resulted from brilliant public relations campaigns; and Oral Roberts and Pope John Paul II are media personalities, not spiritual leaders (9). Christianity is not so much a religion as a business, with Paul as the chief fund raiser whose travels recorded in The Acts of the Apostles are referred to as "working the circuit" that has Jerusalem as its "central office"; Christianity, Timothy observes, is "a wonderful religion, cash-flow-wise" (27). Satirizing Robert Viguerie's means of making the Christian Right into a significant force in recent American politics, Timothy refers to "the names on the Holy Rolodex" as "our Holiest of Holies, and never to be revealed to profane eyes, particularly those of tax gatherers" (57). Throughout the novel Vidal satirizes modern media's power to create opinion and to control the thinking of the masses, thus allowing a neon-lighted, besequined, spiritually shallow Christianity to dominate American political discourse. At novel's end, live coverage of the events at Golgotha is being heavily promoted as the ultimate Christian extravaganza in order to deliver to NBC a Sweeps-Week ratings bonanza.

And, third, Vidal destroys the authority of the Bible by offering a character analysis of Saint Paul that is surprisingly true both to biblical scholarship and to modern psychology. Vidal's Paul is a self-hating Jew who chafes at his associates' Semiticness and, worse, a self-hating homosexual who proscribes the very sex acts that he himself compulsively commits. *Live from Golgotha* is a case study of the religious fanatic who wants to control the very behaviors in others that he is himself most guilty of. As Timothy reveals, Paul

> had this fantastic double standard, but then most saints do. Officially, he hated all sex inside and outside of wedlock on the ground that it

made you unclean in the eyes of God, who is apt to return any minute now, and if you just happen to be pounding away in the sack at the time, woe is you. (45)

"But Saint himself never stopped fooling around," Timothy continues, worshipping Timothy's prodigious sexual equipment as "the true trinity" (47). Like Jim Bakker and a long line of Roman Catholic clergy, Paul is able sexually to exploit spiritually insecure young men "since there was no way you could say no to Saint if you were a Christian lad and wanted to be saved. Saint had us all, literally, as well as figuratively, by the balls" (108).

Vidal's plot hinges upon the possibility of advances in twentieth-century computer technology allowing a first-century bishop to see how Christianity is practiced almost two millennia later. This endows his satire with a double edge, enabling an early Christian to criticize what the religion has become in Vidal's own time, and the modern reader to identify uncomfortably with abuses that compromised the religion from the start. Thus, the attempt of televangelists to exploit people whose lives are miserable and who are desperate for consolation of any kind is both repulsive to Timothy and oddly familiar: Oral Roberts and Pat Robertson are simply doing on a larger, more lucrative scale what Paul himself did. Vidal pulls the curtain back, as it were, and reveals the little man operating the levers to create the Wizard of Christianity's booming voice and intimidating presence. The modern reader cannot take the Bible and its supposed teachings about homosexuality very seriously when he or she sees Paul constantly grabbing the ass of the long-suffering narrator.

The novel's subtitle, *The Gospel According to Gore Vidal,* suggests a further extreme of the satiric impulse: to create an anti-Bible. For the space of the novel Vidal's alternative view of biblical Christianity is not only *as* valid as that of the canonical ones, but is *more* valid. One cannot complain that Vidal plays loosely with gospel kerygma when most televangelists—and, more importantly, Paul and members of the early Christian community—are shown selectively emphasizing details to assign a meaning clearly contrary to Jesus' text or to what history can recover of its context. Vidal exposes the deconstructive impulse which is at the heart of institutional Christianity.

Thus, if Winterson and Vidal both challenge the authority of the Bible and its interpreters, they do so in different ways. Winterson's satire is Horatian, a gentle chiding of the excesses of Christian fundamentalism while still sympathizing with the need for religious guidance in one's life; she does not seem to doubt that the rational minority will prevail spiritually, if at great cost. Vidal's satire, on the other hand, is Juvenalian, as vicious as the abuses that it strips and whips; Vidal wishes to expose the

Bible as a fiction and its believers as dupes or frauds. At the furthest extreme of the satiric-transgressive spectrum, however, are texts which do not simply challenge the Bible's authority, but labor to create a negative reversal of biblical values. Historically, the Sodom story has inspired the greatest effort in this regard, inviting the creation of an anal nihilism that counterblasts The Book of Genesis's heterosexual creationism. In *Les Cent Vingt Journées de Sodome* (1785; translated as *120 Days of Sodom*), for example, the Marquis de Sade imagines a sexuality which is not only nonreproductive, but whose practitioners take supreme pleasure in destroying. Sade associates his action with the Genesis site that gives its name to reproductive sterility, and which by the eighteenth century had become synonymous with sexual–particularly homosexual–excess. Likewise, the characters in John Wilmot, the Earl of Rochester's *Farce of Sodom; or, The Quintessence of Debauchery* (published 1684, but completed circa 1676) persist in practicing sodomy despite certain divine retribution; making a farce of what orthodox morality considers tragedy, Rochester elevates transgression to be the quintessential life-enhancing act. *Salò* (1975), Pier Paolo Pasolini's cinematic treatment of the Sodom story, was initially thought so repulsive that it was shown by the defense at the trial of Pasolini's murderer to suggest that Pasolini deserved to die. And in *The Boys of Life* (1991), Paul Russell creates a Pasolini-like filmmaker whose life and whose film, "The Gospel according to Sodom," both conclude in sexual apocalypse. The casual description of the Mediterranean city of Toulon by the narrator of Jean Cocteau's *Le Livre Blanc* (1928; translated as *White Book*) as "that delightful Sodom where the fire of heaven falls without danger, striking by means of caressing sunshine" (43) seems gentle by comparison.

A demon of the perverse haunts each of the above-mentioned Sodom texts. In each there is a ferociously creative energy coming from the act of transgressing that is analogous to Huck's discovery in Mark Twain's *Adventures of Huckleberry Finn* that if being good and going to heaven means betraying his friend Jim, then the greater heroism lies in reversing the poles of socially ordained morality: Evil, be thou my good. In these self-consciously transgressive texts, the "evil" proscribed by the Bible is transformed into the greatest source of pleasure *when* one is able to envision a higher morality and has the courage to transgress against the quotidian one.

And, curiously, such a need to transgress against divine prohibition may be at the heart of the Fall story in Genesis. The Gnostic tradition's reading of the Eden narrative, for example, holds Adam and Eve's "transgression" to be noble because it is in the pursuit of knowledge, the highest good.[3]

Others as well have read the Creation and Fall story as a representation of the inevitably tragic consequences of heroically pursuing knowledge. Such a reading rejects enclosure within the limited sphere of Eden as living a one-dimensional life, and accepts that knowing a wider, broader realm of experience necessarily involves suffering. For just as goodness without knowledge of evil is not virtue but naivete, so happiness without pain is monotonous and simplistic. Adam and Eve are to be applauded for desiring to go, like Job, beyond the protective hedge that Yahweh has surrounded them with, in order to learn what it means to live a fully virtuous life. Such a reading of Genesis holds that challenging an oppressive, monolithic authority is what humans are *supposed* to do; it is the way to claim a richer, deeper humanity.

By extension, acceptance of unorthodox sexual orientation is more heroic than acceptance of a socially constructed identity. As the narrator in Winterson's *Oranges* comes to understand,

> To eat of the fruit means to leave the garden because the fruit speaks of other things, other longings. So at dusk you say goodbye to the place you love, not knowing if you can ever return, knowing you can never return by the same way as this. It may be, some other day, that you will open a gate by chance, and find yourself again on the other side of the wall. (123)

The form that such an act of transgression takes—whether the comic correction of a Winterson, the satiric challenge of a Vidal, or the dark inversion of a Sade, a Rochester, or a Pasolini—is, thus, paradoxically sanctioned by the Bible itself.

TRANSITION: "GOSPEL FOR A PROUD SUNDAY"

By satirizing or inverting the Bible, the gay and lesbian writer proclaims his/her independence of a society intolerant of, or inhospitable to, difference; the walls of an oppressive tradition are pushed back by the transgressive text to create a space where gay and lesbian readers may breathe more easily. There is a danger to the satiric impulse, however, which is often clear about what it rejects but less certain about what it would create in its place. Juvenalian satire, in particular—whose speaker is compelled by bitterness, resentment, and anger to speak out—may have a nihilism at its heart. Despite a gay/lesbian reader's initial delight in Gore Vidal's brilliantly bitchy invective, Vidal is a lesser talent because he is unable to offer his readers any hope of redemption. And for all his prophet-like denunciations of a government indifferent to AIDS-related gay deaths, of a medical establishment more interested in making money than in saving lives, and of a significant segment of the gay population more eager to pursue pleasure than to practice a saving restraint, Larry Kramer alienates–as the prophet's shrillness of voice is wont to do–but without offering that ultimate vision of reconciliation and renewal that prophets likewise take as an essential part of their mission. Gay and lesbian writers need not only to challenge the oppressive authority of the Bible, but must find ways to appropriate it in the creation of a gay/lesbian spirituality.

The danger of failing to do so is dramatized in Lindsley Cameron's "Gospel for a Proud Sunday." The unnamed narrator, feeling guilty at not marching in the annual Gay Pride Parade, watches near St. Patrick's cathedral as a strikingly beautiful, long-haired young man in a hippie-like robe challenges a bigot carrying a sign that reads "AIDS–GOD'S PUNISHMENT FOR GAYS." When an altercation breaks out and the police are called, the narrator flees to a nearby coffee shop. The hippie, having escaped as well, enters and quickly makes the narrator uncomfortable by opening a conversation in which he challenges the self-justifying rationality which both prevents the narrator from marching in the parade and keeps him from religious faith.

> You're kind of hung up on understanding, aren't you? Haven't you ever noticed how limited it is? Can you tell me why mercy is superior to efficiency? . . . I can't tell you, because it can't be explained. Not everything can. But you know it's true. . . . Would anything that *wasn't* beyond your comprehension be worthy to be called God? Would you really worship a being who had your values? Think about it. Wouldn't you want something . . . superior? . . . Don't you want to get beyond *yourself?* (83)

When the narrator resists the hippie's call to belief in something beyond the self, the hippie proposes to silence his doubt by working a miracle then and there. Turning to the emaciated and heavily perspiring waiter, by whom the narrator has been faintly disgusted, the hippie tells him that if he will believe, he will be cured. Suddenly,

> this waiter–I mean it, it wasn't just that he straightened up and stopped shaking and sweating, but he swelled up. I saw it, I saw this skeletal, pathetic kid round out like someone was inflating him. He must have put on fifty pounds in five seconds–it was like watching a plant grow in a time-lapse movie. Or the Incredible Hulk on televi-

sion. Muscles popped out on his arms, on his chest. All of a sudden, he was a gorgeous kid, the kind it breaks your heart to pass on a beach. He looked extremely, glowingly, radiantly healthy, and a little dazed. I don't think he knew what had happened. (85)

However, rather than accepting the hippie as Jesus, and being converted to belief after witnessing first-hand that the biblical accounts of His healing the sick and raising the dead are true, the narrator feels outrage. "It's goddamned obscene," he yells.

You *could* save them, but you'd rather let the innocent suffer, whole nations at a time–did I say *let* them? You get off on it! You know how many people have AIDS right here in this city right now? You could actually cure them all, couldn't you? But no, you won't, will you? . . . I mean, it's so fucking *arbitrary.* (85-86)

After decking the miracle-working hippie, the narrator storms out of the coffee shop, but decides to march in the Gay Pride Parade after all.

Cameron's story is a challenge to both the straight and the gay moral imagination. On the one hand, it suggests that if Jesus were to return today, it would be to minister to the very people whom the church hierarchy most despises and spends so much of its political capital oppressing, rather than to the church and city officials proudly lined up on the front steps of St. Patrick's Cathedral. Disparaging the religious zealots gathered to protest the annual expression of Gay Pride, the hippie notes that "Gays are very dear to God." When the frustrated narrator snaps in reply, "That's not the way I heard it," he is cautioned: "What you heard was wrong" (82). Like Dostoyevsky's "Legend of the Grand Inquisitor," Cameron's story challenges the church hierarchy's perversion of the Word of God whose spirit the church was appointed to keep alive. Reversing the terms of the traditional reading of the Sodom story, which is often used to condemn gay and lesbian sexuality, the hippie dismisses Roman Catholic nuns and priests as "sterile" (82), and asserts that the affliction visited upon the ancient Sodomites was actually a sign of God's love; "He has rewarded gays from the beginning" (83). The morally self-satisfied, proud that God has not afflicted them with a painful disease, do not understand that the *absence* of affliction indicates, rather, that He does *not* love them. Ironically, it is society's misuse of the Bible while attempting to dispossess gays and lesbians of basic civil liberties that guarantees the insulted and injured entrance into the kingdom of heaven from which the self-righteous, self-appointed guardians of public morality will be excluded. In driving the bigots from the steps of St. Patrick's Cathedral, the hippie recapitulates

Jesus' driving the moneylenders from the temple, and church leaders like Cardinal O'Connor, by extension, are dismissed as being so many more Caiaphases.

But "Gospel for a Proud Sunday" is a warning as well to spiritually alienated gays like the narrator who, having lived for the pleasures of the body, feel betrayed by its inevitable mortality and are so angered by injustice in this world that they lose hope in the possibility of miracle. As the hippie points out, reason can explain efficiency, not mercy, and only mercy can eliminate injustice; a rational person seeking justice in this world will only be driven mad with despair. Religion has something to offer gays suffering the holocaust of AIDS–not a cure, but an acceptance of pain and suffering that allows transcendence. The narrator may be converted at story's end in that he is outraged enough by the arbitrariness of divine mercy to join the Pride parade that he was originally avoiding, but he remains so imprisoned by his own rationality that he is insensitive to miracle. As the hippie warned him at the start, the narrator is so rational that even "if you saw God intervene in human history, perform a miracle right before your eyes, you still wouldn't worship Him" (84). He will never understand that one is redeemed by suffering, that the embrace of God is so powerful that it destroys the body of those whom He loves, that no one was more dear to Yahweh than His faithful servant Job, whom He afflicted almost past endurance.

Organized religion *has* abandoned and betrayed gays, the story suggests, but it is gays' loss of faith which not only allows bigots to dominate public discourse on religion-based values but blinds gays themselves to their difference as the sign of their being God's chosen people. Salvation is near for gays, who must not lose hope by losing their sense of miracle. At the end of the story, the ironic application of Christ's words on the cross–"Father, forgive them, for they know not what they do"–highlights the story's drama of varying levels of consciousness and awareness. The narrator believes that he does indeed understand, and that God's refusal to cure the AIDS-afflicted when He has the power to do so justifies the rejection of God. But it is not so much God that the narrator rejects as it is the operation of miracle. The narrator is right to reject the delusive belief of the spiritually smug that if one prays, God will answer; but he fails to see that a hedonistic life centered on pleasuring the body is just as vacuous. The "gospel" contained within the story teaches that being open to the possibility of miracle–being aware of life beyond the physical–is the only way to feel pride and self-worth. It is, in short, the only way to redeem oneself and one's people.

What Cameron has done is to reclaim the Bible from its perversion by the orthodox, in the creation of a gay spirituality. When read unencumbered by homilistic tradition, the Bible proves deeply unorthodox. As Robert Goss shows in *Jesus Acted Up: A Gay and Lesbian Manifesto* (1993), Jesus challenged the shallow, legalistic religiousness of the Sadducees and Pharisees, denounced "traditional family values" ("who is my mother? who is my brother?"), and embraced the socially marginalized; in general, He reversed the values and priorities of society, making the first last and the last first. Gays and lesbians need to go beyond reasoning about AIDS (which will only drive a sensitive person mad), to mercy, compassion, love—go beyond the self. That is the miracle of redemption.

Finally, the story suggests—and much to the narrator's confusion—that sex is holy. Sex is a religious experience because it transcends reason, allowing a person to go beyond him/herself in a merging with another; significantly, the word "ecstasy" in English has a sexual as well as a spiritual reference. The mistrust and disdain that the orthodox have of sex is a sign of their own sterility. The religion of sex that the hippie teaches in "Gospel" is similar to that of Father Dan in Paul Rudnick's *Jeffrey* (1994), whom Jeffrey meets after withdrawing from emotional and physical intimacy because AIDS has made life suddenly "radioactive" (48):

> Of course life sucks; it always will—so why not make the most of it? How dare you not lunge for any shred of happiness? . . . There is only one real blasphemy—the refusal of joy! Of a corsage and a kiss! (69)

And:

> I'm telling you, the only times I really feel the presence of God are when I'm having sex, and during a great Broadway musical! (67-68)

Sex is important for the joy it allows one to share with another person, not for the pleasure that it allows one to take for oneself. Sex that lacks this sacramental, life-enhancing quality is profanation.

Gays and lesbians need to create a vibrant, life-affirming religion that is not simply a parody of heterosexual Judeo-Christianity. Anger at and resentment of orthodox, institutionalized religion must eventually be replaced by an acceptance of gay and lesbian life as holy. One must have a sense of miracle and a sense of sex as sacrament if one is to have life to the full. Otherwise, one risks becoming as shallow and as self-hating as Larry Kramer's "Faggots," or as strident and as incapable of the joy of human communion as Kramer himself often seems to be.

CONSTRUCTING A GAY/LESBIAN SPIRITUALITY: THE APPROPRIATIVE IMPULSE

In Fannie Flagg's *Fried Green Tomatoes at the Whistle Stop Cafe* (1988), Rebecca Alpert notes (92), one of the characters uses biblical Ruth's vow to Naomi "as the secret message sent . . . to let her 'friend' know that she wishes to leave an abusive marriage and come live with her":

> And Ruth said, Intreat me not to leave thee, or to return from follow-ing after thee: for wither thou goest, I will go; and where thou lodgest, I will lodge: thy people shall be my people, and thy God my God. (Ruth 1: 16)

The allusion imports to the novel the biblical ethos of the strong caring for the weak, while validating a relationship that other characters find ques-tionable, and provocatively raising to the surface the biblical model's submerged lesbianism.[4] Similarly, in the short story "Marty," Richard Davis figures Stanley's loss of his boyhood friend and lover to a childhood illness that his evangelical parents would not allow to be treated medically as Elijah's assumption into heaven in a fiery chariot, his mantle of proph-ecy descending to Elisha who is forced to remain on earth.[5] Davis's con-cluding the story by quoting in full the passage from Kings about Elijah's apotheosis leaves the reader with a sense of inconsolable loss: with Marty's death, the sacred is fled from the earth, and all one can do is mourn. But the analogy hints as well at something about Stanley's future. At this moment in the story the boy cannot see how, like Elisha, he will grow to assume the strength, compassion, and independence of his departed friend; nevertheless, a double portion of Marty's spirit is upon him.

In each of these two examples, a gay/lesbian writer finds in the Bible a figure that enables him/her to construct a same-sex relationship of extraor-dinary resonance and spirit. Neither text argues with the Bible or its believers, contests the Bible's authority, or lapses into spiritual indiffer-ence before a seemingly inhospitable authority. Rather, each reclaims for the homosexual imagination a possibility intrinsic in the biblical text that is unavailable to or is denied by orthodox readers. The end result of such an operation is the reassertion of the sacral quality of gay and lesbian relationships.

Richard Howard's poem "The Giant on Giant-Killing: Homage to the bronze *David* of Donatello, 1430" suggests one way in which the Bible can be reclaimed for gay and lesbian use—by allowing a voice to sound that the Bible and subsequent tradition have suppressed. Goliath of Gath, champion of the Philistines, is not permitted to speak in 1 Samuel 17 except to offer his initial challenge to the Israelites and then to scoff at the seemingly inappropriate adversary that they send to meet him. Howard's poem ventriloquizes Goliath's voice from the grave, allowing him to explain that he was overcome not by David's martial strategy but by the beauty of the boy, who is described in 1 Samuel 16: 12 as being "ruddy, and withal of a beautiful countenance, and goodly to look to."

> No need for a stone! My eyes
> were my only enemy, my only weapon too,
> and fell upon David like a sword. (41-43)

Howard is able to recover Goliath's previously unrecorded voice because, as is testified by the title of the volume in which the lyric appears, the poet shares "fellow feelings" with Goliath; he too knows what it is to be overcome by the sight of a handsome youth. But, as the subtitle of the poem suggests, the "fellow feelings" extend further than this, the poet recognizing in the bronze *David* of Donatello a similar understanding of the David-Goliath relationship.[6] The poem records its own "genealogy of transformation," much as Bergman calls for, by which a potentially homophobic trope is made into a celebratory one. The reader of Howard's poem will never be able to read the Bible episode—or look at Donatello's bronze—the same way again.

For an operation more complex—and one with even further-reaching consequences—consider the implications of Dale Peck's using Song 3: 1-3 as the epigraph to the "Three Night Watchmen" chapter of *Martin and John* (1993). The biblical passage in question bespeaks urgent desire and frustration:

> Upon my couch at night
> I sought the one I love—
> I sought but found him not.
> "I must rise and roam the town,
> Through the streets and through the squares.
> I must seek the one I love."
> I sought, but found him not.
> I met the watchmen
> who patrol the town.
> "Have you seen the one I love?" (Peck's trans.)

Indeed, The Song of Songs is a parable of desire, a drama of seeking and finding, of pursuit and delayed gratification. As Harold Fisch notes, in

Song "love is something to be struggled and striven for more than it is something to be celebrated. The terror of loss and emptiness, the longing for fulfillment are more central to the poem than fulfillment itself or descriptions of beauty." The "forward movement" of the passage chosen by Peck, in particular,

> suggests the unremittingness of the search, a longing ever increasing, an intensity of devotion seeking but never quite finding its embodiment in language. Greek and Roman pastoral knows desire (usually of the swain), but the yearning of the loved one whose lover is absent and whose soul is empty of content is something different. (85)

And, as Fisch further shows, an allegorical imperative drives the text. Desire–intensified by having the object of one's fulfillment momentarily within one's grasp only to see him disappear as one tries to embrace him–is not simply the condition of love, but of religious experience as well. God is never fully available; all one can experience is an intimation of transcendence that is as frustrating as it is delicious. In Song, sexual longing figures religious faith.

What does this signify for Peck's novel? Like Song, the novel is concerned with the elusiveness of love; the narrator, we learn only at the end of the story, has lost Martin to AIDS. Thus, the elusiveness of love dramatized in the biblical text is intensified in *Martin and John* by a disease that erases the beloved as the relationship progresses. What Fisch calls "the agony of yearning" expressed in Song in the metaphor of "an unremitting *search* as the lover, or more specifically, the *beloved* . . . , seeks him whom her soul loves, seeks him and does not find him" (85) is in Peck the agonized search for coherence as the loss of Martin renders John's world incoherent.

Furthermore, the elusive nature of love in Song is implicated in *Martin and John*'s "consciously 'decentered'" narrative (Cady 19). The ages of the characters and their social circumstances–even the specific dynamic of their relationship–change from chapter to chapter. Are Martin and John blue-collar workers struggling to escape a dead-end existence, or members of the upper crust who meet, as in a Noel Coward play, while flirting at the piano at a cocktail party? The narrator's images of his past–his self-construction–recedes from the reader's grasp as well: how did his mother die? what is his relationship with his father? The reader is uncertain what pieces of information are reliable. Iterated motifs gather a haunting significance as they recur from chapter to chapter, suggesting a key to the action's meaning, but the reader is uncertain finally what that meaning is. The elusive text–with its shifting perspective, narrative imbalance, and exasperating mix of uncertainty and suggestive emphasis–mimes the nature of love. The final effect of the novel is of a significance too deep to be rationally or consciously verbalized as John struggles to make sense of what it means to love and lose Martin.[7]

What Peck does, then, is to raise in his text the great biblical justification for erotic love and transfer this divinely revealed guarantee for the sacramental character of eros to a homosexual relationship. Passages from Song, other than the one Peck uses as a chapter epitaph, resonate in the novel, increasing its passionate urgency: "Let him kiss me with the kisses of his mouth: for thy love is better than wine" (1: 2); and "Stay me with flagons, comfort me with apples: for I am sick of love" (5: 8). The haunting appropriateness of the Shulamite Maiden's words to the situation of Martin and John is far more persuasive than any number of polemical arguments might be that love is love, so it makes no difference whether a love is heterosexual or homosexual. "Many waters cannot quench love" (8: 7); the thirst of an amorous soul is moving in and of itself, but particularly so when the lover seeks a partner he has lost to AIDS.

The application of Song to Martin removes his aching loss from the realm of the profane, transforming it into something transcendent. Peck's appropriation of Song's images of the search for the beloved and of the hand reaching out, grasping but uncertain, to talk about AIDS is a daring gesture. Even more powerful, though, is his transformation of the dramatic function of the watchmen. In Song the speaker seeks guidance from the night watchmen assigned to preserve the calm of the city and guarantee its safety while the community sleeps. The watchman himself is a recurring biblical figure (for example, Isa. 21: 8-12) who signals the human need to be on guard, to study the skies for evidence of God, to be alert and to listen with a "circumcised" ear. Here, however, the narrator himself is both the watchman and the love-hungry maiden who seeks the watch's help, for in this chapter John is working as a night watchman at a factory; as he walks the perimeters of the industrial complex, he can see the light shining in the window of the house that he shares with Martin. Returning home after his shift, he sits watching over the sleeping Martin. The image collapses with others in the novel into the watch that he keeps at dying Martin's bedside. "Set me as a seal upon thine heart, as a seal upon thine arm," the maiden in Song says to her beloved; "for love is as strong as death" (8: 6). *Martin and John* dramatizes a love that, however distraught the surviving partner is, proves to be as strong as death.[8]

As extraordinary as is such a maneuver to survive the imponderable devastation of AIDS, one final instance of gay appropriation of biblical voice and vision in the creation of a new spirituality demands attention.

Tony Kushner's two-part *Angels in America* (1993-94) dramatizes the calling of a gay prophet, Prior Walter, as the millennium approaches and an uncertain new world order is coming into being. The excesses of the Reagan administration, the self-deluded morality of American civic religion (in this case, Mormonism), and the hypocrisy of public figures like Roy Cohn have conspired to bring America to the brink of collapse; apocalypse carries the satiric writer's darkest vision. "[T]here are no gods here, no ghosts and spirits in America, there are no angels in America, no spiritual past, no racial past, there's only the political," Louis complains to Belize (*Millennium* 92). This is why, as Ethel Rosenberg says to Roy Cohn, "History is about to crack wide open. Millennium approaches" (*Millennium* 112).

But in addition to the imagery of biblical apocalypse, Kushner appropriates the language of biblical prophecy to bring the viewer/reader to "the very threshold of revelation" (*Millennium* 33); the message that prophet Prior delivers at the conclusion of *Perestroika* is a blessing, "*More Life.*" Kushner's play, like the biblical institution of prophecy, aims at nothing less than the spiritual revitalization of a depleted world. Deep inside his AIDS-ravaged body, Prior is told, "there's a part of you, the most inner part, entirely free of disease" (*Millennium* 34); likewise, there remains in America the promise of a redemptive "softness, compliance, forgiveness, grace" (*Millennium* 100). The prophet who testifies against "this Sour Little Age" (*Perestroika* 14) is also able to show us how, like the snake that sheds its skin, we can change–how we may begin the Great Work. For, no matter how much we fear millennium's approach, the prophet's presence allows us to be "also full of, I don't know, Joy or something. Hope" (*Perestroika* 24). While the viewer/reader is devastated by the moral corruption of America and the apocalypse of which AIDS is just one part, he is at the same time both comforted and exhilarated by Prior's promise that "The Great Work [of renewal] Begins" (*Perestroika* 148) in which gays will take the lead.

The biblical prophet traditionally speaks from a liminal zone in which one world is collapsing but the new world has not yet been brought into being. Speaking at the Princess Grace Awards ceremony in 1994, Kushner exhorted his audience:

> These are hard times in America. Generosity, compassion, justice, fairness, the very notion of the social, of culture, of our interrelatedness are under attack. Artists have voices and visions, and God help us if our artists fail to seek the truth–to sing it, shout it, dance it, film it, and invent new ways that the truth can insist itself on a too-blind world. . . . To paraphrase Herman Melville, we are supposed to be

diving deep, returning from the depths with bloodshot eyes holding in our hands the truth–proof against the false magicians who have bewitched our world. That's the only hope and grace that we have. (qtd. in "About the Author" 3)

Angels offers just such a message of "hope and grace" even as it testifies against "the false magicians who have bewitched our world." Men dying of AIDS are prophets (*Perestroika* 55) because they are able to offer us the blessing of more life that men like Joe's father have withheld from us (*Perestroika* 82); they bring us through suffering to the threshold of revelation. Traditional religion has failed in America; its vision was exhausted when the church became more concerned with exercising power than with healing and comforting the afflicted. The queens who themselves suffer from AIDS yet who continue to minister to the dying are the persons left to practice "Forgiveness. Which is maybe where love and justice finally meet. Peace at last" (*Perestroika* 124). They teach us a way of living past hope, of finding a way to desire more life even *after* hope is gone (*Perestroika* 136). *Angels in America* is as extraordinary in its denunciation of those who abuse the Bible's authority in order to oppress gays as it is in its creation of an entirely gay rhetoric of prophecy–one that sees heaven as "A City Much Like San Francisco" (*Perestroika* 50), understands prophetic revelation in terms of sexual orgasm, and laments the *deus abscondus* in the same terms as Judy Garland sings of "The Man That Got Away." Like Jacob who wrestled with the angel until the breaking of day in order to receive its blessing (Gen. 32: 24-32), Prior struggles with a god who has abandoned his creatures, demanding–in the face of the horrible apocalypse of AIDS–the blessing of "more life." Kushner creates a prophet who testifies, not on behalf of God, but of life itself. If one cannot believe in a god who blesses gay and lesbian life, then one must be bold and pronounce the blessing oneself.

Other writers can be cited who, like André Gide and James Baldwin, are so familiar with the Bible that it becomes the lexicon with which they express their most basic ideas, investing their writing with the power of religious witness. But space does not permit. It remains simply to repeat that, whether attempting to reclaim the gay/lesbian spirituality implicit in the Bible (as Flagg and Howard do), or using the Bible to sanctify gay and lesbian sexuality (as Peck and Kushner do), such writers create a faith in the rightness of gay and lesbian life, dignifying the gay and lesbian struggle against immolation. It is not an orthodox spirituality which results, but one the deeper and more brilliant for its inventiveness in reclaiming the sacred in gay and lesbian life.

*   *   *

The essays that follow are organized according to chronology of topic, but can be divided into three categories.

First, there are those essays that analyze a comparatively neutral use made of the Bible by gay and lesbian writers. Claude J. Summers shows how, even though the temptation is rejected, John Milton's incorporating homosexual temptation into his rewriting of Christ's retreat to the desert provides evidence of the poet's "sophisticated recognition of the range of fully human sexual responses." Gregory Bredbeck considers how in the short story, "The Life to Come," E. M. Forster challenges "prohibitional readings of the Bible" concerning homosexuality by positing Vedic scripture as an alternate religious authority, one that sanctifies same-sex love. And George Klawitter demonstrates the inescapable influence of the Bible on even a self-declared agnostic like poet Thom Gunn.

Second, there are three essays that analyze satiric-transgressive uses of the Bible. Armando Maggi considers "the ironic reversal of the relationship between rhetoric, sodomy, and the Bible" in *L'Alcibiade fanciullo a scola* (circa 1650) in which Antonio Rocco "performs the discourse of Sodom" while "erasing its source, the Bible itself." Similarly, Raymond-Jean Frontain analyzes how sodomy is carnivalized in *Sodom, or the Quintessence of Debauchery,* a farce attributed to John Wilmot, the Earl of Rochester, thus successfully undercutting both the Bible's authority and the presumptive morality that it is otherwise used to sanction. And Ellis Hansen demonstrates how Oscar Wilde appropriated the language of both The Song of Songs and The Book of Revelation to mime the paradox of biblical sensuality and construct a subversive identity for himself as "a poet enamored of the Scarlet Woman, a would-be convert who exposed the scandal of Christianity as art.'"

Finally, there are those that analyze specific appropriations of the biblical text in the attempt to create a gay/lesbian spirituality. Margaret Soenser Breen considers how the Bible functions as the "epistemological anchor" for the lesbian *Bildungsroman*. Amy Benson Brown demonstrates that Jeanette Winterson's articulation of a lesbian subject is inseparable from her revisionary engagement with the Bible. Gayle M. Seymour shows that during the formative stages of his sexual development, Pre-Raphaelite painter Simeon Solomon turned to the biblical David story as the primary means of constructing a homosexual identity that Victorian society could not impugn. And Ed Madden shows how "by writing the life of a lesbian as a kind of gospel of inversion, [Radclyffe] Hall turns a language of condemnation into a language of validation, making her use of biblical language a kind of Foucauldian 'reverse discourse.'"

I am grateful to Claude Summers for commissioning for *Gay and Lesbian Literary Heritage* the essay on the Bible from which the idea for this volume evolved, and for his helpful advice in assembling these essays; his is a gentle voice in gay and lesbian studies, and he is an ever-gracious presence. I want also to thank John De Cecco for the generous leeway he allowed me in framing and organizing this collection, and for his warm encouragement at every step of the way. Manuscript editor Hubert Kennedy possesses a sharp eye and corrected the many lapses of my own. Ben Robertson prepared the index.

Two personal debts require acknowledgement as well. Outings with the late Ruth Gillah Rothenberg to the sand hill crane migration preserve in north central Indiana first alerted me to the creative power of a multiplicity of discourses; and after I first shared with her my interest in "alternative" biblical traditions, she regularly called my attention to references uncovered in the course of her own indefatigable reading. Of more immediate consequence, Myron Dean Yeager's generous good nature allowed him to accept a collaboration other than the one originally envisioned, and so it is to him that I would like to dedicate these efforts.

Raymond-Jean Frontain, PhD

NOTES

1. The stories in Lev Raphael's *Dancing on Tisha B'av* (1990), for example, poignantly show how orthodox Jewish believers have difficulty seeing the connection between local hate crimes against gays and an anti-Semitic group's desecration of their synagogue; and how survivors of Nazi concentration camps are offended, even, that the massive AIDS-related deaths in the gay community should be termed a "holocaust," lest their own tragedy be "cheapened" by comparison. "But the Bible says . . . ," protests one student in a classroom discussion of campus antigay graffiti in "Abominations," the collection's final story. Similarly, Martin Dubsky's collage documenting religiously justified homophobia, *Tom Pilgrim's Progress Among the Consequences of Christianity 1977/8,* was inspired by the artist's anger "at the way the Church and State [could] operate together" in the *Gay News* trial for blasphemy (Cooper 274).

2. None of the canonical gospels was written down at the time of the events it purports to describe; the gospel narratives, rather, derive from the sayings of, and anecdotes regarding, Jesus that had been circulating orally in different Jewish communities. The history of the gospels' transmission was additionally complicated by variations in manuscript tradition (Mark's resurrection chapter, for example, is a late addition) and by the problem of translating dead languages–such as Jerome's mistranslating the Greek word for a young, unmarried woman as "vir-

gin," an error that resulted in the influential medieval doctrine of the Virgin Birth. There is no way of knowing, however, how close to the original biblical texts are the ones recovered by the Reformers and Counter-Reformers in the sixteenth and seventeenth centuries that were eventually stabilized in print. Little wonder that in Vidal's novel none of the principals can be certain of who said what when, and that remarks made by the principals in casual conversation are unnervingly close to statements attributed to Jesus in canonical Scripture.

3. See, for example, Pheme Perkins's analysis of Eve as Wisdom in Gnostic tradition.

4. For other lesbian uses of Ruth, see Frontain, "Bible" 97. I am grateful to Prof. Alpert for supplying me with references to recent scholarship on the Bible and homosexuality.

5. Because of the buzz cut that his macho father inflicts on him, Stanley is tormented–like Elisha–by boys who call him "Baldy."

6. On the division in interpretive tradition over the sexuality of biblical David, and the division among art historians concerning the homoerotic associations of Donatello's bronze *David,* see Frontain, "Fellow Feelings."

An operation similar to Howard's can be found in Guy Hocquenghem's novel *La colère de l'Agneau* (1985), which is a recreation of the last days of Jerusalem told from St.-Jean's point of view. Hocquenghem, a leading French gay activist and the influential theoretician of *Le désir homosexuel* (1972), emphasizes the special relationship that developed between Jesus and Jean ("les entretiens nocturnes, privilège du coeur, puisqu'il [Jean] est le plus jeune"–75) and the "trinité de chair" (134-35) that Jean and the prophet formed with "la Magdaléenne." There is nothing satiric or transgressive about Hocquenghem's novel, which is a fascinating recreation of biblical times that quietly pursues the leads provocatively provided by the biblical text.

7. In an extraordinary reading of the seventeenth-century English religious lyric, William Sessions borrows from Julia Kristeva's dialectical structure of desire: "Against one side that opens to structure and logic, action and consummation, this dialectic of desire posits its ŏther firmly not only in an experience of its own deconstructing of its own meaning but also in an experience even greater than its own deconstruction: the absence of meaning of any kind in the dialectic, of being abandoned or being *as* abandonment, the death of dialectic, a lover without a beloved" (3). Although Sessions finds the biblical analogues to this dialectic in Psalms rather than in Song, his conclusion that in the lyrics ecstasy is constantly qualified in terms of abandonment (12) creates a significant point of entry into Peck's complex and difficult text.

8. Song has been used by other gay artists for similar purpose. For example, in *El Hadj* André Gide uses a motif from Song to legitimize his hero's search for the elusive male ideal (see Pollock 320-21). And Benjamin Britten set Francis Quarles's recension of Song 2: 16, "My beloved is mine, and I am his," to music in *Canticle I,* one of the first pieces written specifically for his lover, Peter Pears, to sing. Biographer Humphrey Carpenter (261-62) concludes that the song was composed as a reconciliation gesture after Pears had an affair while on tour. The

composition, then, is Britten's way of reaffirming and cementing their love after a traumatic disruption, and Pears's vocalization of it is both an effacement of his erring self as he gives himself up to become the vehicle of his lover's words and music, and an assertion of his faithful self who returns like the Bridegroom to the Shulemite Maiden after a winter's absence, fostering the spring-like regeneration of their shared world.

WORKS CITED

"About the Author." *Repartee: The Voice of the Arkansas Repertory Theatre* (March 1996): 3.

Alpert, Rebecca. "Finding Our Past: A Lesbian Interpretation of the Book of Ruth." *Reading Ruth: Contemporary Women Reclaim a Sacred Story.* Ed. Judith A. Kates and Gail Twersky Reimer. New York: Ballantine, 1994. 91-96.

Bergman, David. *Gaiety Transfigured: Gay Self-Representation in American Literature.* Madison: U of Wisconsin P, 1991.

Cady, Joseph. "AIDS Literature." *Gay and Lesbian Literary Heritage.* Ed. Claude J. Summers. New York: Holt, 1995. 16-20.

Cameron, Lindsley. "Gospel for a Proud Sunday." *The Prospect of Detachment.* New York: St. Martin's P, 1988. 78-86.

Carpenter, Humphrey. *Benjamin Britten: A Biography.* New York: Scribner's, 1992.

Cocteau, Jean. *The White Book.* Trans. with an intro. by Margaret Crosland. San Francisco: City Lights, 1989.

Cooper, Emmanuel. *The Sexual Perspective: Homosexuality and Art in the Last 100 Years in the West.* 2nd ed. London: Routledge, 1994.

Davis, Richard. "Marty." *Waves: An Anthology of New Gay Fiction.* Ed. Ethan Mordden. New York: Vintage, 1994.

Fisch, Harold. *Poetry with a Purpose: Biblical Poetics and Interpretation.* Bloomington: Indiana UP, 1988.

Frontain, Raymond-Jean. "The Bible." *Gay and Lesbian Literary Heritage.* Ed. Claude J. Summers. New York: Holt, 1995. 92-100.

_____. "Fellow Feelings: Richard Howard, Donatello, and the Homoerotic David Tradition." Unpublished manuscript.

Hocquenghem, Guy. *La colère de l'Agneau.* Paris: Albin Michel, 1985.

Howard, Richard. "The Giant on Giant-Killing: Homage to the Bronze *David* of Donatello, 1430." *Fellow Feelings.* New York: Atheneum, 1976. 53-55.

Kushner, Tony. *Angels in America. Part One: Millennium Approaches.* New York: Theatre Communications Group, 1993. *Part Two: Perestroika.* New York: Theatre Communications Group, 1994.

Peck, Dale. *Martin and John.* New York: Farrar, Straus, Giroux. 1993.

Perkins, Pheme. "The Gnostic Eve." *Old Testament Women in Western Literature.* Ed. Raymond-Jean Frontain and Jan Wojcik. Conway, AR: U of Central Arkansas P, 1991. 38-67.

Pollock, Patrick. *André Gide, Homosexual Moralist.* New Haven: Yale UP, 1991.

Rudnik, Paul. *Jeffrey.* New York: Plume, 1994.

Sessions, William A. "Abandonment and the English Religious Lyric in the Seventeenth Century." *"Bright Shootes of Everlastingnesse": The Seventeenth-Century Religious Lyric.* Ed. Claude J. Summers and Ted-Larry Pebworth. Columbia: U of Missouri P, 1987. 1-19.

Vidal, Gore. *Live from Golgotha: The Gospel according to Gore Vidal.* New York: Random House, 1992.

Winterson, Jeanette. *Oranges Are Not the Only Fruit.* 1985. New York: Atlantic Monthly P, 1987.

The Discourse of Sodom in a Seventeenth-Century Venetian Text

Armando Maggi, PhD

University of Pennsylvania

SUMMARY. This essay examines *L'Alcibiade fanciullo a scola,* a seventeenth-century text written in Venice. *L'Alcibiade* is a sort of Platonic dialogue between a sodomite teacher and his young and attractive pupil. The teacher tries to convince his student to let him penetrate him. The discourse of the sodomite teacher is similar to Lacan's "discourse of the master." Maggi brings to the fore the intrinsic ambiguities of the sodomite discourse. On the one hand, since he posits himself outside society, the sodomite is able to manipulate and distort any sort of discourse. The sodomite teacher believes that women embody the religious/political power that oppresses sodomites. The master knows that any discourse exclusively aims to acquire a certain power. On the other hand, the sodomite discourse is nothing but another form of power/oppression. The master subjugates the other through his "sodomite rhetoric," based on lies and puns. *[Article copies available for a fee from The Haworth Document Delivery Service: 1-800-342-9678. E-mail address: getinfo@ haworth. com]*

Armando Maggi received his PhD from the University of Chicago. He is currently teaching at the University of Pennsylvania in the Department of Romance Languages. His areas of specialization are the following: late Renaissance, female mystical literature, comparative studies, and gender studies. He has published extensively on Italian, Portuguese, and French literature.

Correspondence may be addressed: Department of Romance Languages, 521 Williams Hall, University of Pennsylvania, Philadelphia, PA 19104-6305.

[Haworth co-indexing entry note]: "The Discourse of Sodom in a Seventeenth-Century Venetian Text." Maggi, Armando. Co-published simultaneously in *Journal of Homosexuality* (The Haworth Press, Inc.) Vol. 33, No. 3/4, 1997, pp. 25-43; and: *Reclaiming the Sacred: The Bible in Gay and Lesbian Culture* (ed: Raymond-Jean Frontain) Harrington Park Press, an imprint of The Haworth Press, Inc., 1997, pp. 25-43. Single or multiple copies of this article are available for a fee from The Haworth Document Delivery Service [1-800-342-9678, 9:00 a.m. - 5:00 p.m. (EST). E-mail address: getinfo@haworth.com].

L'Alcibiade fanciullo a scola (Alcibiades Boy at School), an anonymous text published in Venice circa 1650, is "the most obscene book of the Italian literature."[1] Although its author remained a mystery until the end of the nineteenth century, *L'Alcibiade* has always been considered a product of the so-called "Accademia degli incogniti" (Academy of the Unknown), which was notorious for its libertine ideology and its aggressive anticlericalism.[2] The most prominent figures of this Academy were Alberto Loredan, its actual founder and author of an interesting series of erotic short stories (*Novelle amorose*), Ferrante Pallavicino, who is still remembered for his outrageous *Retorica delle puttane* (Rhetoric of the Whores), and Antonio Rocco, a friar who wrote two philosophical works influenced by the Aristotelian Cesare Cremonini, well-known professor of the university of Padova. Borrowing Cremonini's theories, in *Animae rationalis immortalitas simul cum ipsius propagatione ex semine* Rocco writes that the human soul is intrinsically connected to the body, and thus is mortal.[3] Although all the above members of the Venetian Academy were denounced to the Inquisition for their libertinage, they were protected by the Venetian government, and none were put on trial.[4]

The actual author of *L'Alcibiade fanciullo a scola* is Antonio Rocco. In two letters, published by Achille Neri in 1888, Alberto Loredan, the founder of the Academy of the Unknown, states that the author of *L'Alcibiade* was Antonio Rocco and that he, Loredan, had received the original manuscript of the text in 1650.[5] Antonio Rocco was born in 1586. He studied at Padova, where he was intrigued by Cesare Cremonini's heretical thought. Nonetheless, he became a friar and taught philosophy at the convent of San Giorgio Maggiore in Venice. Throughout the years the Holy Inquisition collected an impressive dossier against Rocco, who was repeatedly accused of being a heretic and a libertine (Spini 163-164). But the Academy of the Unknown, composed of the most affluent members of the Venetian society, could afford to ignore the constant threats of the Catholic Church.

In *L'Alcibiade,* the discourse of/about sodomy is structured as a dialogue between a teacher and his student, and is set in ancient Greece. Filodemo, a renowned Athenian teacher, attempts to convince Alcibiades, his beautiful and young disciple, to let him penetrate him.[6] Although the adolescent allows his mentor to kiss and to caress him, he denies Filodemo his virgin ass. *L'Alcibiade* revolves around this denial; its discourse is triggered by a negation. Indeed, the first pages focus on the teacher's frustrated desire. He cannot sleep, nor eat, nor even teach anymore. His despair is driving him insane; he *must* have Alcibiades's ass. When he cannot sustain his frustration any longer, the master engages his disciple in a dramatic and hopefully conciliatory discussion.

As we will see in detail, in *L'Alcibiade* the discourse of/about sodomy is essentially the discourse of the master. We may say that the sodomite/ master speaks because the other denies him his asshole–that is, the fulfillment of his desire. The other's "hole" is the actual source of the master's discourse. The master speaks in order to "fill" that denied hole. As Lacan would say, the master is in fact an "impostor." The master "is somebody who, upon finding himself at the place of the constitutive lack in the structure, acts as if he holds the reins of that surplus, of the mysterious X which eludes the grasp of the structure" (Zizek, *Enjoy* 103; Lacan, *Le séminaire* 19-27). Although the "hole" that founds his discourse lies in the other, the master pretends to possess/dominate it. The teacher must succeed in convincing his student that he, the master, already "knows the hole," that he already has power over it.

As an impostor, the teacher performs an ironic reversal of the relationship between rhetoric, sodomy, and the Bible. In *L'Alcibiade,* Genesis 19 is an unspoken reference; even the term "Sodom" is absent from the text. As we will see, Rocco does not allow the Bible to articulate its mythic discourse against homosexuality. Being aware of the powerful and destructive force inherent in any myth, the author "silences" the biblical narration. Whereas Genesis 19 alludes to the sin "against nature" without articulating it explicitly, Rocco performs the discourse of Sodom "erasing" its source, the Bible itself.

In *Amore è puro interesse* (Love is Sheer Interest), a discourse delivered to the "Accademia degli Incogniti" (Academy of the Unknown), Rocco had made clear that for him love is nothing but a longing for power. "When one loves," Rocco states, "one loves oneself and not the other" (165). According to Rocco, if love "is nothing but an internal quality, a feeling, a desire, and the effect of the loving soul, he [the lover] longs for his own satisfaction and not for the other's" (Rocco, *Amore* 166). Rocco believes that there are four forms of love: natural love, civic love, lascivious love, and divine love. Each of these alleged kinds of love is nothing but a camouflaged form of selfish cravings. The actual source of each of these "loves" is personal interest. For instance, natural love is that affection that a father has for his son. In fact, Rocco reminds us, a father loves his son as long as the child realizes his father's own expectations. Through his son the father actually aims to become eternal. If the son does not respect his father's desires, the same nurturing father turns into a vengeful enemy (166-167). That civic love is sheer interest is confirmed by history. Indeed, the origin of the Roman Empire lies in a fratricide (168-169).

Rocco justifies lascivious love, the third kind of love, by saying that if to know lust means to be lustful, God Himself would be the most lascivious being:

> My material soul desires palpable food, it does not feed on light or vague opinions; it leaves this food to higher and sublime spirits. However, in order to justify myself, I could say that, if to know lust and vices means to be lustful and depraved, the divinity itself would be the worst intelligence. (170)

Love language itself, Rocco holds, clearly expresses the lover's longing for power over the beloved. "My love," "my treasure," "my soul": all these and other expressions bear out Rocco's theory according to which a lover focuses exclusively on his own needs. To gain power over the beloved, Rocco concludes, lovers manipulate any form of discourse. Love discourse is the discourse of an impostor (174).

In *L'Alcibiade,* Rocco applies this theory to sodomite love. Being the discourse of an impostor, sodomite love is intrinsically ironic–that is, it constantly distances itself from its own saying. Its goal being the fulfillment of a desire for power, sodomite discourse interprets, falsifies, and nullifies any previous discourse. In *L'Alcibiade,* the Bible, history, human anatomy, philology, philosophy, go through a farcical reinterpretation/distortion. Rather than expressing a given ideology, the sodomite master speaks in order to destroy. We may apply Gregory W. Bredbeck's definition of male-male sexual behavior in Renaissance England to the discourse of the master in *L'Alcibiade*:

> [male homosexuality was] the mark of subjective erasure, as a movement from the "rational" world of social subjectivity to the "irrational world" of the *contra naturam* . . . a formulation that turns the sodomite . . . into a sort of freewheeling or sublinguistic subject who exists *despite* the society–and language–around him. (144)

In other words, since the sodomite "exists" outside the social order of "rational" language, he is free to manipulate any possible discourse in order to realize his personal power. In *L'Alcibiade,* the identity of the sodomite master is primarily his ironic, self-contradictory, and seductive discourse.

What genre does this book belong to? It is clearly a parody or a spoof of the Platonic dialogue. *L'Alcibiade,* one might say, is simply a satire.[7] The fake Athenian setting, the wise and well-read sodomite who is in fact a caricature of Socrates, the cute and timid disciple, and their aborted erotic encounters might be the major aspects of a postmodern reading of a traditional and "serious" literary genre. Moreover, at the beginning of *L'Alcibiade,* Rocco inserts a preface and sonnet, both mocking the way masters usually "introduce" their knowledge into their students' minds. As Rocco says, instructors usually impart their knowledge by sticking it, their "knowledge," into their students' assholes. But nowadays, Rocco argues, this "vice" (vizio) has acquired huge proportions. It is not uncommon that these "lascivious" teachers end up breaking their students' asses (37).

The author, himself a sodomite and a teacher, apparently denigrates and supports sodomitical encounters between mentors and disciples. *L'Alcibiade* is both a satire of sodomy in the form of a Platonic dialogue and an actual treatise on sodomy. Assuming irony as stylistic cipher of his work, Rocco, at the same time author and indirectly main character of his book, both hides and reveals himself in his writing. Indeed, as Bruce Smith reminds us, "when we read [a] satire, we take sides with the speaker, who smugly distinguishes *us* from *them*" (162).[8] However, in *L'Alcibiade* the "us" is also the "them." Unlike traditional satirists, Rocco seems to use irony against himself. To write about his sodomitical identity, Rocco cannot help but take up a double standpoint. Sodomy equals irony; a sodomite is himself and the other who denies/derides him. By appropriating the other's slander against sodomitical practice, the sodomite nullifies it. This is the sense of the third "preface" to the text, entitled "The Publisher to the Reader," which states that the actual goal of *L'Alcibiade* is to teach parents how "to protect their kids from their evil and depraved teachers" (38).[9] Is *L'Alcibiade* against its own author?

The narration starts off by describing the amazing beauty of the young Alcibiades. The very first sentence reminds us that Alcibiades was of that age when nature "blurs" (*confonde*) the distinctions between the two sexes. Alcibiades looks like a charming girl (39).[10] According to Rocco, Ganymede himself, when Jupiter fell in love with him, probably resembled more a young woman than a man. On the other hand, Filodemo, Alcibiades's teacher, is the quintessence of masculinity. He combines physical virility with profound wisdom. The most influential families in Athens ask him to let their kids "drink from his limpid source." Thus, the opposition masculine/feminine seems to be clearly stated: Filodemo equals masculinity/knowledge/power; Alcibiades seems to be synonymous with passivity/femininity/ignorance.

However, what makes Alcibiades irresistible is less his feminine aspect than his voice and his eloquence: "With a melodious diction he clearly articulated each word and ended every sentence with such harmonious pauses, that no one could resist the siren-like sweetness of his discourse" (41).

Here Rocco reverses Plutarch's well-known description of Alcibiades, according to which Socrates' young lover actually stuttered.[11] Rocco thus grants Alcibiades both an active and a passive character. Whereas his physical appearance makes him a woman and thus a receptacle of male desire, his voice manifests his strength, his virile being, his power of persuasion.

Contradicting the tradition again, whereas in Plato it is Alcibiades who is desperately in love with his master, in Rocco's text it is Filodemo/Socrates who pursues his disciple. The actual dialogue begins when Filodemo, after fondling, caressing, and kissing the young student, asks Alcibiades why he does not want to stick his tongue in his, the master's, mouth. "The kisses that are not received in the mouth are not signs of a devout friendship . . . the kisser's tongue necessarily wants to enter in the mouth of the kissed one" (43). Playing with the double meaning of "lingua" (tongue/ language), Rocco now presents the masculine pole of the forthcoming relationship/dialogue as the actual "receiver," the passive receptacle of the feminine tongue/discourse. "Here, here, I take it," says the teacher inviting Alcibiades to insert his tongue in his mouth. As Filodemo clearly states, he will not be able to impart his teaching unless Alcibiades's tongue "merges" with his own (44). In order to speak his wisdom, the teacher needs to dominate/master the feminine tongue/eloquence. Although Alcibiades is the kisser, the one who "inserts" his tongue/language in the other's mouth, he actually surrenders his "tongue" to his teacher. The discourse about/of Sodom "takes place" in this blurred region of language, where the subject's eloquence/voice is dominated by/surrenders to the master.

In Rocco's text, "feminine" eloquence precludes sodomy. As we will see later, the master considers women the embodiment of power and oppression. According to Filodemo, political/religious power defends women because through women this power attempts to stifle man's natural attraction for boys.[12] Heterosexual intercourse signifies repression. Whereas the disciple speaks the language of morality and "female" power, the sodomite master reverses the traditional topos that connects masculinity with power, articulating a discourse of "masculine" passivity/oppression. We may say that in *L'Alcibiade* "masculine" discourse equals irony that equals sodomy that equals reversal/imposition of power that equals negation of any discourse.

After talking his student into "giving" him his tongue, the master starts fondling the pupil's back with the clear intention of inserting his erect penis in his asshole. When Alcibiades sees the master's hard-on, he goes off on a long, enraged tirade against his teacher's sordid desire:

I did not know that . . . you had such indecent thoughts. I cannot believe that the gravity you show in your countenance could dare to defile the modesty of honored pupils, who are committed to your trust and are subjugated to your discipline. . . . If you teach us that, who will be able to make up for it? Who will be a good model for the others? . . . Do you do these things to the other students as well? And, if this is the case, what do their parents say about it? (47)

Although Filodemo tries to justify his lust for the student by saying that Alcibiades's "divine appearance" has taken up a "vital form" in his soul, the student rejects this Neoplatonic cliché and vigorously states that the most pious men and the Law itself condemn this "abominable vice against nature" (47-48, 50). Alcibiades concludes his argument with an indirect reference to Sodom: "and they say that the gods chastised with sulphur and bitumen the cities that had committed that sin, in order to destroy and to submerge them forever" (50).

Alcibiades, both feminine subject and object of the other's desire, enunciates the discourse of divine Law, which contradicts the discourse of the master. Filodemo attacks what we called the "feminine discourse of Law" by saying that politicians misinterpret the sacred texts in order to keep sodomy for themselves, since it is the most precious thing on earth. The master believes that his primary duty is "to open" Alcibiades's "mind" to "what is possible, and so doing make [him] able to understand everything" (50-51). We may say that the master attempts to modify the pupil's "gaze" on sodomy. The teacher must teach Alcibiades how to look at sodomy. However, although the master presents his discourse as an act of unveiling the truth, his eloquence actually merges facts with lies, rigorous rationalizations with amusing puns, reality with fiction. As we will see later, whereas Alcibiades articulates the passive/feminine gaze of divine Law, the sodomite master nullifies that very gaze through his "sodomitical rhetoric."

The discourse of the sodomite/master aims to appropriate the power of feminine discourse/Law. However, a crucial difference distinguishes the two discourses. Whereas the allegedly divine discourse presents itself as the embodiment of truth and does not acknowledge its being inevitably an "awry" gaze, sodomitical discourse signifies an act of awareness.[13] The sodomite/impostor manipulates any possible discourse, since he knows that every discourse is intrinsically "perverse." As a consequence, the sodomite subject never identifies with his own saying. The sodomite speaker is aware of the fact that his identity does not coincide with how he says/sees himself. If the sacred texts grant the feminine subject with a "blind" gaze upon his/her self, the master/sodomite's irony says that the subject is never what/where he speaks. Whereas heterosexual drive, meant in its broadest sense, "means" as long as it is part of a "feminine" discourse–that is, it responds to the divine request for procreation–sodomite desire is "empty."[14] Sodomy as a signifier points to/springs from a "hole," and it thus fails to "say" what a sodomite is. The fundamental perversion of sodomy is that its language annihilates the subject that speaks it.[15] Referring to the biblical image of Sodom burnt by divine fire, we may say that sodomy "burns" any image of the self.

Responding to his pupil's remarks, the master points out that the expression "contra naturam" has been misinterpreted. "Cunt being called '*natura*,'" the teacher argues, "asshole has been called '*contra naturam*,' simply because it is on the side opposite cunt" (51).[16] The teacher also stresses that cunt is called "natura" not because ass is "contra naturam," but only because cunt generates man. According to the master, the act of giving birth is usually called "natura." However, Filodemo hastily adds that desire is multifaceted. Man does not look for pleasure only to generate other human beings. Every kind of desire is natural. Making use of an argument that he will contradict later, the master also reminds his pupil that man's desire for a boy is superior to that for a woman because a man and a boy are more similar to each other (51-53). Boys are also more precious than women because their beauty is much more transient. Filodemo is convinced that divine and social laws support heterosexual intercourse exclusively to protect women. In fact, if they were not forced to abide by the laws, men would neglect female company (56).

After attacking the alleged perversity of man's desire for boys, Filodemo tackles the primary argument of his pupil's discourse, his indirect reference to Genesis 19. According to the master, a misinterpretation has caused the hatred against homoerotic desire. Filodemo narrates that Solon, while marching with his army through the Arabic deserts, comes across an immense lake whose water, due to some mysterious but natural cause, has turned into inflammatory bitumen (59).[17] Solon's army is composed primarily of exhausted, and thus quite unattractive, women. Since his few male soldiers seem to prefer boys to these "deformed" women, Solon makes his men believe that the boiling lake of bitumen originally was a prosperous city that had been destroyed by God's wrath because of its partiality for sodomy.

Alcibiades does not buy his teacher's story. He wonders why no Greek or Latin author reports such an important event. Filodemo claims that nobody has ever spoken about it because of fear. To unveil the actual origin of the biblical condemnation of sodomy would have meant to undermine the foundations of all political and/or religious power. Articulating an incredibly modern argument in favor of homosexuality, the master says that Solon actually did not state "those cities" had been burnt because they supported sodomite practices, but because they were inhospitable:

> the author of this invention [Solon] . . . does not say that those cities were submerged because of their natural use of boys, but because they were impious, cruel, stingy, greedy, violent, and what brought about their end was their violence against the angels. (61)[18]

A crucial element of this passage must be noted. As is well known, sodomy has been traditionally considered the "crime not to be named among Christians."[19] Even Genesis 19 *does not tell* sodomy; rather it constructs a narration around a silenced core, a narrative "hole," which seems to deny/transcend language.[20] Although it was a silent/silenced event, sodomy was believed to bring about unnameable calamities and misfortunes, effects of God's outraged revenge (Chiffoleau 290). Venetian governments, for instance, interpreted the recurrent plague that troubled the city in the fifteenth century as a direct result of Venetians' widespread, albeit hidden, practice of sodomy. Contrary to what Foucault states, for the Venetian authorities sodomy was not a "confused category," but a rather clear synonym for anal intercourse between two men (Foucault 101). The plague, Guido Ruggiero reminds us, "proved that the same God and the destructive threats of the Old Testament were real" (Ruggiero 112). In other words, sodomy worked as Lacan's *sinthome,* that kernel of enjoyment that simultaneously attracts and repels us (Ragland, "Relation" 188-191). The plague was that "hole" or "wound" in the *real* which had been opened by the unspoken practice of sodomy. Sodomy, we may say, was/is that unbearable, and thus inexpressible, request for pleasure that *might* cause the destruction of one's self.

In *L'Alcibiade* Rocco practices an ironic reversal of the relationship between language, sodomy, and the Bible. The Venetian friar/sodomite turns Genesis 19 into an unspoken, albeit well-known and negative, reference. Even though at the end of his story about Solon and his homosexual soldiers the teacher briefly alludes to the angels/visitors, Filodemo never mentions the sacred text. In *L'Alcibiade,* even the term "Sodom" is absent. Rocco knows that words are never neutral references to things. He understands that the use of "sodomy" or "Sodom" would contradict his deeply auto-ironic, and thus tremendously powerful, discourse on homosexual desire.

Unlike, for instance, Rocky O'Donovan, Rocco is convinced that the mythical narration of the destruction of Sodom is not something "to reclaim" (O'Donovan 247-248). Unlike Lesbos, the myth of Sodom was created to annihilate those who reflect themselves in that very mythic image. Sodom, as we have already said, is a myth that narrates its own destruction. Although it is true that "Sodom [is] the symbol of what heterosexism and homophobia do to us, like [what] the holocaust has become for the Jewish people," a crucial difference distinguishes Genesis 19 and the holocaust. Whereas the "homosexual holocaust," the physical and emotional violence/abuse that gay people have always been subject to, is constantly activated by a myth that signifies a repressed relation to the *real,* the holocaust is a historical event, something that happened in a given time and a given space. It would be a mistake to confound mythic imagery and actual occurrences, because, whereas even a tragic event like the holocaust in the long run can be "digested" and removed, a myth like Sodom never recedes from its virulent effects.[21]

Rocco "silences" the biblical narration by bringing to the fore its unspoken core, sodomy itself, and by turning the sacred text into an implicit point of reference. Even though he directly attacks Genesis 19 through his ironic interpretation, Rocco does not allow the Bible to speak its condemnation of sodomite practice.[22] Certainly, the master argues, the cities of that "fairy tale" (*favola,* myth) deserved to be burnt because of their violence. But are not the social/religious laws violent themselves, when they prevent human beings from pursuing their free choices? Is it not true that "violence kills the soul in a cruel manner" (61)? Social/religious laws are *contra naturam* if they do not allow two human beings to take pleasure from each other even when both of them desire to be together. You are not violent to your neighbor, if your neighbor appreciates and finds delight in what you do to him/her (62).

If what the master says is true, Alcibiades interjects, why are young boys who respond to men's sexual requests despised and called *bardassa* (young male prostitute; 63)? Prostitutes are only those boys, the teacher points out, who "sell themselves," who have sex with older men exclusively for money. In other words, if pederasty is nothing but the imposition of the power of an older "top" over a much younger and inexperienced "bottom," young prostitutes break this rule because they abandon their bodies to such domination only for money. Money renders any sexual intercourse a parody of itself, because the "top" can never tell whether the "bottom" actually enjoys his getting fucked. Indeed, contradicting the traditional view of Greek homosexuality the master holds that both the older man and the passive boy take pleasure in the act of sodomy. Only if the boy has no interest other than a sheerly sexual one can the "top" be sure that he is succeeding in dominating the young "bottom." "Natural" sex between two men only occurs when one dominates and the other is dominated.[23] Is then sex between two adult men natural or not? The master's answer is peremptory: men who engage in same-sex intercourse are "rebels to love," "feral and corrupt beasts," because "male love" can only be "young" (75). Adult homosexuals are "corrupt beasts" and "rebels" because they question the master's "sodomite rhetoric," that is, their consensual sexual encounters are not based on the exertion of power. In other words, adult homosexuality is "feral" because it does not enact the persuasive power of language. Like "beasts," homosexuals act on their desire without "speaking."[24]

The master feels compelled to explain further why male "young love" is superior to any other form of love. Filodemo lists three major kinds of sexual pleasure: heterosexuality, masturbation, and pederasty. According to the teacher, only the last form of sex is beneficial to man's psychological and physical health. A passionate lover, Filodemo explains, longs to "fill any hole either with his hand, or his tongue," or his member, in order to ejaculate and thus to extinguish the "heat" that is consuming his body (65-66).[25] Filodemo claims that woman's body is notoriously very warm, and therefore unsuitable to man's need. One cannot overcome fire with fire, but rather with "mild" ice. Only boys' sweet "coolness" helps an adult male sedate his passion/heat.

According to the sodomite/master, women are dangerous because they embody masculine/religious/political power. Their body's heat suffocates man's weaker warmth. Moreover, a man's penis enjoys a boy's asshole much better than a vagina (66-67). Whereas during penetration a tight young asshole caresses the male member, giving it undescribable delight, a vagina is too large a hole for the member's pleasure. Finally, even if a man is partial to the vagina, he should be disgusted by its "hot and repulsive excrements," which can be fatal to him (72). In other words, the female body is not a passive receptacle of man's pleasure; woman allures man with her deceitful frailty in order to harm him and dominate him. Woman's body speaks a "masculine" discourse, which is camouflaged in a "feminine" form. Sexual intercourse with a woman is even more harmful from a psychological standpoint:

> A secret conversation with them [women] . . . gives you the negative reputation of being a base, effeminate, slothful, and intemperate man. They [women] wish to dominate over man. Moreover, they want you to abandon any serious activity and to lose yourself. . . . (72)

The intimate company of women simply annihilates man. His freedom, reputation, and existence are jeopardized by women's "masculine" vehemence. Young boys (*putti*), on the other hand, are absolutely harmless. Who could ever complain about them? Whereas woman's passive body exclusively aims to deceive man, boys' gentle forms respond to and interact with man's desire. When a man holds it in his hands, a boy's penis "awakes, shakes, moves, shivers a little, weeps, smiles sweetly. . . . " On the contrary, female breasts are like "swollen blisters, empty bags, hanging sacs" (69). A boy's member signifies that the boy, similar to a "young roebuck," is prey of the other. Whereas woman's body is silent to man's sexual rhetoric, the boy's penis authenticates the sodomite's seductive discourse. In other words, the sodomite/master must arouse the boy in order *to see* the power of his rhetoric. If every sexual practice/discourse aims to establish a power, only in pederasty is the subject/master able to see how his seduction takes place in the other.[26]

The master interprets man's seductive discourse as a signifier whose signified is both the arousal and the defeat of the other. In a heterosexual encounter, however, man can never be sure whether his voice has given birth to a signified. Woman's "masculine" body denies any evidence. Woman's body does not say anything.[27] In a sense, Filodemo argues, female sexuality is similar to masturbation, the third and final form of sex. When he masturbates, man in fact mistakes an image for reality (73-74).[28] Like masturbation, intercourse with a woman raises doubts, uncertainties, fatigue.

Rather than assuaging man's lust, images actually stimulate it more and more. This is why masturbation is a sort of addiction that tires, weakens, and even kills man. Man, Filodemo explains to his pupil, needs to reach the "real object"–that is, a young boy's asshole. According to the teacher, anatomy itself says that the asshole is the primary source of pleasure both for the "giver" and the "receiver." Presenting again woman's sexuality as essentially "masculine" and domineering, Filodemo states that the vagina is nothing but a "penis reversed" (*membro virile riversato,* 83). When they are pregnant, women often stick their vagina/penis in the ass of their fetus, who thus starts enjoying sodomy even inside the womb. As a consequence, after birth the baby longs for that pleasure theretofore received from the mother's "member." Sodomy, the master stresses, is the primary and fundamental form of sexuality. The most lascivious women know very well that anal pleasure is much more intense than vaginal.

The pupil starts showing a certain interest in his mentor's discourse. Alcibiades blushes, as if he somehow recalls that original pleasure he had tasted in his mother's body. Filodemo has one final, decisive argument reserved to destroy his pupil's doubts. For the master, not only is sodomy a natural drive, it is also a highly educational practice. It is scientifically proved, Filodemo holds, that sperm and the brain are made of similar fluids. It is also a fact, the teacher continues, that the sperm which has been spilled in the boy's ass for its intrinsic warmth moves up toward the boy's brain, thus enriching the boy's mental faculties (84-85).

Alcibiades finally smiles at his teacher. Filodemo has convinced him. The student bends to receive the member of his impatient master. Filodemo contemplates the pupil's cheeks for a while, unable to say anything. It is his tongue/language (*lingua*) that first tastes the boy's marvelous asshole:

> Almost passing out for the sudden joy, the lucky master fell when he saw those superb wonders. However, regaining his strength he knelt down and paid them [the boy's cheeks] his first tribute with his tongue which, exhausted by the long talk, . . . eager and anxious longed for a refuge in that place. Here, it [the master's tongue] furiously immersed itself and greedier than a hungry baby when he sucks milk from his mother's breast it [his tongue] licked, sucked, drank, swallowed those sweet liquors of ambrosia. (85-86)

The master's tongue eats the pupil's asshole with ardor, preparing it to be penetrated. Slowly inserting his member in Alcibiades's ass, Filodemo finally fills that hole that had triggered his discourse. The student's ass, Filodemo exclaims in his closing hymn to sodomy, is "paradise on earth, where men can enjoy themselves. . . . This will be the center of my thoughts forever. From it my thoughts will originate. It will be the infallible rule of my deeds, goal and aim of all my hopes and happiness" (86).

Rocco states that all the master's thoughts, all his words, derive from his student's asshole. The other's hole is the language spoken by the master and the direct or indirect topic of any of the master's discourses. On the one hand, the master has finally silenced the other; on the other, it is actually the other, as never fulfilled desire, that speaks through the master. The sodomite master, we might say, is at the same time first signifier and first signified of the other's discourse. Alcibiades, the text says, enjoyed the master's dick so much, that from that moment on he couldn't live without Filodemo's cock up his butt (87).

We must keep in mind the radical ambiguity of Rocco's work. The Athenian teacher begins speaking when he perceives the other's denial. However, by distorting/misinterpreting the Bible, anatomy, and history the teacher has awakened the other's desire. The master needs the other's desire to fulfill his own. The "masculine" power of divine Law, which the sodomite sees embodied in the woman, in fact rules over the master. The sodomite is the first signifier of the woman/religious power.

The discourse of Sodom, we may conclude, speaks against itself. Sodom, as we have seen, is a myth/rhetoric which enacts its own destruction. Sodom cannot be defended or "reclaimed," because it signifies against whoever speaks it. The sodomite master fulfills his lust, but he actually becomes prey of the other. The power of the "woman" has imposed itself once again.

L'Alcibiade concludes with a promise. We, the readers, will soon know the rest of the story. A second book will soon come out concerning the lascivious encounters between the master and his pupil. We will hear from the student how he loves to be fucked by his teacher. In fact, Rocco never wrote this book. Once sodomite desire for power is fulfilled, no discourse can subsist. The Bible and sodomy thus share a very similar goal: the oppression/annihilation of the other by means of a silenced/silencing saying.

NOTES

1. This is how Laura Coci defines *L'Alcibiade fanciullo a scola* in the introduction to her recent edition of the text (8). See also the accurate and interesting introduction by Louis Godbout to his French translation (117-122).

2. The most comprehensive study of libertinism in seventeenth-century Italy is Spini's *Ricerca dei libertini*. Although Spini's book is crucial for any study of Italian libertinism, it has a rather moralistic and overcritical attitude toward the works of the Italian libertines.

3. See Spini 149-176.

4. As Spini reminds us (15-25), the fundamental elements of libertine thought are present in European culture since the Middle Ages. Deriving in part from a heterodox interpretation of Aristotle's texts, libertine "philosophy" sees any religion as a historical, and thus transient, manifestation of nature, which is the only and true god. Historical religions, Catholicism included, are invented and used by political power as a form of repression. In fact, being part of nature, human being is mortal. For a libertine, to be religious means to respond to one's instincts, because any instinct is natural.

5. However, this manuscript went lost and only two similar editions have survived in less than ten copies. *L'Alcibiade* was translated into French for the first time by Jules Gay in 1866.

6. The description of Alcibiades's physical aspect follows the cliché of Neoplatonic Renaissance literature. The young boy is slim, elegant, the embodiment of youth (see Ariès 67).

7. Bredbeck underscores how in the English Renaissance sodomy was frequently treated as a farce/satire: "The prevalence of homoerotic allusions within Renaissance satires is easily documented" (34). Bredbeck interprets homoerotic satires as "part of a larger strategy of social exclusion" (35). He analyzes specific

texts by Brathwait, Marston, and Middleton. Particularly interesting is Bredbeck's study of Renaissance writings about Edward II (48-77).

8. Bruce Smith examines how Latin satirists, such as Horace, Juvenal, and Martial influenced English satire against sodomites (161-167). For a similar use of satire in Italian Renaissance, see Giovanni Dall'Orto 54-59. Among other texts, including Michelangelo's famous homoerotic poems, Dall'Orto examines how the sonnets written by Benedetto Varchi for his young pupil were satirized by his contemporaries.

9. Rocco, *L'Alcibiade* 38. As Bruce Smith reminds us, during the Renaissance "homosexual activity . . . like illicit sexual activity of all sorts, usually involved a person in a superior position of power exercising his social prerogative over a person in an inferior position" (193). See also Bray 33-57. Ruggiero draws similar conclusions about the situation in fifteenth-century Venice. The Venetian government was particularly suspicious of schools where sodomite teachers were supposed to abound (138-139).

10. For the concept of androgyny in the Renaissance, see Jonathan Goldberg, *Sodometries* 114-115.

11. See Rocco, *Alcibiade* 110.

12. Again, in *L'Alcibiade* the discourse of the master is never totally false. It is a fact that, as Judith Butler writes, "the feminine survives as the *inscriptional space* of . . . phallogocentrism, the specular surface which receives the marks of a masculine signifying act only to give back a (false) reflection and guarantee of phallogocentric self-sufficiency" (39). In other words, female "power," as the master defines it, is nothing but woman's reflection of a masculine inscription. However, in order to pursue his argument the master does not see that that "power" women allegedly possess is only the "masculine" mark on them. Using the master's terminology, we might say that "politicians" impose on femininity the mark of their domination.

13. See Zizek, *Looking Awry*: "if we look at a thing straight on, i.e., matter-of-factly, disinterestedly, objectively, we see nothing but a formless spot; the object assumes clear and distinctive features only if we look at it 'at an angle,' i.e., with an 'interested' view, supported, permeated, and 'distorted' by *desire*" (11-12).

14. See Ellie Ragland-Sullivan, "The Sexual Masquerade": "the ego is . . . a fiction complicitous with its own deceptions. In this sense the ego might be called the site of ideology in the sense that ideology is narcissistic" (71).

15. In *Sodometries* Goldberg reminds us that seventeenth-century English critics of Marlowe's *Edward II* underscored that a sodomite was "a being beyond any ontological category; to be a sodomite mean[t] to be damned, a being without being" (121-122). Compare Bruce Smith: "Against homosexual acts . . . the Renaissance satirists's ultimate argument was its vacuousness. To act on homosexual desire was to give up one's social and even one's psychological identity" (185). Edelman articulates this point with uncommon clarity. Referring to Genesis 19, "the text that constitutes our cultural Constitution far more than any legal document of state," Edelmann holds that "the gay male anus [is] the site of pleasure

[that] gives birth to AIDS as a figuration of death . . . the nihilism of the anus thus threatens to annihilate all creation" (99).

16. Other Renaissance texts follow the same argument. See the "ninth question" in *La cazzaria* by Antonio Vignale (Rocco, *Alcibiade* 111).

17. The primary source of this passage is Plutarch (I 6); Rocco, *L'Alcibiade* 19.

18. See Goss: "Genesis 19 . . . is the story of a phallic violence and aggression against two sojourners or messengers from God. . . . Ancient societies frequently subjected strangers, the conquered, or trespassers to phallic anal penetration as an indication of their subordinate status" (91-92). Comstock has a quite different approach to the biblical texts: "During the past ten or twenty years many lesbian/ gay Christians have attempted to reexamine and reread those passages that have traditionally been offered up as evidence that the Bible condemns us. We have questioned traditional interpretations, identified the heterosexism of biblical scholars, and searched for positive links between us and the Bible. . . . We have argued that the sin of Sodom was not homosexuality, but rather inhospitality or gang rape. . . . [In] the interest of convincing ourselves and the church that the Bible does not condemn us, we have brought our own bias to our reading of it. . . . I would suggest that our approach to the Bible become less apologetic and more critical–that we approach it not as an authority from which we want approval, but as a document whose shortcomings must be cited" (38-39).

19. Goldberg, *Reclaiming Sodom* 5.

20. As another example of Sodom's silenced/silent discourse see Alan Smith 84-106. Smith examines the poetry of the fifteenth-century Italian poet Domenico di Giovanni, commonly called Burchiello. Smith focuses on Burchiello's "non-sense" poetry and convincingly proves that in Burchiello's sonnets the obscure metaphors, expressions, and words have a hidden meaning which often refers to the practice of sodomy. Burchiello speaks of sodomy hiding it under convoluted figures of speech. Sodomy cannot be told.

21. Compare Edelman 93-117. In his seminal text Edelman questions the various forms of discourses on AIDS. My essay has been inspired in particular by what Edelman says concerning the "Rhetoric of Activism."

22. For instance, *L'Alcibiade* contains no reference to Leviticus 18:22 and 20:13: "You shall not lie with a male as with a woman; it is abomination. If a man lies with a male as with a woman, both of them have committed an abomination; they shall be put to death; their blood is upon them." For an interesting discussion of these passages, see Martin Samuel Cohen 4. Although Leviticus 18:22 defines homosexuality as "abominable behavior," Cohen believes that that does not mean unnatural: "the Torah is tacitly admitting that homosexual intercourse is something which some people would, under normal circumstances, find attractive . . . [but it] divide[s] the world down into two realms, one like God (i.e., the clean, the pure, the unleavened, the sabbatical) and one antithetical to God" (7). See also Schmidt 32-33. Although Schmidt's book is openly homophobic, it contains a clear interpretation of the above biblical passages concerning homosexuality.

23. In "Is the Rectum a Grave?" Bersani holds that "women and gay men spread their legs with an unquenchable appetite for destruction" (251). Being

penetrated essentially responds to the subject's desire for annihilation. "Male homosexuality advertises the risk of the sexual itself as the risk of self-dismissal, of *losing sight* of the self" (262). See also Bersani, "The Gay Outlaw" 5-18.

24. It is interesting to notice that in *Three Essays on the Theory Of Sexuality* Freud himself connected homosexuality to "savage and primitive people." See Fuss 159.

25. In this passage Rocco borrows Galenus's theory on human anatomy. See Galenus, *De semine libri duo* in *Galeni librorum prima classis* (Venice, 1609), 328v-340v; Galenus, *De locis affectis libri sex* in *Galeni librorum quarta classis* (Venice, 1609), 2r-42v; Rocco, *L'Alcibiade* 30-31.

26. In *L'Alcibiade* the master must identify with his student in order to perceive the student's pleasure and thus also his own. "Identification," Diana Fuss reminds us, "is the psychical mechanism that produces self-recognition. Identification inhabits, organizes, instantiates identity" (2).

27. As is well known, Lacan has written extensively on this subject. See Lacan, "God and the *Jouissance* of the Woman. A Love Letter."

28. As Bennett and Rosario remind us (3), "[t]he Roman Catholic condemnation of the mortal sin of 'pollution' or *mollities* (softness or effeminacy) was elaborated in the Middle Ages. Self-pollution was considered a 'sin against nature' and its biblical condemnation was traced back to God's condemnation of Onan for having spilt his seed on the ground rather than conceiving an heir by his widowed sister-in-law Tamar as Levirate law demanded (Genesis 38:7-10)." It is interesting to note that in the Middle Ages "*mollities*" "was a common term for effeminacy, sodomy, and voluntary pollution" (15).

WORKS CITED

Ariès, Philippe. "Thoughts on the History of Homosexuality." *Western Spirituality: Practice and Precept in Past and Present Time.* Ed. P. Ariès and A. Béjin. Oxford: Basil Blackwell, 1985. 60-84.

Bennett, P., and Rosario II, V. A. *Solitary Pleasures: The Historical, Literary, and Artistic Discourses of Autoeroticism.* New York: Routledge, 1995.

Bersani, Leo. "Is the Rectum a Grave?" *Reclaiming Sodom.* Ed. Jonathan Goldberg. New York: Routledge, 1994. 249-264.

――――. "The Gay Outlaw." *Diacritics* 24, 2-3 (1994): 5-18.

Bray, Alan. *Homosexuality in Renaissance England.* London: Gay Men's P, 1982.

Bredbeck, Gregory W. *Sodomy and Interpretation. Marlowe to Milton.* Ithaca: Cornell UP, 1991.

Butler, Judith. *Bodies That Matter: On the Discursive Limits of Sex.* New York: Routledge, 1993.

Chiffoleau, Jacques. "Dire l'indicible: Rémarques sur la categorie du *nefandum* du XIIe au XVe siècles." *Annales* 45 (1990): 289-384.

Cohen, Martin Samuel. "The Biblical Prohibition of Homosexual Intercourse." *J of Homosexuality* 19.4 (1990): 3-14.

Comstock, David Gary. *Gay Theology Without Apology.* Cleveland: Pilgrim P, 1993.

Dall'Orto, Giovanni. "'Socratic Love' as a Disguise for Same-Sex Love in the Italian Renaissance." *J of Homosexuality* 16.1-2 (1988): 38-59.

Edelman, Lee. *Homographesis: Essays in Gay Literary and Cultural Theory.* New York: Routledge, 1994.

Foucault, Michel. *History of Sexuality: An Introduction.* Trans. Robert Hurley. New York: Pantheon Books, 1978.

Freud, Sigmund. "Three Essays on the Theory of Sexuality" 1905. *Standard Edition of the Complete Psychological Works of Sigmund Freud.* Oxford: The Hogarth P, 1953-64. 7:135-243.

Fuss, Diana. *Identification Papers.* New York: Routledge, 1995.

Goldberg, Jonathan. *Sodometries.* Stanford: Stanford UP, 1992.

_____. "Introduction." *Reclaiming Sodom.* Ed. Jonathan Goldberg. New York: Routledge, 1994. 2-25.

Goss, Robert. *Jesus Acted Up: A Gay and Lesbian Manifesto.* New York: Harper-SanFrancisco, 1993.

Lacan, Jacques. *Le séminaire. Livre XX. Encore.* Paris: Seuil, 1975.

_____. "God and the *Jouissance* of the Woman: A Love Letter." *Feminine Sexuality: Jacques Lacan and the école freudienne.* Ed. Juliet Mitchell and Jacqueline Rose. New York: Norton, 1985. 137-148.

Neri, Achille. "Intorno a due libri curiosi del sec. XVII." *Giornale storico della letteratura italiana* 12 (1888): 219.

O'Donovan, Rocky. "Reclaiming Sodom." *Reclaiming Sodom.* Ed. Jonathan Goldberg. New York: Routledge, 1994. 247-248.

Plutarco. *La vita di Solone.* Ed. M. Manfredini. Milan: Mondadori, 1977.

Ragland-Sullivan, Ellie. "The Sexual Masquerade." *Lacan and the Subject of Language.* Ed. E. Ragland-Sullivan and Mark Bracher. New York: Routledge, 1991. 49-80.

_____. "The Relation Between the Voice and the Gaze." *Reading Seminar XI. Lacan's Four Fundamental Concepts of Psychoanalysis.* Ed. Richard Feldstein, Bruce Fink, and Maire Jaanus. New York: State U of New York P, 1995. 187-204.

Rocco, Antonio. *L'Alcibiade fanciullo a scola.* Ed. Laura Coci. Rome: Salerno, 1988.

_____. *Alcibiade enfant à l'école.* Trans. Louis Godbout. Montréal: Les Editions Balzac, 1995.

_____. "Amore è un puro interesse." *Discorsi dell'Accademia degli Incogniti.* Venice: Sarzina, 1635. 164-177.

Ruggiero, Guido. *Boundaries of Eros: Sex Crime and Sexuality in Renaissance Venice.* Oxford: Oxford UP, 1985.

Schmidt, Thomas. *Straight and Narrow? Compassion and Clarity in the Homosexual Debate.* Downer Grove, IL: InterVarsity P, 1995.

Smith, Alan. "Fraudomy: Reading Sexuality and Politics in Burchiello." *Queering the Renaissance.* Ed. Jonathan Goldberg. Durham: Duke UP, 1994. 84-106.

Smith, Bruce R. *Homosexual Desire in Shakespeare's England.* Chicago: U of Chicago P, 1991.

Spini, Giorgio. *Ricerca dei libertini. La teoria dell'impostura delle religioni nel seicento italiano.* Turin: La Nuova Italia, 1983.

Zizek, Slavoj. *Looking Awry: An Introduction to Jacques Lacan Through Popular Culture.* Cambridge: MIT P, 1991.

_____ . *Enjoy Your Symptom! Jacques Lacan in Hollywood and Out.* New York: Routledge, 1992.

The (Homo)Sexual Temptation
in Milton's *Paradise Regained*

Claude J. Summers, PhD

University of Michigan-Dearborn

SUMMARY. While the sexual temptation of *Paradise Regained* is tactful, it is also characteristically Miltonic in its daring. Despite its decorous presentation, the temptation is exceedingly bold in that it is not merely a heterosexual temptation but a homosexual one as well. Acknowledgment of the homosexual lure in the brief epic is essential to understanding the dynamics of the celebrated banquet scene and to appreciating the comprehensiveness of Milton's trial of the Son's humanity. Such a recognition also helps place in perspective the alleged misogyny of *Paradise Regained,* even as it also reveals the complexity of Milton's poetic technique, particularly his ability to work by indirection and implication and to exploit classical and biblical sources. Although Jesus rejects the homosexual temptation (as He does the heterosexual one), He does not condemn homosexuality. Milton's incorporation of a homosexual temptation provides evidence of his sophisticated recognition of the range of fully human sexual responses. *[Article copies available for a fee from The Haworth Document Delivery Service: 1-800-342-9678. E-mail address: getinfo@haworth. com]*

Claude J. Summers is the William E. Stirton Professor in the Humanities and Professor of English at the University of Michigan-Dearborn. Among his books are *Gay Fictions: Wilde to Stonewall; Homosexuality in Renaissance and Enlightenment England: Literary Representations in Historical Context;* and *The Gay and Lesbian Literary Heritage.*

Correspondence may be addressed: Department of Humanities, University of Michigan-Dearborn, Dearborn, MI 48128-1491; or by e-mail: csummers@umich.edu.

[Haworth co-indexing entry note]: "The (Homo)Sexual Temptation in Milton's *Paradise Regained.*" Summers, Claude J. Co-published simultaneously in *Journal of Homosexuality* (The Haworth Press, Inc.) Vol. 33, No. 3/4, 1997, pp. 45-69; and: *Reclaiming the Sacred: The Bible in Gay and Lesbian Culture* (ed: Raymond-Jean Frontain) Harrington Park Press, an imprint of The Haworth Press, Inc., 1997, pp. 45-69. Single or multiple copies of this article are available for a fee from The Haworth Document Delivery Service [1-800-342-9678, 9:00 a.m. - 5:00 p.m. (EST). E-mail address: getinfo@haworth.com].

45

The sexual temptation in *Paradise Regained* is introduced with great tact. Indeed, so decorously does Milton include it within the larger lure *voluptaria* that many readers have failed to note its existence, and even those who have recognized its presence have failed to explore fully its implications.[1] Milton's discretion is understandable. Despite a rich body of religious verse that incorporates the conventions of secular love poetry, a tradition of mysticism that readily adopts the language of sexual desire, and the persistent allegorization of heavenly love in terms of earthly love, Christianity has been so dominated by the antisexual sentiments of Paul and of many Church fathers as to make almost any explicit, nonallegorical representation of Jesus as a sexual being potentially heretical and blasphemous. This reluctance to associate the historical Jesus with sexual impulses continues even into our own secular age, as witnessed, for example, by the hostility directed against the film *The Last Temptation of Christ* and by the 1977 prosecution of the British newspaper *Gay News* for blasphemy for publishing a poem that uses homosexual imagery to *praise* Christ.[2] Clearly, any depiction of a sexual temptation of the Messiah is rife with dangers of sensationalism and with the potential for blasphemy.

But however greatly Milton may have felt the need for delicacy of expression, the sexual temptation is essential to *Paradise Regained*. For the very reason that made it so problematic–the Christian tradition's emphasis on sexual morality and its idealization of virginity–Milton could hardly have avoided or evaded a sexual temptation in a brief epic that explores the mystery of the Incarnation by dramatizing the temptations faced by a Messiah who, in the words of Hebrews 4:15, was "touched with the feeling of our infirmities . . . was in all points tempted like as we are, yet without sin." Assuming the doctrine of *kenosis,* as derived from Philippians 2:5-8–

> Let this mind be in you, which was also in Christ Jesus: Who, being in the form of God, thought it not robbery to be equal with God: But made himself of no reputation, and took upon him the form of a servant, and was made in the likeness of men: And being found in fashion as a man, he humbled himself, and became obedient unto death, even the death of the cross

–Milton presents Jesus as emptied of his divinity. He is a "perfect Man" who is confronted by (and triumphs over) the common temptations of mankind and thereby earns salvation for humanity. In a poem that is structured around the "triple equation" of the flesh, the world, and the devil; that in effect charts Jesus' initiation rite; and that is itself a contribution to Renaissance art's participation in the *humanation* of God, it would

have been inconceivable for Milton not to have included a sexual temptation.[3]

My purpose in this essay is to argue that while the sexual temptation of
Paradise Regained is tactful, it is also characteristically Miltonic in its
daring. Despite its decorous presentation, the temptation is exceedingly
bold in that it is unsanctioned by specific biblical authority; is (unlike
some contemporaneous analogues, including Fletcher's *Christ's Victory
and Triumph*) realistic rather than allegorical; and, most strikingly of all, is
not merely a heterosexual temptation but a homosexual one as well. The
homosexual temptation is proffered subtly and obliquely but is nonetheless significant for that. In exploring the (homo)sexual temptation of *Paradise Regained,* I hope to illuminate Milton's subtle poetic technique, particularly his penchant for meaningful allusion and concealed premises,
while casting new light on the poem, including its alleged misogyny.
Acknowledgment of the homosexual lure of the brief epic is essential to
understanding the dynamics of the celebrated banquet scene and to appreciating the comprehensiveness of Milton's trial of the Son's humanity. My
procedure is, first, to examine the infernal consult in which the sexual
temptation is broached and the banquet scene in which it is executed; then
to explore the means by which Milton incorporates a homosexual counterplot and to consider its consequences for the poem; and, finally, to place
the homosexual temptation of *Paradise Regained* within the context of
Milton's other references to homosexuality.

The first observation to be made about the sexual temptation of *Paradise Regained* is that it is introduced indirectly and apparently only to be
rejected. After Satan's initial failure to tempt Jesus to turn stones into
bread–a temptation actually for the Messiah to mistrust his faith in his
divine origins–Satan confers with his fellow rebellious angels in the
poem's second infernal consult. He has, he reports, discovered this second
Adam to be a far greater challenge than the original one:

> I, as I undertook, and with the vote
> Consenting in full frequence was impowr'd,
> Have found him, view'd him, tasted him, but find
> Far other labour to be undergon
> Then when I dealt with *Adam* first of Men,
> Though *Adam* by his Wives allurement fell,
> However to this Man inferior far,
> If he be Man by Mothers side at least,
> With more then humane gifts from Heaven adorn'd,
> Perfections absolute, Graces divine,
> And amplitude of mind to greatest Deeds.

> Therefore I am return'd, lest confidence
> Of my success with *Eve* in Paradise
> Deceive ye to perswasion over-sure
> Of like succeeding here: I summon all
> Rather to be in readiness, with hand
> Or counsel to assist; lest I who erst
> Thought none my equal, now be over-match'd. (2.129-146)

This speech is notable both for Satan's political anxiety, as he pointedly establishes his confrontation with Jesus as fully authorized by the congregation of fallen angels, and for his uncharacteristic humility, as he openly pleads for help from his colleagues. Significant, too, is Satan's frank acknowledgment of the sexual element in Adam's fall "by his Wives allurement." Moreover, while he intimates that the temptation of the Son will demand some greater or further enticement than the one that proved so successful in Eden, Satan also sees it as basically analogous to the original temptation, which involved uxoriousness as a central element. Although Satan recognizes Jesus as a serious challenge to his preeminence, he by no means despairs of success.

Taking seriously his leader's request for help, Belial, the "dissolutest" and "sensuallest" of the fallen angels, forthrightly proposes a rather crude sexual temptation, one consonant with his description in *Paradise Lost* as the least of the rebel crew, "then whom a Spirit more lewd / Fell not from Heaven, or more gross to love / Vice for itself" (1.490-492):

> Set women in his eye and in his walk,
> Among daughters of men the fairest found;
> Many are in each Region passing fair
> As the noon Skie; more like to Goddesses
> Expert in amorous Arts, enchanting tongues
> Perswasive, Virgin majesty with mild
> And sweet allay'd, yet terrible to approach,
> Skill'd to retire, and in retiring draw
> Hearts after them tangl'd in Amorous Nets. (2.153-162)

For Belial, the lure of women is a highly promising solution to the fallen angels' dilemma. So great, he believes, is the seductive power of women and so universally susceptible are men to their charms that a sexual enticement by beautiful women is certain to be effective:

> Such object hath the power to soft'n and tame
> Severest temper, smooth the rugged'st brow,

Enerve, and with voluptuous hope dissolve,
Draw out with credulous desire, and lead
At will the manliest, resolutest brest,
As the Magnetic hardest Iron draws. (2.163-168)

Belial's faith in the charms of women is based on long experience. After all,
as he points out, when nothing else worked, women "beguil'd the heart / Of
wisest *Solomon*" (2.169-170).

Satan, however, peremptorily rejects Belial's proposal on the grounds
that it is simplistic and unworthy of his great opponent. Recognizing that
the plan is deeply revealing of the proposer's character, Satan rebukes
Belial for weighing everyone in his own uneven scale, ironically a tendency to which he himself inclines:

          because of old
Thou thy self doat'st on womankind, admiring
Thir shape, thir colour, and attractive grace,
None are, thou think'st, but taken with such toys.
(2.174-177)

Inasmuch as Belial and the sons of Belial are particularly associated with
homosexuality in Judges 19ff. and in *Paradise Lost* 1.500-505, he is
clearly not unaware of an alternative to the lure of women, yet he offers no
such possibility. Satan, on the other hand, specifically points out that not
all men are susceptible to the attractions of women. He reminds his subordinate that the pastoral and courtly scenes of classical seductions attributed
to Belial and his "lusty Crew" of mythological figures "Delight not all"
(2.178, 191).

By posing a rhetorical question, Satan disputes Belial's naive assumption that men are universally attracted to feminine beauty:

          among the Sons of Men,
How many have with a smile made small account
Of beauty and her lures, easily scorn'd
All her assaults, on worthier things intent? (2.191-195)

He specifically cites Alexander the Great and Scipio Africanus (the younger) as examples of mortal men who were impervious to the blandish-
ments of female charms:

Remember that *Pellean* Conquerour,
A youth, how all the Beauties of the East,

> He slightly view'd, and slightly over-pass'd;
> How he sirnam'd of *Africa* dismiss'd
> In his prime youth the fair *Iberian* maid. (2.196-200)

He reminds Belial and the other fallen angels that Jesus is wiser than Solomon and not likely to fall prey to superficial beauty, which "stands / In the admiration only of weak minds / Led captive" (2.220-222).

Ostensibly regarding an erotic temptation as beneath the dignity of the Son, Satan concludes that he must be tested with "manlier objects":

> Therefore with manlier objects we must try
> His constancy, with such as have more shew
> Of worth, of honour, glory, and popular praise;
> Rocks whereon greatest men have oftest wreck'd;
> Or that which only seems to satisfie
> Lawful desires of Nature, not beyond. (2.225-230)

Thus, the sexual temptation is apparently present in *Paradise Regained* only by virtue of its rejection. By including a sexual temptation in his poem only in the guise of denying one, Milton seems to be adopting the rhetorical figures of *apophasis* and *praeteritio,* in which one makes an assertion while pretending to suppress it, much as a politician might call a press conference to announce that he or she will not use scurrilous gossip about an opponent in an election campaign.

The sexual temptation of *Paradise Regained* consists not merely of Belial's repudiated proposal, however. Despite Satan's putative rejection of Belial's plan, the archtempter actually incorporates a thinly disguised erotic temptation into the banquet scene that follows. Echoing Comus's argument in the *Masque,* Satan presents–allegedly as Nature's homage to her Lord–a splendid repast. In the narrator's description, the banquet is remarkable for its exquisite delicacy and luxury:

> Our Saviour lifting up his eyes beheld
> In ample space under the broadest shade
> A Table richly spred, in regal mode,
> With dishes pil'd, and meats of noblest sort
> And savour, Beasts of chase, or Fowl or game,
> In pastry built, or from the spit, or boyl'd,
> Gris-amber-steam'd; all Fish from Sea or Shore,
> Freshet, or purling Brook, of shell or fin,
> And exquisitest name, for which was drain'd
> *Pontus* and *Lucrine* Bay, and *Afric* Coast. (2.338-347)

The banquet's conflation of the appeals to the related but separate bodily and sexual appetites is made apparent in the narrator's remark, "Alas how simple, to these Cates compar'd, / Was that crude Apple that diverted *Eve!*" (2.348-349). This comparison, Barbara Lewalski remarks, "suggests that the banquet is to be seen at one level as a magnification of the sensual appeal of the apple" in *Paradise Lost* (225). As in both *Paradise Lost* and the *Masque,* so here too the test of temperance is figured forth as a temptation to gluttony, in which the excess of food symbolizes sexual excesses as well. As John Shawcross explains, "The interrelationships between sex and eating can be evidenced by natural observation and thus their mutuality is recognized by myth and religion, not only by Freud" (*"Paradise Regain'd"* 53). Moreover, as Edward Le Comte points out, in numerous Renaissance poems, including works by Tasso and Marino that Milton undoubtedly knew, banquets serve as a prelude to sex (105), as they also do in several classical poems that Milton also surely knew.

Most pointedly, however, the interrelationship of sex and food in the banquet scene depends not merely on symbolic association or literary analogues. The banquet is made obviously and specifically sexual in the description of the servers, who are compared to mythological and romance figures noted for their sexual allurement:

> And at a stately side-board by the wine
> That fragrant smell diffus'd, in order stood
> Tall stripling youths rich clad, of fairer hew
> Then *Ganymed* or *Hylas,* distant more
> Under the Trees now trip'd, now solemn stood
> Nymphs of *Diana's* train, and *Naiades*
> With fruits and flowers from *Amalthea's* horn,
> And Ladies of th' *Hesperides,* that seem'd
> Fairer then feign'd of old, or fabl'd since
> Of Fairy Damsels met in Forest wide
> By Knights of *Logres,* or of *Lyones,*
> *Lancelot* or *Pelleas*, or *Pellenore,*
> And all the while Harmonious Airs were heard
> Of chiming strings, or charming pipes and winds
> Of gentlest gale *Arabian* odors fann'd
> From their soft wings, and *Flora's* earliest smells.
> (2.350-365)

The sensual ambiance and seductive intent of this *tableau vivant* are obvious. What Satan has done is to disguise, modify, and refine the sexual temptation suggested by Belial and incorporate it into the banquet scene.

More to the point, Milton has included the erotic temptation as part of a deliberate strategy, not as the result of inadvertence or of having forgotten Satan's earlier speech, as William Riley Parker somewhat lamely speculated (2:1141).

To understand Satan's machinations here it is necessary to place his actions in the infernal consult in context. Satan's apparent rejection but actual adaptation of Belial's suggestion is a predictable consequence of his intensely competitive nature and acute political self-consciousness. He may indeed recognize Jesus' superiority to Adam and he probably does realize that the temptation of the Messiah will be far more challenging than the seduction of Adam and Eve, but Satan's primary motivation in the infernal consult is political rather than tactical. His purpose in the consult is not to seek advice from his followers, but to underline the difficulties of the task that he has undertaken and thereby both add luster to his heroic endeavor and prepare an excuse should he fail. His request for aid is merely a gesture to emphasize the greatness of the difficulty that he faces and to solidify his own position as leader of the infernal crew. Just as Satan calls the great consult in *Paradise Lost* to ratify a plan on which he has already decided, so here too the consultation is largely a pro forma exercise. And just as in *Paradise Lost* Satan is careful not to permit any of his confederates (and potential rivals) to share in his enterprise or even to volunteer to accompany him on his necessarily solitary journey, thereby "winning cheap the high repute / Which he through hazard huge must earn" (*PL* 2.472-3), so here too he is careful not to allow Belial any credit for suggesting the sexual temptation. Thus, he rebukes the subordinate for proposing a plan similar to one that he has either already decided upon or that he quickly adapts in a form sufficiently different as to incur no obvious indebtedness. In fact, the association of the "sons of Belial" with homosexuality may well inspire the actual temptation.[4] Despite Satan's apparently unequivocal rejection of Belial's original plan, the banquet scene subsumes the erotic temptation, though in a disguised and altered form.

The actual temptation is, to be sure, considerably different from the blatant one proposed by Belial. Whereas Belial would have Jesus accosted by accomplished courtesans, Satan more subtly includes the sexual lure within a broader appeal to bodily appetite, as indeed part of a temptation that seems only to "satisfie / Lawful desires of Nature, not beyond" (2.229-30). The banquet materializes soon after the Son first becomes aware of physical hunger, "which declares, / Nature hath need of what she asks" (2.252-253), and soon after he dreams "as appetite is wont to dream / Of meats and drinks, Natures refreshment sweet" (2.264-265). Occurring in a pastoral landscape that suggests natural innocence—"a woody Scene, / Natures own work it seem'd (Nature taught Art)" (2.294-295)–the banquet is offered as Nature's own gift. Falsely claiming that the banquet includes no "Meats by the law unclean . . . Nor proffered by an Enemy" (2.327, 330), Satan represents the lavish table as merely a "sweet restorative delight" (2.373), designed only to assuage natural appetite. But for all its ostensible naturalness and innocence, the sumptuous banquet is actually analogous to those offered to the Israelites in the Wilderness by the false prophet Balaam, who enticed them to "eat things sacrificed unto idols, and to commit fornication" (Rev. 2:14). The presence of the beautiful women, Lewalski points out, recalls "the Moabite women who enticed the Israelites to feasting and whoredom as a prelude to idolatry" (202). Recognizing the banquet as the devil's table, Jesus sees through Satan's pretense to innocence. He asks, "with my hunger what hast thou to do?" (2.389). And he rejects both the excess and the concupiscence represented by the banquet: "Thy pompous Delicacies I contemn, / And count thy specious gifts no gifts but guiles" (2.390-91). In rejecting the banquet, Jesus rejects a temptation to idolatry and to gluttony, both of which encompass sexual excess.

But Satan's erotic lure differs from Belial's proposed temptation not only in its greater subtlety and richer symbolic import, but also, and most significantly, in the fact that it includes beautiful males as well as the Circean romance heroines.[5] Satan's recognition that not all men are susceptible to the charms of women has as an unstated corollary the premise that some men are susceptible only (or primarily) to the attractions of their own sex. Hence, the presence of "Tall stripling youths rich clad, of fairer hew / Then *Ganymed* or *Hylas*." Ganymede, the beautiful Trojan boy abducted by Jupiter and made cupbearer to the gods, and Hylas, the young companion beloved of Hercules, were in the Renaissance not only archetypes of male adolescent beauty but also bywords for male homosexuality, or more specifically, for pederasty, the love of an older man for a youth.

The centrality of Ganymede and Hylas to Renaissance conceptions of homosexuality is indisputable. As James Saslow observes, the myth of Ganymede

> played a particularly important role throughout the Middle Ages and the Renaissance as an embodiment of homosexuality. The recurring Latin term *catamitus* is supposed to have resulted from a corruption of his name, and to medieval writers the word *ganymede* meant the same thing: a boy used for sexual pleasure. Although occurrences of the term declined in the Quattrocento, its sexual meaning was never

lost; *ganymede* reappeared in the sixteenth and seventeenth centuries as a synonym for male concubine. (29)[6]

The homosexual relationship of Jupiter and Ganymede is explicit, for example, in the opening scene of Marlowe's *Dido, Queen of Carthage* (lines 1-121). Hylas was similarly adduced as a symbol of male homosexuality, particularly of the power of a male youth to conquer amorously an adult male, as illustrated succinctly in Angelo Polizano's verse drama *Orfeo* (1480): "To this holy love [of homosexuality] did Hercules concede, / He who felled giants till Hylas made him fall" (qtd. in and trans. by Saslow 31). In Canto X of Book IV of the *Faerie Queene,* Spenser ensconces "great *Hercules,* and *Hylas* deare" among the lovers "lincked in true harts consent" in the garden of the Temple of Venus (xxvii.1 and xxvi.5), while in Canto XII of Book III both Hylas (that "daintie lad") and Ganymede (that "ympe of Troy") are cited as beautiful love objects of Hercules and Jove, respectively (vii. 5, 3). Similarly, Hercules and Hylas, as well as Jove and Ganymede, are included in the rollcall of famous homosexual lovers in Marlowe's *Edward II* (lines 690, 476). Perhaps most significantly, even in Elegy VII, the poem in which he recounts his own (hetero)sexual awakening, Milton cites both Ganymede and Hylas as examples of love's transforming power.

The homosexual (or perhaps more accurately, ambisexual) temptation is not simply added as an afterthought in Satan's conjuration of the banquet. Rather, it is carefully prepared for in his rejection of Belial's exclusively heterosexual proposal. Satan's decision to try the Messiah's constancy with "manlier objects" than the female courtesans proposed by Belial is meant quite literally as well as metaphorically. In fact, the phrase may punningly allude to another Renaissance term for homosexuality, *masculine love,* which Joseph Cady has identified in Bacon's *New Atlantis* and Heywood's *Pleasant Dialogues and Dramas* (where it specifically refers to the relationship between Jupiter and Ganymede) among other places. Most tellingly, however, Satan's citation of Alexander the Great and Scipio Africanus as notable examples of individuals unsusceptible to heterosexual lures is evidence of Milton's deliberate and careful execution of the homosexual temptation.

Satan might naturally compare Alexander and Scipio with Jesus, since each was rumored to be of divine origin, born as a result of unions between a divine father and a mortal mother (Plutarch 298-300, Livy XXVI.19).[7] They each embarked on a spectacularly successful public career at a very young age and, like Jesus, they were known for their chastity and restraint. But Alexander and Scipio were legendary not only for their temperance, but also for their masculine attachments and devotion to homoerotic friendship. While both "made small account" of female charms, both were highly appreciative of male beauty. Hence, by invoking them to repudiate Belial's proposal, Satan also prepares for the homosexual temptation of the banquet scene, creating in effect a homosexual counter-plot barely concealed beneath the heterosexual surface plot.

Alexander was famous for slighting female beauty. In Plutarch's words, he preferred "the beautie of his continencie, before [the sweet faces of the ladies of Persia]: he passed by without any sparke of affection towardes them, more then if they had bene images of stone without life" (4:322). Thus, Walter MacKellar may be right to state in the *Variorum Commentary* that lines 196-198 probably refer specifically to Alexander's "treatment of the mother, wife, and daughters of Darius, whom he captured after the battle of Issus"; but he is surely wrong in his endorsement of E. C. Blakeney's disingenuous explanation of "slightly" in line 196: "he was moved by compassion rather than by *contempt*" (119). Although he married for dynastic purposes, Alexander consistently displayed indifference toward female attractions, and all of his most intense emotional and physical relationships were with men. His greatest and most enduring attachment was to his companion and lieutenant Hephaestion, who loved him for being Alexander, whereas his other chief advisor, Craterus, loved him for being king (Plutarch 4:353). The relationship of Alexander and Hephaestion was frequently celebrated as an example of elevated homosexual love, as in Marlowe's *Edward II* (line 689).

Alexander was famed for his bodily temperance, for thinking "it more princely for a king . . . to conquer him selfe, then to overcome his enemies" (Plutarch 4:322), a phrase that Jesus echoes when he rejects the lure of earthly kingdoms by declaring that "he who reigns within himself, and rules, / Passions, Desires, and Fears is more a king" (2.466-467). As Plutarch observes, Alexander was "hardly moved with lust or pleasure of the body, and would moderately use it" (4:301). Yet two episodes in his life in which he abandoned his customary self-restraint may be especially pertinent in understanding Satan's purpose in citing him as a prelude to the sexual temptation.

The more famous of the two involves Alexander's relationship with Hephaestion. When the latter died, his friend grieved extravagantly:

> Alexander unwisely tooke the chaunce of [Hephaeston's] death, and commaunded all the heares of his horse and mules to be presently shorn in token of mourning, and that al the battlements of the wals of cities should also be overthrown, and hong up pore Glaucus his Phisitian upon a crosse, and commaunded that no minstrel should be heard play of any kind of instrument within his campe: until that

there was brought him an oracle from Iupiter Hammon, commaunding that Hephaestion should be worshipped and sacrificed unto, as a demy god. In the end, to passe over his mourning and sorow, he went unto the warres, as unto a hunting of men, and there subdued the people of the Cossaeians, whom he pluckt up by the rootes, and slue man, woman, and childe. And this was called the sacrifice of Hephaestions funeralls. (Plutarch 4:380-381)

It was this notoriously irrational response to the death of Hephaestion that prompted Donne's remark in the "Obsequies to the Lord Harington" that "in no degree I can expresse / Grief in great Alexanders great excesse / Who at his friends death, made whole townes devest / Their walls and bullwarks which became them best" (lines 251-254). The excessiveness (and destructiveness) of Alexander's mourning for Hephaestion illustrates how even someone famous for moderation may be induced by love to irrational and idolatrous behavior.

The other episode teaches a similar lesson, but in a context particularly relevant to the banquet scene in *Paradise Regained*. When Alexander invaded India, he and his army traveled painfully some sixty days through a barren wilderness, suffering great privations. Finally arriving in the bounteous country of Carmania, however, they devoted seven days to unrestrained luxury and riotous banqueting. This excess was unusual, for Alexander was customarily "nothing curious of dainty dishes: for when any did send him rare frutes, or fishe, from the contries nere the sea side, he would send them abroad unto his frendes, and seldom kepe any thinge for him selfe" (Plutarch 4:324-325). In Carmania, however, Alexander abandoned such restraint, as Plutarch memorably describes:

> For night and day, he was feasting continually with his friends apon a scaffold longer then broad, rising up of height, and drawn with eight goodly horse. After that scaffold followed divers other charrets covered over, some with goodly rich arras, and purple silk, other with trim fresh boughes which they renued at every fields end: and in those Alexanders other frends and captaines made mery together. In all this armie, there was neither helmet, pike, dart, nor target seene: but gold and silver bowles, cups, and flagons in the souldiers hands, al the way as they went, drawing wine out of great pipes and vessels which they caried with them, one drinking to another, some marching in the fields going forward, and others also set at the table. About them were the minstrels playing and piping on their flutes and shalmes, and women singing and daunsing, and fooling by the way as they went. In all this dissolute marching through the country, and

in the middest of their dronkennes, they mingled with it sport: that every man did strive to counterfeat all the insolencies of Bacchus, as if god Bacchus him self had ben there in person, and had led the mommery. (4:375)

One day, during this period of Dionysian revelry, Alexander went to observe the dancing and became enchanted with a young man named Bagoas. "This Bagoas being in his daunsing garments, came through the Theater, and sat him down by Alexander," Plutarch reports. "The Macedonians were so glad of it, that they showted and clapped their hands for joy, crying out alowde, to kisse him: So that in fine he toke him in his armes, and kissed him, before them all" (4:376).[8] Although Alexander was ordinarily chaste and temperate, this precedent of his becoming infatuated with a beautiful young man in the midst of culinary excesses probably inspires Satan's hope that Jesus might similarly become besotted with one of the "Tall stripling youths" poised to dispense wine at the banquet.

Scipio Africanus, who encouraged comparisons of himself with Alexander (Livy XXVI.19), was also renowned both for moderation and for intense masculine friendships. Scipio's greatest friendship was with Laelius, and it is their relationship that forms the basis of Cicero's *De Amicitia*. They were, Frank O. Copley writes, "the Damon and Pythias, the Jonathan and David of Roman tradition" (xvi). From a very young age, Scipio acquired a reputation for chastity. As Polybius observes, however,

> This was a glory which, great and difficult as it generally is, was not hard to gain at that period in Rome, owing to the general deterioration of morals. Some had wasted their energies on favourite youths; others on mistresses; and a great many on banquets enlivened with poetry and wine, and all the extravagant expenditure which they entailed, having quickly caught during the war with Perseus the dissoluteness of Greek manners in this respect. (XXII.11)

Scipio's continence and single-minded devotion to the pursuit of glory are explained by Silius Italicus in terms of the appearance to the young Roman of two allegorical figures, Pleasure and Virtue. Despite the allurements of a lavishly bedecked and bountiful Pleasure, Scipio chose the privations of Virtue, who promised him "not garments stained with Tyrian purple nor fragrant perfumes that a man should blush to use, but victory–victory over the fierce foe who is now harassing the empire of Rome; you shall destroy the Carthaginians and place your proud laurel upon the knees of Jove" (XV.116-120). So indifferent to material possessions and the trappings of luxury was Scipio that, according to Polybius, when he conquered Carthage, "reckoned the wealthiest city in the world," he "took absolutely nothing from it for his own private use, either by purchase or by any other manner of acquisition whatever, although he was by no means a very rich man, but very moderately so for a Roman" (XVIII.35).

Satan's reference to Scipio's dismissal of the "fair *Iberian* maid" alludes to an incident that occurred during the Roman's celebrated Spanish campaign. After having captured New Carthage, Scipio granted the request of an elderly matron to protect the honor of the hostages. Then a young woman captive, possessed "of a beauty so extraordinary that, wherever she went, she drew the eyes of everyone" (Livy XXVI.50), was brought to him. Scipio magnanimously restored the young woman to her fiancé, assuring him that "Your betrothed has been in my camp with the same regard for modesty as in the house of your parents-in-law, her own parents" (Livy XXVI.50). But a later incident on Scipio's Spanish campaign, one that Satan does not cite, is especially important in the formulation of the homosexual temptation. After having defeated Hasdrubal, Scipio took possession of the enemy's camp and some twelve thousand captives, among whom was "a well-grown boy of conspicuous beauty" named Massiva (Livy XXVII.19). Scipio was so taken with Massiva's beauty that he not only granted him freedom, but also presented him "with a gold ring, a tunic with a broad stripe, and a Spanish cloak, a golden brooch and a horse with his equipment" (Livy XXVII.19). The point is that Satan knows that Scipio was not merely indifferent to the charms of the Iberian maid, but also highly susceptible to male beauty, as illustrated by his generosity to Massiva.

Although presented in the surface plot as negative examples of individuals who are impervious to heterosexual temptations, Alexander and Scipio also simultaneously function positively in the homosexual counterplot as examples of notable historical figures who were homosexually inclined. Despite their characteristic temperance, they both, at pivotal moments in their careers, succumbed to the lure of masculine beauty. Surely Satan's (and Milton's) detailed but strategically suppressed knowledge of their history of erotic responses shapes the ambisexual temptation of the banquet scene, directed at a young man who shares with Alexander and Scipio both a reputedly divine origin and a reputation for chastity, but who has not yet been tested. The proclivity of the historical figures toward masculine love prompts the presence at the banquet of the beautiful young men. Milton constructs the homosexual counterplot with great subtlety, primarily by means of unstated premises and implicit allusions. Even the romance heroines (who hover in the background "distant more / Under the Trees") serve to conceal partially the primary (homo)erotic temptation, which is embodied in the "Tall stripling youths rich clad, of fairer hew / Then *Ganymed* or *Hylas*" in the foreground. But for all its subtlety of presentation, the homosexual temptation of *Paradise Regained* is nevertheless significant in the poem. Indeed, its importance to the poem is actually underlined by the delicacy, obliquity, and self-consciousness of Milton's artistry.

To recognize the homosexual temptation in Milton's brief epic is both to understand more clearly the comprehensiveness of the series of temptations to which the Son is exposed and to appreciate more fully the complexity of Milton's poetic technique, particularly his characteristic ability to work by indirection and implication, suggesting more than he actually says. But recognition of the homosexual counterplot of the banquet scene also helps place in perspective the alleged misogyny of *Paradise Regained.* W. B. C. Watkins has complained that the descriptions of women in the brief epic reveal "underneath the surface a violent crosscurrent of ambivalent emotions, which while producing [Milton's] finest poetry and drama temporarily wreck the poem" (119). Similarly, other readers have objected to the contemptuous characterization of female beauty as a "trivial toy" (2.222), considering it a gratuitous and misogynistic comment on women (Parker 2:1139). Shawcross has rightly defended Milton against such charges, pointing out that those comments reflect not the opinions of Milton but those of Belial and Satan and forcefully arguing that "Milton is not casting any aspersion on moral sexual experience or woman or women" (*"Paradise Regain'd"* 111).

But what has not been noticed is that Satan's disparagement of female beauty as unworthy of those "of more exalted mind, / Made and set wholly on the accomplishment / Of greatest things" (2.206-208) itself contributes to the development of the homosexual counterplot, for it echoes a Renaissance defense of male homosexuality that was rooted in the assumption of male superiority. Ficino, in his commentary on Plato's *Symposium,* for example, makes an argument similar to Satan's, when he paraphrases Pausanias's famous distinction between heavenly Eros, or homosexuality, and common Eros, or heterosexuality. "Some men," Ficino writes,

> either on account of their nature or their training, are better equipped for offspring of the soul than for those of the body. Others, and certainly the majority of them, are the opposite. The former pursue heavenly love, the latter earthly. The former, therefore, naturally love men more than women, and those nearly adults rather than children, because the first two are much stronger in mental keenness, and this because of its higher beauty is most essential to knowledge, which they naturally wish to cultivate. (207)

The elitist idea that homosexual relationships are the only ones worthy of truly philosophical men derives from Plato and is a recurrent feature of medieval and Renaissance defenses of homosexuality.[9] It is present in *Paradise Regained* not as an expression of Milton's misogyny but as an element in Satan's homosexual temptation.

Since Luke 4:13 ("when the devil had ended all the temptation") implies that Jesus was exposed to all the temptations to which human beings are subjected, it is not surprising that Milton includes a sexual temptation in *Paradise Regained*. William B. Hunter Jr. may be right to contend that the human temptations of the poem are authorized by the baptismal service, in which in Milton's day "every person baptized, or, if a baby, his adult representative, was asked, according to the Book of Common Prayer, 'Dost thou renounce the devil and all his works, the vain pomp and glory of the world, with all covetous desires of the same, and the sinful desires of the flesh: so that thou wilt not follow, nor be led by them?'" (186). Still, the incorporation of a specifically homosexual temptation remains rather startling, if not entirely unprecedented.[10] In an essay attempting to explain Islam's violent reaction to Salman Rushdie's novel *The Satanic Verses*, Ali A. Mázrui compares Rushdie's blasphemy to the comparable blasphemy of a hypothetical Western work of literature "based on the thesis that the twelve apostles were Jesus' homosexual lovers" and speculates that such a work would find no defenders among those who protested Rushdie's death sentence (356). Ironically, despite the intended shocking nature of Mázrui's comparison, Milton may indeed have been prompted in his decision to depict the Son's exposure to a homosexual temptation by a little-known and even less frequently acknowledged heresy that posits a homosexual relationship between Jesus and John the Beloved Disciple, who describes himself throughout his gospel as the best loved of the apostles. This heresy may have influenced or, perhaps more likely, been influenced by the association of St. John with an idealized Ganymede, as in the fourteenth-century *Ovidius moralizatus* by the monk Petrus Berchorius (Saslow 6).

This heresy has not, to my knowledge, been carefully explored, probably because of the virulent prejudice against homosexuality in the Christian tradition, which has commonly characterized it as the sin not to be named among Christians. But in the twelfth century, the remarkable St. Aelred of Rievaulx "gave love between those of the same gender its most profound and lasting expression in a Christian context" (Boswell, *Christianity* 221); and, significantly, he buttressed his idealization of love between men in *De speculo caritas* with the example of Jesus and John, even referring to their relationship as a "marriage":

We can enjoy this [union of two men in which soul mixes with soul and they thereby become one] in the present with those whom we love not merely with our minds but with our hearts; for some are joined to us more intimately and passionately than others in the lovely bond of spiritual friendship. And lest this sort of sacred love should seem improper to anyone, Jesus himself, in everything like us, patient and compassionate with us in every matter, transfigured it through the expression of his own love: for he allowed one, not all, to recline on his breast as a sign of his special love, so that the virgin head was supported in the flowers [*sic*] of the virgin breast, and the closer they were, the more copiously did the fragrant secrets of the heavenly marriage impart the sweet smell of spiritual chrism to their virgin love.

    Although all the disciples were blessed with the sweetness of the greatest love of the most holy master, nonetheless he conceded as a privilege to one alone this symbol of a more intimate love, that he should be called the "disciple whom Jesus loved." (Qtd. in and trans. by Boswell, *Christianity* 225-226)

Closer to Milton's own time, the iconoclastic Christopher Marlowe expressed this heresy more crudely, and in specifically sexual terms, in the infamous "Baines libel," where he asserted "That St John the Evangelist was bedfellow to Christ and leaned alwaies in his bosome, that he vsed him as the sinners of Sodoma" (qtd. in Kocher 35). Milton was probably also aware that James I defended his homoerotic attachment to George Villiers, Duke of Buckingham by reference to the relationship of Jesus and John. As James told his council, "Christ had his John, and I have my George" (qtd. in Willson 384). The homosexual temptation of *Paradise Regained* may have been inspired, at least in part, as a refutation of this heresy that alleged Jesus to be homosexual. At the very least, the heresy gives point to Milton's inclusion of the temptation.[11]

    It is important to emphasize that in rejecting the sexual temptation, Jesus does not condemn homosexuality, any more than he condemns heterosexuality or women or food, which are also important components of the temptation. What he condemns is the gluttony of the banquet scene, in which lust and idolatry are implicit elements. Moreover, just as the Lady in the *Masque* rejects the bounty of nature as offered by Comus on the grounds that "none / But such as are good men can give good things, / And that which is not good, is not delicious / To a wel-govern'd and wise appetite" (lines 701-704), so the Messiah weighs the temptations proffered by Satan "Thereafter as I like / The giver" (2:321-322), and spurns the banquet because it is the devil's table. That Jesus refuses the banquet because of the giver, rather than because food or sensual beauty are suspect in themselves, is clear from the fact that following his triumph over Satan on the pinnacle of the Temple of Jerusalem, he is rescued by angels, who, in a truly Edenic setting, present him a sumptuous repast (4:586-595).

In having the Son refrain from condemning homosexuality, Milton follows biblical precedent, for the historical Jesus nowhere remarked on homosexuality. The Christian tradition's antipathy toward same-sex relationships derives not from Jesus but from the Judaic tradition and from the writings of Paul.[12] Equally significant is the fact that Alexander and Scipio are not stigmatized for their homosexuality in the poem, but are instead presented as admirable historical figures, whose homosexuality is an expression of their humanity. Indeed, the very point of their comparison with Jesus is their customary moderation and self-restraint. Not being perfect men, they are revealed as less than the Messiah, who, possessing a "temperance invincible" (2.408), withstands temptations to which they are susceptible, but they are not on that account condemned. Alexander and Scipio are censured in Book III for their destructive military exploits, not their homosexuality. Milton's attitude toward homosexuality in *Paradise Regained* is both sophisticated and humane.

Although a full discussion of the issue is beyond the scope of this paper, Milton's inclusion of a homosexual temptation in *Paradise Regained* needs also to be seen in the context of his biography and of his other treatments of homosexuality. In a seminal 1975 essay, John Shawcross analyzed Milton's intense friendship with Charles Diodati as a homoerotic relationship, concluding that "The total view of Diodati seen from the extant evidence certainly points to a homosexual nature; of Milton, to a latent homosexualism which was probably repressed consciously (as well as subconsciously) from becoming overt except with Diodati" ("Milton and Diodati" 157).[13] My interest here is not in whether Milton was homosexual, but in whether Milton's relationship with Diodati, coupled with the poet's difficulty in achieving a satisfactory heterosexual adjustment, might help explain his attitudes toward homosexuality in *Paradise Regained.* In this regard, the homosexual allusions of Elegy VII, the epigraphs on the title pages of the *Masque* and the *Poems* of 1645, which are from Virgil's homoerotic second eclogue, and the charged homoeroticism and homosexual allusions of *Epitaphium Damonis* are all pertinent, suggesting both Milton's deep familiarity with the literature of homosexuality and his capacity for discovering in it emotions correlative to his own. Thus, it is quite unlikely that the Son's censure of Greek poets for singing "The vices of Thir Deities, and thir own / In Fable, Hymn, or Song, so personating / Thir Gods ridiculous, and themselves past shame" (4.340-342) is meant as a reflection on the pervasive homoeroticism of Greek poetry. Or, perhaps more pertinently, that Jesus' rejection of the homosexual temptation is intended as a condemnation of homosexuality.

Milton's various references to sodomy and his treatments of the Sodom myth, which has provided the foundation for the civil and religious persecution of homosexuality, are also revealing of his attitudes. He unremarkably lists sodomy among the numerous offenses against chastity in *Christian Doctrine* (6:726, 756), but there is no evidence there that he has in mind anything like a committed homosexual relationship. In *Reason of Church-Government*, Milton compares "the offences of those peccant Cities [i.e., Sodom and Gomorrah] with these enormous rites of ungodly misrule that Prelaty hath wrought both in the Church of Christ and in the state of this Kingdome," implying that the cities of the plain were more worthy of mercy than the Anglican bishops (3:861). Similarly, in *Eikonoklastes*, Milton compares those who persist in their infatuation for the executed King Charles with the inhabitants of Sodom: they "have none to blame but thir own folly, if they live and dye in such a strook'n blindness, as next to that of *Sodom* hath not happ'ned to any sort of men more gross, or more misleading" (3:342). In both these instances, Sodom is merely evoked as a precedent of God's anger with the ungodly, and as a means of execrating Milton's antagonists.

More interesting are the notes recorded in the Trinity manuscript for a proposed dramatization of the Sodom story, which was to be entitled "Cupids funeral pile. Sodom burning." In this unwritten drama, Milton planned to depict the residents of the city "every one with mistresse, or Ganymed, gitterning along the streets, or solacing on the banks of Jordan, or down the stream" and to feature an angelic debate about "love & how it differs from lust" (*Poems* 40). What is clear from these notes is that, on the one hand, Milton recognized homosexuals and heterosexuals as distinct classes of people, but that, on the other hand, he did not conceive of the Sodom story as referring exclusively to homosexuality, since he planned to portray heterosexual as well as homosexual lust.[14] Indeed, the issue that God's destruction of Sodom suggested to Milton was the generalized question of lust rather than of homosexuality, as is also clear from the citation of "that bituminous Lake where *Sodom* flam'd" (*Paradise Lost* 10.562) in connection with the bitter ashes tasted by the fallen angels after the seduction of Adam and Eve.

In *Paradise Lost*, the Sons of Belial, "flown with insolence and wine" are witnessed in "the Streets of *Sodom*," but, with greater elaboration, associated with "that night / In *Gibeah*, when the hospitable door / Expos'd a Matron to avoid worse rape" (1.502-506). The reference is to the grisly tale recounted in Judges 19 of the Levite concubine who is gang-raped to death in Gibeah and her body later hacked into pieces. The "worse rape" of line 506 is the threatened (homosexual) rape of the concubine's master, but in juxtaposing these allusions, Milton obviously recognized the story of Gibeah as "the exact heterosexual companion-piece to the story of Sodom" (Alter 356). He seems to have interpreted both stories as warnings against rape and against violations of hospitality, as well as against unbridled lust. This suggests that Milton interpreted the Sodom story in accord with a much earlier tradition (now revived by theologians and biblical exegetes). John Boswell expertly summarizes the history of this interpretation:

> The notion that Genesis 19–the account of Sodom's destruction–condemned homosexual relations was the result of myths popularized during the early centuries of the Christian era but not universally accepted until much later and only erratically evoked in discussions of the morality of gay sexuality. Many patristic authors concluded that the point of the story was to condemn inhospitality to strangers; others understood it to condemn rape; most interpreted it in broadly allegorical terms, only tangentially related to sexuality. (*Christianity* 113-114)

Thus, Milton, for all his pervasive concern with chastity and temperance, consistently fails to single out homosexuality as in itself a particularly grave sin or to associate Sodom (and sodomy) exclusively with homosexuality. It is, then, perhaps not so surprising that he was able to incorporate the homosexual temptation into *Paradise Regained* with such poise.

As Northrop Frye observed many years ago, "The conflict in *Paradise Regained* is ultimately a spiritual one, but the basis of the human spirit is the physical body, and the body is the battleground of the spirit" (230). Thus, it is crucial to understand precisely the nature of the physical temptations to which Milton exposes the Messiah. Significant among those physical temptations is the hitherto unexplored homosexual lure, which figures prominently in the banquet scene. A part of the poem's larger lure *voluptaria,* the erotic temptation is depicted with great tact, yet it is also thoroughly Miltonic in its daring. Creating a homosexual counter-plot by means of concealed premises and subtle allusions, Milton presents the homosexual enticement deliberately and with enormous care. Its presence is neither gratuitous nor accidental. The obliquity of its execution is particularly interesting for the insight it provides into Milton's poetic technique, but the temptation functions primarily to expand the comprehensiveness of Milton's vision in the brief epic and to register the uniqueness of his interpretation of familiar material, including most specifically the Bible. Recognition of the homosexual counterplot helps to explain the apparent misogyny of the poem, to clarify more fully the nature of the banquet scene, and to illustrate concretely Milton's masterful exploitation of received classical and biblical traditions for his own purposes. Yet it is also important in its own right, as evidence of Milton's sophisticated recognition of the range of fully human sexual possibilities.

NOTES

1. This essay was originally written as a contribution to a proposed festschrift for the late J. Max Patrick that never materialized. I am happy to dedicate the essay to his memory. Because I circulated the manuscript to some colleagues who then mentioned it to other colleagues, this essay has been widely cited as "forthcoming in *'Grateful Vicissitude': Essays in Honor of J. Max Patrick.*" The essay was written about the same time as (but independently of) the work of Gregory Bredbeck, who also concludes that *Paradise Regained* "views the temptation of Jesus as an interrogation of male sexual temptation instead of as a correction of original female weakness" (213). Although our conclusions are similar, our approaches are very different, and my work and Bredbeck's should be seen as complementary rather than duplicative. Outside of Bredbeck's, the fullest discussions of the sexual temptation are the sensitive analysis of Lewalski (193-227) and the superficial one of Le Comte (101-108). Other critics mention a sexual lure in passing, most notably Cullen (144-55) and Hunter (186-87). Perhaps the most irrelevant recognition of the sexual temptation is that of Broadbent, whose psychoanalytic approach reduces the banquet scene to evidence "of hunger for a love which is ultimately maternal (it feeds), and for a power which is incestuous" (90). All quotations in my text from Milton's poetry are from *The Student's Milton.*

2. Admittedly, the ludicrous prosecution of *Gay News* had far more to do with homophobia than with any genuine concern for blasphemy. But precisely because charges of blasphemy may so easily be used to harass authors and publishers, the threat of such charges creates a chilling effect and enforces self-censorship.

3. On the "triple equation" of gluttony, vainglory, and avarice, see especially Pope (51-69) but also Lewalski (177-78, 222-27), Cullen (125-181), and Shawcross (*"Paradise Regain'd"* 45-58); on the poem as initiation rite, see Shawcross (*"Paradise Regain'd"* 83); on the *humanation* of God, and on Incarnational theology's debate about Christ's sexuality, see Steinberg (9-23). Most recent critics of *Paradise Regained* agree that, at least to some degree, Jesus is tempted as a human being (see, for example, Lewalski 133-163 and Marilla 56-67), as do I, but for a recent contrary view, see Jordan.

4. On the association of Belial with homosexuality, see Bredbeck (214-25).

5. For identification and discussions of the Circean romance heroines, see Lewalski (224-25) and Le Comte (106-107). For a discussion of Milton's relationship to romance literature, see Patterson.

6. There was also an idealistic version of the Ganymede myth, derived from Xenophon, and Christianized by early Christian mythographers, who interpreted the rape of Ganymede as a religious allegory (Saslow 4-6). But this version was not nearly so influential or so prevalent in the Renaissance as the homosexual interpretation. The context in which Milton cites Ganymede makes it abundantly clear that he is drawing on the homosexual version.

7. Lewalki discusses Alexander and Scipio in their roles as Herculean figures and world conquerors (236-39).

8. The relationship of Alexander and Bagoas is the basis of Renault's fine historical novel, *The Persian Boy.* In a postscript to her novel, Renault cites as her sources both Curtius and Athenaeus, as well as Plutarch (463-469). She quotes Curtius's description of Bagoas as "a eunuch of remarkable beauty and in the very flower of boyhood, who had been loved by Darius, and who was afterwards to be loved by Alexander" (463).

9. Because Ganymede displaced Hebe as cupbearer to the gods, and because Juno strenuously objected to Jupiter's relationship with Ganymede, treatments of the Ganymede myth are often tainted by misogyny, with Ganymede exalted at the expense of Hebe (or sometimes Helen or Juno) in debates about the relative merits of men or women as sexual partners of men. See Saslow 115-25; and Boswell (*Christianity* 255-66).

10. In *Michael and the Dragon, or Christ Tempted and Satan foyled* (1635), Daniel Dyke implied a homosexual temptation of Jesus when he advised his readers to develop "this same Stoicall eye of our Saviour, that we may see eye-pleasing and tempting objects, and not be set a-gogge, . . . as he with the beauty of a young boy, to whom it was answered, that the Praetor must have continent eyes, as well as hands" (318). I am grateful to Joseph Wittreich for calling my attention to this reference.

11. Michael Schoenfeldt calls attention to the homoeroticism of Herbert's *Lucus* 34, "To John leaning on the Lord's breast," a Latin poem based on John 21:20. In 1817, the great utilitarian philosopher Jeremy Bentham began making notes for a book that would openly confront Pauline attitudes toward homosexuality and the way those attitudes encourage bigotry. In these notes, he too considers the question of whether Jesus and John might have been lovers, but finally decides that "good taste and self-regarding prudence would require us to turn aside" from this "topic of extreme delicacy" (qtd. in Crompton 278). More daringly, Bentham develops a countermyth based on the account of Jesus' arrest in Mark 14:50-52, where a young lad, whom Bentham identifies as a homosexual temple prostitute, is more faithful than the disciples (Crompton 280-83). Unfortunately, Bentham's book was never completed or published.

12. On the development of Christian antipathy toward homosexuality, see Boswell (*Christianity*), who demonstrates that ecclesiastical and civil hostility toward homosexuality becomes dominant only in the twelfth century, but that by the end of the Middle Ages, it is almost unchallenged.

13. Shawcross's essay is reprinted and its implications extended in *John Milton.*

14. Milton's failure to connect the Sodom story specifically to homosexuality supports Bray's point that in the Renaissance the term *sodomy* did not denote a specific identity but was considered a symptom of universal dissolution and a temptation to which all men were subject (25-26). On the other hand, insofar as Milton recognizes homosexually and heterosexually inclined persons as belonging to separate classes on the basis of their different erotic responses, he challenges the idea that such a distinction is a recent phenomenon. On the debate about the construction of sexual identity in earlier ages, see, in addition to Bray and Bredbeck, Foucault, Greenberg, Weeks, Gerard and Hekma, Boswell ("Revolutions" and "Gay History"), Cady, and Summers ("Homosexuality"). Milton's recourse to classical sources indicates that his construction of homosexuality was not exclusively sodomitical—that is, construed solely in terms of the biblical prohibition that justified the destruction of the Cities of the Plain. On the tension in the Renaissance between sodomitical and classical constructions of homosexuality, see Summers ("Marlowe").

WORKS CITED

Alter, Robert. "Proust and the Ideological Reader." *Salmagundi* 58-59 (fall 1982-winter 1983): 347-57.

Boswell, John. *Christianity, Social Tolerance, and Homosexuality: Gay People in Western Europe from the Beginning of the Christian Era to the Fourteenth Century.* Chicago: U of Chicago P, 1980.

_____. "Gay History." *Atlantic* (February 1989): 74-78.

_____. "Revolutions, Universals, Categories." *Salmagundi* 58-59 (fall 1982-winter 1983): 89-113.

Bray, Alan. *Homosexuality in Renaissance England.* London: Gay Men's P, 1982.

Bredbeck, Gregory W. *Sodomy and Interpretation: Marlowe to Milton.* Ithaca, NY: Cornell UP, 1991.

Broadbent, J. B. "The Private Mythology of *Paradise Regained.*" *Calm of Mind: Tercentenary Essays on "Paradise Regained" and "Samson Agonistes."* Ed. Joseph A. Wittreich, Jr. Cleveland: P of Case Western Reserve U, 1971. 77-92.

Cady, Joseph. " 'Masculine Love,' Renaissance Writing, and the New Historiography of Homosexuality." *Homosexuality in Renaissance and Enlightenment England: Literary Representations in Historical Context.* Ed. Claude J. Summers. New York: The Haworth Press, Inc. 1992. 9-40.

Copley, Frank O. "Introduction." *Cicero: On Old Age and On Friendship.* Trans. Frank O. Copley. Ann Arbor: U of Michigan P, 1967. ix-xvi.

Crompton, Louis. *Byron and Greek Love: Homophobia in Nineteenth-Century England.* Berkeley: U of California P, 1985.

Cullen, Patrick. *Infernal Triad: The Flesh, the World, and the Devil in Spenser and Milton.* Princeton: Princeton UP, 1974.

Donne, John. *The Complete English Poems of John Donne.* Ed. C. A. Patrides. Everyman's Library. London: Dent, 1985.

Dyke, Daniel. *Michael and the Dragon, or Christ Tempted and Satan foyled.* London: John Beale, 1635.

Ficino, Marsilio. *Commentarium in Convivio Platonis.* Trans. and ed. by Sears R. Jayne. Columbia: U of Missouri P, 1943.

Foucault, Michel. *The History of Sexuality. Volume I: An Introduction.* New York: Pantheon, 1978.

Frye, Northrop. "The Typology of 'Paradise Regained.'" *Modern Philology* 53 (1956): 227-38.

Gerard, Kent, and Gert Hekma, eds. *The Pursuit of Sodomy: Male Homosexuality in Renaissance and Enlightenment Europe.* New York: The Haworth Press, Inc., 1988.

Greenberg, David F. *The Construction of Homosexuality.* Chicago: U of Chicago P, 1988.

Hunter, William B., Jr. "The Double Set of Temptations in *Paradise Regained.*" *Milton Studies* 14 (1980): 183-93.

Jordan, Richard Douglas. "*Paradise Lost* and the Second Adam." *Milton Studies* 9 (1976): 261-75.

Kocher, Paul H. *Christopher Marlowe: A Study of His Thought, Learning, and Character.* Chapel Hill: U of North Carolina P, 1946.

Le Comte, Edward. *Milton and Sex.* New York: Columbia UP, 1978.

Lewalski, Barbara Kiefer. *Milton's Brief Epic: The Genre, Meaning, and Art of "Paradise Regained."* Providence, RI: Brown UP, 1966.

Livy. *Livy with an English Translation.* Trans. Frank Gardner Moore. Loeb Classical Library. 14 vols. Rev. ed. Cambridge: Harvard UP, 1950.

MacKellar, Walter. *A Variorum Commentary on the Poems of John Milton. Volume 4: Paradise Regained.* New York: Columbia UP, 1975.

Marilla, E. L. *Milton and Modern Man.* University: U of Alabama P, 1968.

Marlowe, Christopher. *The Works of Christopher Marlowe.* Ed. C. F. Tucker Brooke. Oxford: Clarendon P, 1910.

Mázrui, Ali A. "Is *The Satanic Verses* a Satanic Novel?" *Michigan Quarterly Review* 28 (1989): 347-71.

Milton, John. *Christian Doctrine.* Ed. Maurice Kelley. Trans. John Carey. *Complete Prose Works of John Milton.* Ed. Don M. Wolfe et al. 8 vols. New Haven: Yale UP, 1973. Vol. 6.

_____ . *Eikonoklastes.* Ed. Merritt Y. Hughes. *Complete Prose Works of John Milton.* Ed. Don M. Wolfe et al. 8 vols. New Haven: Yale UP, 1973. 3:335-601.

_____ . *Poems. Reproduced in Facsimile from the Manuscript in Trinity College, Cambridge.* Menston, England: Scolar P, 1972.

_____ . *Reason of Church-Government.* Ed. Ralph A. Haug. *Complete Prose Works of John Milton.* Ed. Don M. Wolfe et al. 8 vols. New Haven: Yale UP, 1973. 1:736-861.

_____ . *The Student's Milton.* Ed. Frank Allen Patterson. Rev. ed. New York: Appleton-Century-Crofts, 1933.

Parker, William Riley. *Milton: A Biography.* 2 vols. Oxford: Clarendon P, 1968.

Patterson, Annabel M. *"Paradise Regained*: A Last Chance at Romance." *Milton Studies* 17 (1983): 187-208.

Plutarch. "The Life of Alexander the Great." In *Plutarch's Lives of the Noble Grecians and Romans Englished by Sir Thomas North.* Intro. by George Wyndham. 6 vols. London: Nutt, 1895; New York: AMS, 1967. 4:298-386.

Polybius. *The Histories of Polybius.* Trans. Evelyn S. Shuckburgh. 2 vols. London: Macmillan, 1889.

Pope, Elizabeth Marie. *"Paradise Regained": The Tradition and the Poem.* Baltimore: Johns Hopkins UP, 1947.

Renault, Mary. *The Persian Boy.* New York: Pantheon, 1972; New York: Bantam, 1974.

Saslow, James M. *Ganymede in the Renaissance: Homosexuality in Art and Society.* New Haven: Yale UP, 1986.

Schoenfeldt, Michael. *Prayer and Power: George Herbert and Renaissance Courtship.* Chicago: U of Chicago P, 1991.

Shawcross, John T. *John Milton: The Self and the World.* Lexington: UP of Kentucky, 1993.

_____. "Milton and Diodati: An Essay in Psychodynamic Meaning." *Milton Studies* 7 (1975): 127-163.

_____. *"Paradise Regain'd": Worthy T'Have Not Remain'd So Long Unsung.* Pittsburgh: Duquesne UP, 1988.

Silius Italicus. *Punica.* Trans. J. D. Duff. Loeb Classical Library. 2 vols. Cambridge: Harvard UP, 1934.

Spenser, Edmund. *The Poetical Works of Edmund Spenser.* Ed. J. C. Smith and E. de Selincourt. London: Oxford U P, 1912.

Steinberg, Leo. *The Sexuality of Christ in Renaissance Art and in Modern Oblivion.* New York: Pantheon, 1983.

Summers, Claude J. "Homosexuality and Renaissance Literature, or the Anxieties of Anachronism." *South Central Review* 9.1 (1992): 2-23.

_____. "Marlowe and Constructions of Renaissance Homosexuality." *Canadian Review of Comparative Literature / Revue Canadienne de Littérature Comparée* 21 (1994): 27-44.

Watkins, W. B. C. *An Anatomy of Milton's Verse.* Baton Rouge: Louisiana State UP, 1955.

Weeks, Jeffrey. *Coming Out: Homosexual Politics in Britain, from the Nineteenth Century to the Present.* London: Quartet Books, 1977.

Willson, David Harris. *King James VI and I.* London: Jonathan Cape, 1956.

Bakhtinian Grotesque Realism and the Subversion of Biblical Authority in Rochester's *Sodom*

Raymond-Jean Frontain, PhD

University of Central Arkansas

SUMMARY. Rather than signalling Rochester's agreement with the presumptive biblical imprecation against sodomy and consequent divine vengeance, the apocalyptic denouement of *The Farce of Sodom* bespeaks defiance of divine judgment and a willingness to persevere in the pleasure of homosexual anal sex *despite* what might seem certain divine retribution. A Bakhtinian reading of the play's carnivalesque features concludes that it is the failure of all sexual endeavor, rather than of sodomy per se, that is dramatized in the farce's concluding scene. *Sodom* anticipates both the modern attitude towards the open male body that has come to dominate contemporary gay discourse, and the transgressive uses to which modern writers have put the Bible by which they undercut its authority and the presumptive morality that it is otherwise used to sanction. *[Article copies available for a fee from The Haworth Document Delivery Service: 1-800-342-9678. E-mail address: getinfo@haworth.com]*

Raymond-Jean Frontain is an associate professor of English at the University of Central Arkansas. The editor of three previously published collections of essays on biblically inspired literary traditions, he has published articles on gay literary appropriations of the David story, contributed the "Bible" essay to *Gay and Lesbian Literary Heritage* (Holt, 1995), and is a regular contributor to *The James White Review.*

Correspondence may be addressed: Department of English, 317 Irby Hall, University of Central Arkansas, Conway, AR 72035-0001, or electronically at raymondf@cc1.uca.edu.

[Haworth co-indexing entry note]: "Bakhtinian Grotesque Realism and the Subversion of Biblical Authority in Rochester's *Sodom*." Frontain, Raymond-Jean. Co-published simultaneously in *Journal of Homosexuality* (The Haworth Press, Inc.) Vol. 33, No. 3/4, 1997, pp. 71-95; and: *Reclaiming the Sacred: The Bible in Gay and Lesbian Culture* (ed: Raymond-Jean Frontain) Harrington Park Press, an imprint of The Haworth Press, Inc., 1997, pp. 71-95. Single or multiple copies of this article are available for a fee from The Haworth Document Delivery Service [1-800-342-9678, 9:00 a.m. - 5:00 p.m. (EST). E-mail address: getinfo@haworth.com].

The only attempt at a systematic interpretation of John Wilmot, the Earl of Rochester's *The Farce of Sodom, or the Quintessence of Debauchery*[1] remains Richard Elias's 1978 essay on *Sodom* as political satire which argues that Rochester drew upon the episode recorded in Genesis 19 to criticize court politics in the years immediately following the 1672 Declaration of Indulgence. The biblical narrative's failure to specify exactly what vice aroused the wrath of God, argues Elias, allowed it to "be fitted to the realities of Restoration court politics as its enemies saw them: an indolent, pleasure-loving king who surrounded himself with titled whores as mistresses and noble satyrs as companions" (429). What is more, "the events of 1666–war, plague, and fire–only seemed to confirm" the Sodom story's suggestion "that the moral corruption that spread outward from the court would eventually culminate in similar ruin" for England (429). The rise to power in 1667 of Buckingham, who was often accused of sodomy by his political enemies, "added some point to these metaphoric comparisons" (430). In issuing the Declaration of Indulgence, Charles aroused resentment both of the royal prerogative powers and of the men like Buckingham who were seen to "shelter under them" (435). Thus, Elias concludes, in *Sodom* Rochester lampoons Charles as Bolloximian who,

> despite his wishes, . . . but fully in line with the intentions of his council, . . . becomes an absolute monarch, a tyrant in fact. *Sodom* thus delineates in sexual terms the degeneration of a benign king to a raging dictator who, in Act V, threatens to invade heaven and bugger the gods. In this light, sodomy becomes a grisly metaphor for popery, or rather for the way it was to be imposed on the English. (434)

The fire and brimstone that sweep down upon Bolloximian and his councilors at the conclusion of the play suggest what will happen to England if the Country Party that came to power after the fall of Clarendon continues to control the king. For Rochester, Elias concludes, the perversions of Roman Catholicism were as dangerous to the national health as the alleged sexual perversions of the biblical Sodomites were to Lot and his family.[2]

The political context that Elias establishes seems, in general, to be an accurate one. The Rochester who concludes "Verses for which he was Banished" by claiming "I hate all monarchs with the thrones they sit on, / From the hector of France to the cully of Britain" would no doubt have been as outraged by the prerogatory action of the king in issuing the Declaration of Indulgence as Elias suggests. And Elias's initial identification of characters and events in the farce with specific personalities and happenings within Charles's inner circle has been confirmed by J. W.

Johnson (135-36) and placed within the context of Rochester's biography.[3]

But Elias can be faulted on three major counts: for misreading the tone of the play; for implicitly ascribing to the Bible an authority which it clearly did not possess for Rochester; and for mistaking the import that sodomy had for him. A festive aura pervades *Sodom,* one that might best be described in terms of the Bakhtinian sexual carnivalesque. And sodomy in other works by Rochester is equated, not with perversion, but–as in *Sodom*–with liberation from the tedious effort of having to "drudge in fair Aurelia's womb."[4] What is more, *Sodom*'s deployment of the biblical narrative can be used to map the Bible's transformation in the late seventeenth century from the ultimate social and moral authority to a secular grab bag of allusions on a par with Shakespeare's plays and the Greco-Roman classics. For rather than signaling Rochester's agreement with the presumptive biblical imprecation against sodomy and consequent divine vengeance, the conclusion of the play bespeaks defiance of divine judgment and a willingness to persevere in the pleasure of homosexual anal sex *despite* what might seem certain divine retribution. When the essentially transgressive function that sodomy had for Rochester is taken into account, Bolloximian's desire to "heaven invade, and bugger all the gods" (5.1.13) becomes an instance not of tragic hubris but of comic panache.

I propose to read *Sodom* in terms of Mikhail Bakhtin's theory of the carnivalesque grotesque. During carnival, Bakhtin claims, the world–and especially the body–is turned upside down as attention that is traditionally reserved for the head is transferred to the material bodily lower stratum, and the bodily acts most subject to the rules of social decorum–eating, drinking, elimination, and copulation–are performed publicly and with gusto. The grotesque body of carnival realism dominates Rochester's farce, investing the play with the satiric power that Elias identifies, but in a festive–if, admittedly, not fully celebratory–way that Elias fails to recognize. That such festivity ultimately fails is inevitable in Rochester; as he wrote to his wife, the great misfortune of human existence is that there is "soe greate a disproportion t'wixt our desires & what it [no referent provided] has ordained to content them" (*Letters* 241-42). But while that failure may qualify the value that sodomy holds in the farce, it does not undercut its transgressive power; indeed, it reinforces it. In Rochester's *Sodom,* in effect, one finds one of the earliest expressions of the modern attitude towards the open male body that has come to dominate contemporary gay discourse, as well as a telling anticipation of the transgressive uses to which modern authors have put the Bible by which they undercut its authority and the presumptive morality that it is otherwise used to sanction.

"THE CHOICE OF BUGGERY"

The plot of *Sodom* turns upon King Bolloximian's libertine complaint that heterosexual, vaginal intercourse is no longer satisfying: "No longer I my cunts admire. / The drudgery has worn out my desire" (1.1.26-27). Bolloximian elaborates upon the specific reason for his frustration later in the play when, explaining why other animals are aroused to even greater lust by frequency of intercourse while the human male's appetite is lessened, he complains that female animals'

> cunts by use improve their influence
> Whilst ours grow void of pleasure and of sense.
> By oft formenting, cunt so big doth swell,
> That pintle works like clappers in a bell:
> All vacuum. No grasping flesh doth guide
> Or hug the brawny muscles of its side,
> Tickling the nerves, the prepuce or glans,
> Which all mankind with great delight entrance.
> (3.1.69-76)

The reason for the vacuum-like condition of the court women's vaginas becomes clear in the second scene when Queen Cuntigratia is "frigged with a dildo" by one of her maids of honor and complains about the inefficacy of the lady's ministration only to be told that the fault lies not with the swiftness or hardiness of the strokes that Lady Officina is supplying, but with the instrument that she has been given to work with: the dildo should have been made "of a larger size. / This dildo by a handful is too short" (1.2.69-70). In Act 4, the women, frustrated, complain directly to Virtuoso, "Dildo and Merkin Maker to the Court" (*Dramatis Personae*), that his dildos "are not stiff" "nor long enough," and "the muzzle is too small" (4.1.3-4): "Oh fie! They scarce exceed a virgin's span, / Yet should *exceed* what Nature gives to man" (11-12, emphasis added).[5]

The action of *Sodom*, then, is propelled by the lessening of heterosexual pleasure that results when, paradoxically, by employing oversized dildos, women only further alienate the men in whose absence such devices have been pressed to serve. "Products [like dildos] spoil cunts," Bolloximian complains of his former mistress, the "Grand Cunt" Officina; "what like woman was, it makes like cow" (3.1.157-58). The king's favorite, Pockenello, agrees: "fruitless cunts by frigging may be spoiled / When they use dildos big as new-born child" (159-60). To relieve the king's frustration, his councilors propose that he adopt a sexual alternative.

> Boras.   The choice of buggery, sir, is wanting *now.*
>   I would advise you, sir, to make a pass
>   Once more at Pockenello's loyal arse.
>   Besides, sir, Pene has so soft a skin
>   'Twould tempt a saint to thrust his pintle in.
> Tooly.   When last, good sir, your pleasure did vouchsafe
>   To let poor Tooly's hand your pintle chafe,
>   You gently moved it to my arse–when lo!
>   Arse did the deed which light hand could not do.
>   (1.1.41-49, emphasis added)

Borastus's "now" suggests that "the choice of buggery" was not wanting at some former time and deserves to be recovered since heterosexual vaginal sex currently proves so unsatisfying. Reminded of the pleasure he'd formerly enjoyed in homosexual anal intercourse, Bolloximian turns to his Buggermaster-General and commands:

> Bollox.   Henceforth, Borastus, set the nation free.
>   Let conscience have its force of liberty.
>   I do proclaim, that buggery may be used
>   O'er all the land, so cunt be not abused.
>   That's the provision. This shall be your trust.
> Boras.   All things shall to your orders be adjust.
> Bollox.   To Buggeranthus let this grant be given,
>   and let him bugger all things under heaven.
>   (1.1.67-74)

An ambivalent hierarchy is maintained here. Men are free to "bugger all things *under* heaven," thus insisting that a limit of some kind be respected, but "under" suggests the anal region of the body and a sexual position as well.

Bolloximian's proclamation is enthusiastically received by the men of the land, the transgressive power of sodomy being celebrated with mock-heroic enthusiasm. "May as the gods his name immortal be," Borastus exclaims, "That first received the gift of buggery" (3.1.89-90). Anal intercourse has been recovered as the primal pleasure, a gift from the gods themselves in that the gods have not only provided mortals with the example of sodomy but have oftentimes initiated mortals into it by imposing their sexual will upon defenseless, if not always unwilling, mortal males (for example, Zeus's ravishment of Ganymede). Buggeranthus reports that the army in particular is delighted.

> If lust presents, they want no woman's aid.
> Each buggers with content his own comrade.
> . . . . .
> It saves them, sir, at least a fortnight's pay.
> But arse they fuck, and bugger one another,
> And live like man and wife, sister and brother.
> (3.1.113-18)

The proclamation unleashes a mood of extraordinary sexual festivity in which the men, relieved of their sexual tedium, enjoy a sexual holiday. The golden age of peace, harmony, and sexually ambivalent but universal brotherhood has seemingly been reestablished on earth.

This gaiety, however, is interrupted by the arrival of Flux, the court physician, who informs the king of "the crying pains" of a venereal epidemic that has been raging for ten days time.

> The pricks are eaten off, the women's parts
> Are withered more than their despairing hearts.
> The children harbour heavy discontents,
> Complaining sorely of their fundaments.
> The old do curse and envy all that swive,
> And yet–in spite of impotence–will strive
> To fuck and bugger, though they stink alive.
> (5.1.25-31)

When Bolloximian asks what redress the doctor proposes, Flux insists that the king should revoke his edict and:

> To Love and Nature all their rights restore,
> Fuck no men, and let buggery be no more.
> It does the propagable end destroy,
> Which Nature gave with pleasure to enjoy.
> Please her, and she'll be kind; if you displease,
> She turns into corruption and disease.
> (5.1.44-49)

Sodomy, according to Flux, is an offense against both Love and Nature, who punish its performance with "corruption and disease." The apocalyptic chastisement of the biblical Cities of the Plain seems about to be repeated at the very end of the play when, just as "The curtain is drawn," the stage direction specifies "Enter FIRE and BRIMSTONE, and a CLOUD OF SMOKE appears." Rochester's farce risks suddenly devolving into tragedy as Bolloximian's kingdom is condemned to repeat the fate of biblical Sodom.

But even in the face of this apparent tragedy, the king refuses to respect the implicit judgment upon his and his nation's sexual activity.

> Then must I go to the old whore, my wife?
> Why did the Gods, that gave me leave to be
> A king, not grant me immortality?
> To be a substitute for heaven at will—
> I scorn the gift—I'll reign and bugger still.
> (5.1.53-57)

Its difficulty of syntax aside, Bolloximian's response to the threat of divine punishment is deeply moving. While he regrets that the gods have not bestowed immortality upon him, the experience of sodomy allows him to feel divine ("To be a substitute for heaven at will"); sexual "will" or desire is conflated linguistically with the sovereign "will" or dominion of kings and gods. In fact, even were the gods to offer him immortality (in exchange for his renouncing buggery, the passage seems to suggest), he would scorn their gift, preferring to reign on earth and exert his sexual will over his male minions.

Thus, even when confronted by death, Bolloximian refuses to repent and instead renews his commitment to sodomy, the most intense pleasure that he has known; and the gusto with which he pursues this pleasure reinforces the play's farcical aspect even in this moment of incipient tragedy. In the last lines of the play, Bolloximian turns to Pockenello, whom the *Dramatis Personnae* has identified as a "Pimp, Catamite, and the King's Favourite."

> Let heaven descend, and set the world on fire—
> We to some dark cavern will retire.
> There on thy buggered arse will I expire.

Bolloximian's sexual appetite proves indefatigable, even in the face of probable death, as his puns indicate. "Dark cavern" is a rural place of retreat to which the king and his minion will flee from the burning city, as well as the rectum of his favorite; similarly, "expire" both anticipates Bolloximian's death and suggests an orgasm of apocalyptic dimensions.

Bolloximian's awareness of the consequences of his actions but continued defiance of divine will in the pursuit of the sexual gratification that he perceives to be the highest pleasure and reward raises him to comic hero-ism, the farce playing itself out as Bolloximian anticipates continuing his sodomitical pleasures despite the world's apparent end. The stage direc-tion notes that Bolloximian speaks these lines "leering all the while" on Pockenello. Whatever "heaven" may think of it, sodomy is for Bolloxi-mian the most important thing on earth, and insofar as audience members laugh at his parting leer they suggest that they approve of, or at least sympathize with, his choice. Sodomy may call down upon his head the wrath of the gods, but for Bolloximian it is a pleasure well worth dying for. If the title *All for Love; or, The World Well Lost* (1677) suggests John Dryden's heroic ideal, then sacrificing "all for buggery" would seem to be Rochester's mock-heroic one.

There is, then, an ambivalence to Bolloximian's "choice of buggery." A festive aura surrounds the privileging of sodomy in the play, a festivity that persists even in the face of the fire and brimstone of divine judgment. But such festivity cannot mute the fact that the licensing of sodomy is mortally dangerous for Bolloximian and his people . . . at least *if* Flux's testimony is to be believed. There are, however, serious problems with Flux's reasoning–problems that identify the ambivalence at the heart of Rochester's *Sodom* with that in grotesque comic realism. It is to Bakhtin's theory of the carnivalesque that we must turn for an understanding both of the creative dynamic of Rochester's ambivalence and of the subversive political significance of his opening the male body as a site of sexual pleasure.

"BUGGER, BUGGER, BUGGER, / ALL IN HUGGER-MUGGER"

Carnival, Bakhtin has taught us, is a necessary act of social renewal in which the hierarchical structure which threatens to inhibit the flow of the life force is momentarily turned upside down. Even though that hierarchy will be reestablished at carnival's end, the hierarch's own perception of his power will have been modified, not to mention the perception of those over whom he rules.[6] In the grotesque realism that dominates the spirit of medieval carnival–and that Stallybrass and White have shown continues to characterize the transgressive spirit from Renaissance through modern times–exaggerated emphasis is placed upon the breasts, belly, buttocks, and genitals in order to reassert the importance of the very "fertility, growth, and a brimming-over abundance" (19) that the strictures of hierar-chy and the workaday world inhibit and are in danger of destroying. "The essential principle of grotesque realism is degradation, that is, the lowering of all that is high, spiritual, ideal, abstract," Bakhtin writes; "it is a transfer to the material level, to the sphere of earth and body in their indissoluble unity" (19-20). In the parodic act of "uncrowning," the body does a cartwheel when what is reserved for the head is transferred to the material bodily lower stratum; it is not reason or understanding which rules society for the season of carnival, but passion and sexual appetite.

Rochester's *Sodom* opens at just such a moment of uncrowning as Bolloximian decrees that sodomy shall replace vaginal intercourse as the officially sanctioned mode of sexual gratification. Bolloximian's proclamation has the paradoxical force of commanding license: "set the nation free. / Let conscience have its force of liberty." The relaxing of laws against sodomy will supposedly free the nation to indulge the mode of sexual pleasure that individuals *would* choose were there no legal constraints prohibiting it; Bolloximian is certain that, allowed liberty, conscience will freely choose sodomy. The world has been turned upside down or, more accurately, backwards/front: the anus replaces the vagina as vaginal intercourse is "uncrowned" in an act that promises renewal of a different sort than the strictly procreative. For the limited time of the farce's enactment, audience members enter a world in which the socially authorized poles of pleasure are reversed, and from which they exit with a modified awareness of what their own sexual possibilities are.

The grotesque bodily realism of Bakhtinian carnival dominates Rochester's farce. Genitals, for example, are conspicuously on display. The queen and her maids of honor freely discuss the size and needs of their vaginas, going so far as to uncover them onstage during the group masturbation activity of Act 1, Scene 2. Male genitalia are represented by the oversized dildos that improbably exceed nature; as in Rochester's lampoon of Charles II, the phallus is the scepter or fool's bauble by which the carnival world of pleasure is ruled. At the opening of Act 2, the stage directions describe a tableau in which

> Six naked women and six naked men appear, and dance, the men doing obeisance to the women's cunts, kissing and touching them often, the women doing ceremonies to the men's pricks, kissing them, dandling their cods, &c, and so fall to fucking, after which the women sigh, and the men look simple [dazed] and sneak off.

The masque is an antimasque, carnival reversing the standards that the masque was originally designed to inculcate at the Stuart court earlier in the century. Here the normally prohibited display of genitalia is made into a public ceremony, just as the socially restraining action of dance is subverted and its underlying sexual significance made explicit. Elsewhere, in Act 4, Scene 1, the women of the court examine Virtuoso's phallus and bring him to a premature ejaculation simply by the heat of their glances. And in Act 2, Scene 1, fifteen-year-old Prince Prickett and his somewhat older sister, Princess Swivia, analyze his genital development before she shuts the door and invites him to examine her "thing." Prickett's first sight of the pudendum is unsettling:

> Strange how it looks–methinks it smells of ling:
> It has a beard, yes, and a mouth all raw–
> The strangest creature that I ever saw.
> And these the beasts that keep men so in awe?
> (2.1.9-12)

Prickett's language is as outrageous as anything to be found in Rabelais, who supplies Bakhtin with his great example of the carnivalesque grotesque.[7]

But it is the statues of naked men and women engaged in lewd acts that adorn the pleasure garden in Act 1, Scene 2, that may best illustrate the challenge that Rochester's grotesque bodily realism offers to the hierarchical construction of sexuality. The "new bodily canon" that Bakhtin notes came to dominate the High Renaissance, and that was further refined in the neoclassical style,

> presents an entirely finished, completed, strictly limited body, which is shown from the outside as something individual. That which protrudes, bulges, sprouts, or branches off (when a body transgresses its limits and a new one begins) is eliminated, hidden, or moderated. All orifices of the body are closed. The basis of the image is the individual, strictly limited mass, the impenetrable facade. The opaque surface and the body's "valleys" acquire an essential meaning as the border of a closed individuality that does not merge with other bodies and with the world. (320)[8]

Rochester's farce, like the Aretine statues, not only emphasizes protuberances and dramatizes the body's merging with other bodies, but it opens that orifice considered *least* penetrable in hierarchical constructions, the male anus. For, traditionally, the open body that is essential to festive discourse is female, a woman's generosity in providing unrestricted access to her vagina marking the essentially sexual spirit of comedy's festival of cakes and ale.[9]

But in Rochester's *Sodom* a male's offering his body to another male for sexual use–far from being yet another instance of comic generosity or another disruptive act of the carnivalesque–threatens to destroy the entire community. The male's body being opened to penetration brings about not renewal but the end of the world, because in *Sodom* Rochester seeks a subversive reorientation of sexual perspectives and reversal of poles of discourse. Although the sinister aspect of the play's conclusion is partly due to the threat of a devouring appetite set loose, Rochester's insistence upon the open male body carries other implications as well.

As Guy Hocquenghem notes in his chapter on "Capitalism, the Family, and the Anus," in a mercantile or capitalist society sublimation is "exercised on the anus as on no other organ, in the sense that the anus is made to progress from the lowest to the highest point: anality is the very movement of sublimation itself" (96). The very thought of sodomy inspires revulsion in people who pride themselves on being socially refined because intimate contact with the fundament suggests a return to a state of being so "fundamental," as it were, that it abrogates the advance associated in culture with clothing, that great signifier of gender and social status as well as the means by which hierarchical society "closes" the body and prevents it–in Bakhtin's terms–from "outgrow[ing] itself, trangress[ing] its own limits" (26). In hierarchical terms, sodomy is the rejection of society's civilizing power, a deliberate defilement or sinking back into the dirt from which the species arose.[10]

For a male to invite penetration by another male is to voluntarily relinquish the power that comes to him naturally through the social structure, and so to effect a permanent (rather than carnival's merely momentary) subversion of that hierarchy. As Hocquenghem observes (103), by relinquishing the power socially invested in his phallus, the male who allows himself to be sodomized calls into question the power of the phallus in general–for, if that power can be renounced so easily, it may not be as valuable as patriarchy asserts. Likewise, because sodomy is performed for the gratification of one or both partners, without any intention or possibility of species reproduction, it is the "purest" form of sexual pleasure and thus undermines in particular the idea of the family, that microcosm of society. So threatening is this subversion of the social order that historically, in the Judeo-Christian West, homosexual sodomy has been identified as the sin or crime that cannot even be named without risk of contaminating the speaker.

Bolloximian's proclamation uncrowning the vagina and privileging the male anus carries with it an unstated exception in that Bolloximian does not himself ever submit to penetration; rather, his courtiers compete to offer themselves to him for sodomization. Desire has been set free, but hierarchy is maintained in this regard at least.[11] Yet by refusing to rescind his proclamation and by personally persisting in his sodomitical desire for Pockenello even after he has been threatened with divine retribution, Bolloximian subverts not simply the patriarchy that governs social intercourse, but the rules of carnival as well. Hierarchy is not reasserted at the end of the play in revised or modified form, but is completely abrogated; indeed, at the conclusion of *Sodom* there appears to be no society left to structure. The male body is being kept open past the close of carnival, as it were; the rectum is the grave in which the family and other political institutions are to be buried.[12] Hence the ambivalent festivity of the play's final scene. Carnival that goes on too long risks becoming a nightmare of excess, losing its essential *jouissance*; the more intense the pleasure, the more nihilistic it risks becoming.

But in its initial festive privileging of the male anus, Rochester's *Sodom* anticipates the subversive use of the open male body made by many twentieth-century self-identified homosexual writers. A telling example is Peter Orlovsky's *Clean Asshole Poems & Smiling Vegetable Songs* (1978), the volume's title indicating Orlovsky's intention both to challenge the American middle class's preference for red meat, and to reclaim the anus as a site of pleasure rather than of shame. The asshole is clean, not dirty; rather than being something that the individual should be reluctant to acknowledge, it is worthy of being celebrated as the site of pleasure and significance, even as the subject of poetry and song. The festive aspect of Orlovsky's anal transgression is developed in lyrics like "Good Fuck with Denise" in which Orlovsky celebrates working construction naked

> in Serra Nevadas
> & quite a few times
> the sun gave me a warm kiss
> on the center of my ass hole
> wile bending deep down doing some funney work. (25-29)

Songs in praise of "my sweet strong dildo" ("Dildo Song"), or that advise the reader to "Keep it clean in your sweet between / Keep it clean night & day when 69's o.k." ("Keep It Clean In Between"), are expressions of what, in the final words of "Frist Poem," the speaker calls "my gay jubilation." They are the effusions of a poetic voice that recalls of a teenaged romance:

> My oh My what a big healthey cock he had
> but I was young & strong

& could take it.
("Woe–Its Waring Time Again in the Armey" 31-33)

Throughout *Clean Asshole Songs* the speaker is plainly aware of the shock value of asserting such an unorthodox standard of "heroic" behavior–the ability to take "a big healthey cock" up the ass. Like Rimbaud, he delights to *épater les bourgeois.*[13]

In a hierarchical culture, asserting the anus as a site of pleasure is the most subversive thing that a man can do sexually. "When a man gets too straight he's just a god damned prick," observes William Burroughs (qtd. in Miles 96), suggesting the limitations of exclusive heterosexuality. "Straight" implies that one is forward-oriented, obsessed with pursuing a single direction, with the additional connotation of being one-sided in the pursuit of pleasure, more concerned with one's own satisfaction than with one's partner's. For a male to be more than his phallus, he must be the opposite of straight, which is "bent"–that is, he must be open to sexual alternatives, willing to give and receive sexual pleasure through organs other than the phallus, most notably the anus. Only when a male is willing to offer his body to others as a feast of cakes (a slang word for buttocks, as it happens) and ale is he truly a man.

Bolloximian refuses at the conclusion of *Sodom,* even when it is clear that the carnival is over, to return to what Rochester's audience would consider orthodox, socially sanctioned sexual relations. Rejecting outright any possibility of reconciling with his wife, and persisting in sodomy even if it means death, he effectively overturns the biblical order that a man should "cleave unto his wife: and they shall be one flesh" if he hopes to enjoy the divine gift of eternal life (Gen. 2: 24). He thus gives witness to the power of sodomy, a pleasure so much more intense than vaginal intercourse, as the Marquis de Sade repeatedly argued, that one persists in it despite the threat of punishment.[14]

But clearly the threat of punishment and the sodomist's awareness of the consequences of his act intensify a related pleasure: the sheer joy of transgressing.

ROCHESTER'S RESTRAINED FESTIVITY

Sodomy's paradoxically nihilistic intensification of sexual pleasure echoes a major theme found elsewhere in Rochester, one that requires a careful reading of Dr. Flux's speech before its full significance can be assessed.

The plight described by Dr. Flux clearly undercuts the festive nature of Rochester's sexual carnival. The women have gone mad with sexual despair; the men are sexually exhausted and riddled with venereal disease; children "complain . . . sorely of their fundaments" after being sodomized by adults; and the elderly are still tormented by lust even though impotence and general physical decrepitude deny them any hope of satisfying their desire. Far from comically expanding into a universe of renewal and joy, Bolloximian's kingdom of Sodom devolves into a world of sexual nightmare.

But despite what Dr. Flux claims, the epidemic is *not* the result of Bolloximian's licensing the men in his kingdom to practice sodomy (a fact which seriously undermines Elias's argument associating sodomy with Roman Catholicism). Anal intercourse proves to be but one of the play's multivarious sexual considerations. Nature makes intercourse pleasurable, Dr. Flux argues, in order to induce males and females to procreate. Thus, according to Dr. Flux, any nonreproductive sexual activity would be equally prone to "corruption and disease"—whether it be the women's "frigging" with dildos, their intercourse with animals, or the men's anal intercourse, with female or with male partners. Among the members of the royal family, as Flux himself reports (5.1.39-41), Queen Cuntigratia dies presumably because of her abuse of masturbation; Princess Swivia is raving mad "with pains and ulcerations in her womb"; and Prince Prickett "has a clap," caught when he was initiated in the rites of vaginal sex by his sister in Act 2, and not as a consequence of practicing anal sex. Flux's own speech betrays the limitations of his understanding of what makes for "natural" behavior.

What is more, Flux's very name implicates him in the license that he castigates, preventing him from serving as the moral center of the play as Elias supposes. The *Oxford English Dictionary* gives as its first meaning of "flux" "an abnormally copious flowing of blood, excrement, etc. from the bowels or other organs; a morbid or excessive discharge." In the sexually charged context of the play, Rochester's use of the word suggests a venereal discharge, implicating Flux in the universal contamination that he fulminates against. His body is clearly as vulnerable to corruption as everyone else's, which exposes as unwarranted his assumption of moral superiority. Rather, he is a self-righteous Malvolio darkening Sir Toby's midnight feast who, because he cannot permit himself to enjoy cakes and ale, would keep others from enjoying them too.

Finally, at no point in the play is the Judeo-Christian heterosexual ideal weighed against the sodomitical one and found to be superior, as Elias silently infers. There is nothing idealistic about nonsodomitical sex in *Sodom*. The court keeps a dildo and merkin maker in residence full-time to supply the tools with which women may gratify themselves, and to provide pubic "wigs" when the women's crotches go bald, either through friction during excessive coitus or as a consequence of venereal disease. Adultery is freely practised, and the soldiers' heterosexual coupling is a commercial transaction, Buggeranthus reporting that his men have saved "a fortnight's pay" after being permitted to take each other as sex partners. In this regard, Rochester seems to be drawing upon the older interpretive tradition that associates the sins of the Cities of the Plain with any kind of sexual license rather than with homosexual sodomy specifically. Understanding biblical Sodom to have been the site of both heterosexual and homosexual license, for example, Rochester's near-contemporary, John Milton, envisioned writing a Sodom drama in which "each evening everyone with mistress or Ganymede [walked] gitterning along the streets" (qtd. in Frontain, "Bible" 94).

Rather, the destruction wreaked upon Bolloximian's kingdom despite the king's transgressive joy in sodomy is an expression of Rochester's natural ambivalence towards any form of sexual excess: he was, finally, as unable to practice restraint as he was painfully conscious of the uselessness of indulgence. This paradox deserves amplification.

Gilbert Burnet observed that "There were two Principles in his [Rochester's] natural temper, that being heightened by that heat [of intemperance] carried him to great excesses: a violent love of Pleasure, and a disposition to extravagant Mirth" (in Farley-Hills, *Critical Heritage* 51). Thus, Rochester would appear to have been as predisposed by nature to Bakhtinian festivity as any of his fellow court wits, and in a letter to Elizabeth Barry he aptly described himself as "the wildest and most fantastical odd man alive" (*Letters* 3). Yet it is the *absence* of festivity that Dustin Griffin isolates as the most telling feature of Rochester's verse:

> Broadly speaking, his response to the body's vulnerability is neither anxious gloom (at one extreme) nor Rabelaisian laughter at the other. His laughter, derisive and sometimes brittle rather than festive, seeks neither to celebrate the body nor nervously to cover its naked weakness. It exposes the ridiculous. ("Holiday Writers" 59)

This seeming paradox is explained by the general problem, first recognized by Carole Fabricant, that Rochester had with *all* sexuality. Borrowing the title of one of his most sexually charged poems, Fabricant notes that because of the vulnerability of the body and its inability to satisfy the demands of imagination and appetite, Rochester's world is *always* one of imperfect enjoyment. "Rochester's writings deal less with orgasm than with its obstruction," she notes; "less with sexuality than with the *failure* of sexuality" (339). Rochester was painfully aware that passion cannot be sustained. Thus, as the time-conscious speaker of Rochester's haunting lyric "Love and Life" exclaims, if "The present moment's all my lot," and if that passes "as fast as it is got," then there is no point in talking about "inconstancy" inasmuch as it is miracle enough to remain true to another for "This live-long minute" (lines 8-15). Barbara Everett has extended Fabricant's analysis to account for "the sense of nothing" that underlies Rochester's work. The title of "The Maim'd [or Disabled] Debauchee," she notes, "compacts into a phrase the theme of impotency or emptiness below the surface of the extreme worldly experience," the last line of the poem showing "reality dissolving, chaos and promiscuity taking over, and sheer nothing opening all around" (21, 23)[15]–much the same way as *Sodom* concludes. The absence of despair in Rochester is the more impressive for his continuing to celebrate the present moment of pleasure even when so acutely aware of its pending failure.[16] Rochester seems to know that although carnival may not last very long, it is mankind's only stay against the void.

Thus, by raising the issue of his own mortality in Act 5, even while preparing to indulge his sodomitical pleasure for perhaps the final time, Bolloximian implicitly underscores how similar his conundrum is to that of the women earlier in the play. All sexual pleasure is brief, and the more ardently we humans strive to obtain and enjoy it, the more dissatisfied we will be when it ends. Although he may appear to momentarily escape the women's sexual despair, Bolloximian is condemned, just as surely as they are, to be frustrated eventually by the very experience that gives him the greatest joy; his anticipated coupling with Pockenello will probably not outlast the pending end of the world. *Sodom* concludes–as Everett notes every work of Rochester concludes–with "Nothing." Bolloximian's glory lies in refusing to be defeated by "Nothing" at the start.

It makes no difference that "The choice of buggery" (1.1.41) proves ultimately a destructive choice, for every choice in Rochester's world will result in "nothing." *Sodom* establishes sodomy as the most intense sexual sensation available to Bolloximian; his adherence to it even in the face of what seems to be divine retribution is witness to its power to provide the most intense sensation that humans can know. What *is* important is that, like Rochester's other libertine heroes, Bolloximian resolves to *enjoy* the farce of sex even while knowing full well that it will come to "nothing."

CONCLUSION:
ROCHESTER'S SECULARIZATION OF THE BIBLE

Sodomy is natural, Rochester's play asserts–so natural that only the strictest social proscription can keep it from universally supplanting vaginal intercourse. Bolloximian's relaxing that proscription, however, calls into question a higher or more authoritative one: the Judeo-Christian biblical injunction that is raised by the controlling allusion in the farce's title.

The biblical narrative of Sodom and Gomorrah suggests that divine punishment will be visited upon a site of sexual subversiveness, a correlation that Rochester's play reenacts only to deconstruct. For there are several problems with too trusting an acceptance of such a correlation as Elias makes. First, despite the biblical allusion contained in the farce's title, the play betrays more an Ovidian than a Christian ethos. Characters speak of "the gods" rather than of "God," as Rochester deliberately invokes a pre-Christian authority. And far from proscribing sodomy, the only gods implicit in the play themselves made a gift of the practice to men. Rochester has created a divinely ordered universe, but not one that is morally proscriptive; he reminds his audience of the biblical threat of punishment in order to render it meaningless.

Second, even if one would follow Elias and accept Flux as the spokesperson for orthodox morality, the Bible's authority can be reasserted at the end of the play only if *Sodom* leads the audience to recognize the seriousness of Bolloximian's transgression, which, as we have seen, *Sodom* clearly does *not* do. Indeed, the play is entitled a "farce," thus erasing even the possibility of tragic consequence for Bolloximian's sexual transgression. What is more, far from asserting that a moral authority governs the universe, *Sodom* questions whether there is any ultimate moral significance to sexual actions at all. *Sodom* dramatizes a world of sensation, outside of which there is nothing.

Finally, the play subverts the biblically authorized theology of marriage and sexual intercourse that James Grantham Turner has shown was used to construct seventeenth-century heterosexual relationships. Bolloximian does not cleave to his wife; far from concluding with a sexual paradise of one flesh on earth, the play suggests that Cuntigratia initiated the division in their married life by overindulging the use of dildos.

What allows Rochester to challenge the single greatest authority of his culture? If *Sodom* is situated at that significant moment in the history of sexuality that initiates the construction of a homosexual identity, it is situated at a significant moment in the interpretive history of the Bible as well. Although the English Revolution, which beheaded the king and temporarily deposed the bishops, was reversed by the restoration of both Charles II and the episcopate, hierarchy's authority was never to be the same. Puritan insistence upon the "inner light of reason" and the "liberty to prophesy" freed the Bible from monolithic interpretation and, paradoxically, significantly lessened its authority. For when there are as many readings of a passage as there are "saints" inspired to comment upon it, the urgency of any single interpretation is all the less commanding. What is more, the century's Baconian scientific movement, which resulted in the founding of the Royal Society in Rochester's day, implicitly challenged the reliability of miracles and mystery as a way of knowing by carefully scrutinizing conclusions deduced from revelation. Thus, when Hobbes examined "The Number, Antiquity, Scope, Authority and Interpreters of the Books of Holy Scripture" in Part III of *Leviathan* (1651), he considered the biblical scrolls as historical documents rather than as inspired texts.[17] Little wonder that when Dryden came to write *Absalom and Achitophel,* he felt free to use "the biblical text as a novel alternative to classical mythology" (Roston 177) rather than as an inspired source that he felt obliged carefully to follow.

Thus, while the Judeo-Christian threat of divine retribution associated with the Sodom story is raised at the end of *Sodom,* Rochester could feel free to transform radically its meaning. In the biblical narrative, Lot is saved by escaping the city where his visitors have been threatened with sodomization by the local men, but there is no corresponding Lot figure in Rochester's *Sodom*; although Bolloximian likewise flees the city, he flees not *from* sodomy but *to* it. Likewise, humans themselves, not an avenging Jehovah, are responsible for their destruction when they exceed what nature provides; their pursuit of more intense sensation leads to the inevitable collapse of the natural organism. Sodomy, nevertheless, is valorized as the most intense sensation available, one's best comfort against the threat of death. Far from making the farce of human sexuality into a tragedy, Rochester reduces the biblical tragedy of human transgression and punishment into a farce.

In doing so, Rochester takes one of the first steps towards the modern reclamation of the biblical narrative most often used to construct–or deconstruct–homosexual identity. *Sodom* anticipates the use made of the Genesis episode by the Marquis de Sade in *Les Cent Vingt Journées de Sodome* (1785), by Pier Paolo Pasolini in *Salò* (1975), and by Paul Russell in *Boys of Life* (1991), whose protagonist, Carlos Reichart (a character clearly based upon Pasolini), films "The Gospel according to Sodom," in which the arrival in the ancient city of a beautiful young male provokes a disturbing sexual apocalypse.[18] Like Rochester, they create worlds where the greater heroism is to transgress against biblical authority by indulging socially proscribed sexual desire even when to do so is fatal; indeed, the threat that hangs over the act guarantees its larger meaning and intensifies the pleasure of performing it. Like Bolloximian, the characters in these works freely choose "buggery" because it enhances their sensation of being alive and allows them to enjoy a sexual carnival even while fully conscious of how dark that carnival may finally prove. Rochester may insist in his title that his vision of "the quintessence of debauchery" is only a "farce," but his inversion of the Book of Genesis's heterosexual creationism makes his homosexual anal nihilism only slightly less heroic for being so festively mock-heroic.

NOTES

1. After noting that Rochester "perhaps . . . collaborated in an obscene farce *Sodom,*" Keith Walker observes that "to assert this twenty years ago would have damaged Rochester's reputation as much as to deny it today" (x). Like Paddy Lyons (314), whose edition of Rochester's verse I follow throughout, I find persuasive the various arguments for Rochester's primary, if not exclusive, authorship of *Sodom* put forward by Larry Carver and J. W. Johnson. As significant, however, are the thematic parallels that I will be calling attention to throughout this essay. It is only for efficiency's sake, however, that I refer to Rochester in this essay as the sole author of the play.

2. Elias's association of sodomy with Roman Catholicism is plausible, a tradition asserting that association having been a staple of militant Protestantism. Thomas Coryate, for example, reports that while touring Switzerland in 1610 he visited Henry Bullingen, the nephew of the great Calvinist divine. Bullingen showed Coryate "one most execrable booke written by an Italian, one *Ioannes Casa* Bishop of Beneventum in Italy, in praise of that unnaturall sinne of Sodomy," which Bullingen claimed to have inherited from his grandfather, who had "kept it as a monument of the abhominable impurity of a papistical Bishop" (391).

3. Marianne Thörmahlen (295-303) analyzes the specific targets of Rochester's political satire in "Verses," effectively qualifying Christopher Hill's assessment of Rochester as "the courtier and friend of Charles II who wrote savage republican verse" (qtd. in Thörmahlen 300 n.50). Indeed, one of the best arguments for Rochester's partial or sole authorship of *Sodom* is how closely it duplicates the subject, if not the tone, of Rochester's court and social satires in which, according to Thörmahlen (308),

> fashionable society activities, Court amours and drunken revels are viewed with cynical distaste, sometimes even with physical revulsion. The impatience and restlessness that could be felt in the love poems have their counterparts in the Court satires, too. Inferior minds express themselves in vile talk, and the realm of the senses is profoundly disappointing; bodies are diseased or unclean, food and drink abysmal. At no level does human intercourse, of whatever kind, afford satisfaction. If true worth and substance reside anywhere in human existence, it is not in that sphere.

Larry Carver's reading of the play would support Elias's general claim in this regard as well. Both the P1 and P2 manuscript versions of *Sodom,* Carver notes, are "propelled by . . . a desire to puncture the sycophancy of the pro-Stuart apologists, particularly Dryden, and to reveal the depravity of the court, political and sexual" (30). As I argue below, the ultimate failure of sexual festivity in *Sodom* is perhaps the farce's most Rochesterian trait.

4. I rely upon Weber in this regard, regretting only that he does not consider *Sodom* in his analysis. Thörmahlen's analysis (20-23) of the pederastic references in Rochester's poetry arrives independently at a conclusion similar to Weber's that for Rochester the sexual activities that occurred between two men depended upon the age and social status of the participants rather than upon any biblical or ecclesiastical injunction. For example, in *Sodom* Bolloximian is never buggered by his courtiers; instead they put themselves sexually at his service. The play, thus, respects the same homosocial "economy of desire" that Weber finds operating in Rochester's verse which, Weber concludes, is "predicated on a system in which boys and women are interchangeable objects circulating between men of equal position" (102). The exclusion of women from this sexual economy at the outset of the play, however, makes *Sodom* the fulfillment of what Weber concludes was Rochester's "goal of masculine self-sufficiency" (110).

5. An analogous situation exists in Rochester's description in "Signior Dildo" of his kinswoman Barbara Palmer, Countess of Castlemaine and Duchess of Cleveland:

That pattern of virtue her Grace of Cleveland
Has swallowed more pricks than the ocean has sand;
But by rubbing and scrubbing so large it does grow,
It is fit for just nothing but Signior Dildo. (37-40)

Rochester's association of dildos with Roman Catholicism in this poem (see Thörmahlen 289, 293-94) offers tangential support to Elias's argument that *Sodom* associates sexual license with unhealthy religious liberty.

6. This important qualification of Bakhtin has been made by Leah Marcus, among others. As Marcus notes, "Some of the most interesting recent theorists have argued for festival's inclusion of both normative and revisionary impulses. Its seemingly lawless topsy-turveydom can both undermine and reinforce–it can constitute a process of adjustment within a perpetuation of order" (7). Bakhtin has also been criticized for drawing upon medieval folk customs to create a context for Rabelais, a Renaissance writer, but as Stallybrass and White have shown, the transgressive functions of carnival and the grotesque body transcend periodization, their stage changing but their function remaining, in general, constant from the medieval period through the modern.

7. This is a feature of the larger Rochester canon as well. As editor Keith Walker observes, "in Rochester's poetry, private parts are always assuming a life of their own, detached from the body" (xviii).

One of the most telling indications in *Sodom* of Rochester's grotesque bodily realism are the sexual fluids that are emitted throughout the play. The body must be "open" and self-control relinquished for such fluids to be released. And, true to the mock-heroic tone of the farce, these fluids do not simply flow, but gush fountain-like, suggesting a brimming over and superabundance of life. This is not a dry and sterile world, but one lush with extravagance and excess.

8. See Stallybrass and White (21-22) on the neoclassical statue elevated on a pedestal as the model for the closed body, and chap. 2 in general on the grotesque, satiric body in eighteenth-century culture. In "Patriarchal Territories," Stallybrass works with the political significance in earlier texts of the closed body as well.

9. Chaucer's Wife of Bath, for example, boasts that she uses "myn instrument / As freely as my Makere hath it sent" ("Wife of Bath's Prologue" 155-56). The opening of the vagina to sexual use is one of the principal actions of festive comedy; see Frontain, "Madame" and "Anatomizing."

10. Paul Hallam analyzes seventeenth- through twentieth-century published objections to sodomy, concluding that critics fear sodomists for three reasons: lest the supposedly secret fraternity or conspiracy of sodomists undermine national security and communal morality; lest they assault the unprotected rears of anxious heterosexual men or the rears of their young; and lest they contaminate the supposedly clean and healthy portion of society by their association with fecal matter. Hallam's shrugging observation, "I'll accept the dirt taboo. I can't imagine a world without dirt" (44), is a good example of the festive acceptance of the world in its fullness.

11. Such an arrangement is in keeping as well with "The Disabled Debauchee" in which the speaker cannot remember whether, during a particularly memorable threeway, "the well-looked link-boy" "fucked" the speaker's mistress, Cloris, or the speaker himself made use of the "boy" (lines 37-40). Hierarchy is maintained in that there is no suggestion of the page possibly penetrating the speaker. But by equalizing vaginal and anal sex, and making interchangeable his male and female partner, the speaker promotes a sexual confusion that challenges the hierarchy from which his own privileges, both sexual and social, derive, even while reasserting his own position in that hierarchy. As David Farley-Hills argues, much of the power of Rochester's poetry is the result of the tension between the "traditional form and ceremonies" that maintained "the ideas of order from which his social privileges derived," and his private loss of belief in a divine order which led him to see "life as ultimately meaningless" and any attempt "at establishing order as arbitrary and unstable" (*Rochester's Poetry* 36).
Obviously, I think grossly misguided Ronald Paulson's conclusion that "in general we must regard the link-boy in Rochester as we would in a satire of Juvenal, as a perversion of normal human activities" (120 n.7). In "The Disabled Debauchee," rather, Rochester seeks to undermine "normal" social *perceptions* of what is sexually fulfilling. I am surprised that Paulson thinks Rochester might even be remotely interested in upholding socially prescribed "norms" of sexual activity.

12. See Leo Bersani's psychoanalytic reading of the rectum's cultural ambivalence as a grave, especially his conclusion that "Male homosexuality advertises the risk of the sexual itself as the risk of self-dismissal, of *losing sight* of the self, and in so doing it proposes and dangerously represents *jouissance* as a mode of ascesis" (262). See, too, Lee Edelman's juxtaposition of the Genesis Creation story with "the gay male anus [as] the site of pleasure [that] gives birth to AIDS

as a figuration of death": "the nihilism of the anus thus threatens to annihilate all creation" (99).

13. Among Rimbaud's more aggressive poems are "*Le Sonnet du trou du cul*" ("Sonnet to the Asshole") and "*Nos fesses ne sont pas les leurs*" ("Our Asses Are Not like Theirs").

14. In discussing Sade's delight in sodomy as "*contresens*"–that is, its value as sexual pleasure lying in the fact that it is "the *antithesis* of propagation"–Maurice Lever (116-17) quotes a speech by Sade's Dolmace on why the "sodomite pleasure" should surpass all others:

> The pleasure is such that nothing can interfere with it, and the object that serves it cannot, in savoring it, fail to be transported to the third heaven. No other is as good, no other can satisfy as fully both the individuals who indulge in it, and those who have experienced it can revert to other things only with difficulty.

Like Rochester's Bolloximian, Sade dismissingly compares vaginal sex to "swim[ming] in a vacuum," and wittily reminds his wife (to whom he was writing at the time) that nature abhors a vacuum, thus suggesting that vaginal sex is actually *less* natural an act than sodomy.

See also Lever 205-6 for a summary of Monsieur de Bressac's explanation to Justine of the rapturous pleasures of being penetrated by another man, and Lever's analysis (585 n.10) of why prosecutions of sodomy were "astonishingly limited" in the eighteenth century despite the repressiveness of the law.

15. The finest writing on Rochester has developed these insights. As Ronald Berman has shown, the defeat of the senses is the inevitable result of heightened sensuality in Rochester; heterosexual pleasures, because the more ordinary, simply wane more quickly than homosexual ones. For Anne Righter, Rochester–like Byron–"persistently asked of sense experience things which were not only in excess of what they could give, but inappropriate to it," and so was condemned to a life of disappointment and frustration (4). Griffin likewise notes that Rochester's poems "never reflect a completely satisfying sense experience" (*Satires* 7); elsewhere he concludes that "In Rochester's world of impotence the worst plight is usually not the death of desire nor even the failure of the body to perform. Rather, it is the persistence of desire, the continued eagerness to perform, when the power of attracting is gone" ("Holiday Writers" 59). Thörmahlen demonstrates that in Rochester's lyrics pleasure is always conditional or unrealized (22-23), Rochester being "a writer who rarely contemplates aspects of love other than the purely physical, but who has little if anything to say about the glories of sexual fulfillment" (29).

16. Berman's insights into this paradoxical aspect of Rochester are particularly strong: "The dandy in the poems of Rochester is involved in decadence because it is a sign of life. Yet the failure of the senses is Rochester's great obsession. If the supreme value remains 'pleasure,' then the failure of that principle is itself the end of a philosophy. Man is estranged from the only experience that he finds meaningful. To be aware of this possibility, in a milieu in which nothing really matters, is to commit an act of morality" (368).

In his introduction to the *Letters,* Treglown (12-13) reads "All my past life is mine no more" in terms of Hobbes's theory of time to explain why the speaker is more concerned with the pleasure of the present moment than with the progenerative aspect of sex.

17. Gerard Reedy has studied the tension between reason and revelation in late seventeenth-century thought. See also the excellent anthology, compiled by John Drury, of mid-eighteenth-century writing that grew from this late seventeenth-century movement. On Rochester's ability to quote the Bible subversively, see Treglown's introduction to Rochester's *Letters* (14).

18. *Lot in Sodom,* a 1930 film made by Melville Webber and James Sibley Watson, seems to have approached this theme but in a more uncertain way. According to Richard Dyer, on whose description of the film I rely, "It shows Sodom destroyed for its gayness and thus may appear morally conventional, but it feels like a celebration of gayness" (109).

WORKS CITED

Bakhtin, Mikhail. *Rabelais and His World.* Trans. Helene Iswolsky. Cambridge, MA: MIT P, 1968.

Berman, Ronald. "Rochester and the Defeat of the Senses." *Kenyon R* 26 (1964): 354-68.

Bersani, Leo. "Is the Rectum a Grave?" 1987. Rpt. *Reclaiming Sodom.* Ed. Jonathan Goldberg. New York: Routledge, 1994. 249-64.

Carver, Larry. "The Texts and the Text of *Sodom." Papers of the Bibliographical Society of America* 73 (1979): 19-40.

Coryate, Thomas. *Coryates Crudities.* London, 1611.

Drury, John, ed. *Critics of the Bible 1724-1873.* Cambridge: Cambridge UP, 1989.

Dyer, Richard. *Now You See It: Studies in Lesbian and Gay Film.* London: Routledge, 1990.

Edelman, Lee. *Homographesis: Essays in Gay Literary and Cultural Theory.* New York: Routledge, 1994.

Elias, Richard. "Political Satire in *Sodom." SEL* 18 (1978): 423-38.

Everett, Barbara. "The Sense of Nothing." *Spirit of Wit: Reconsiderations of Rochester.* Ed. Jeremy Treglown. Hamden, CT: Archon Books, 1982. 1-41.

Fabricant, Carole. "Rochester's World of Imperfect Enjoyment." *JEGP* 73 (1974): 338-50.

Farley-Hills, David, ed. *Rochester: The Critical Heritage.* New York: Barnes and Noble, 1972.

_____ . *Rochester's Poetry.* Totowa, NJ: Rowman and Littlefield, 1978.

Frontain, Raymond-Jean. "Anatomizing Boccaccio's Sexual Festivity." *Approaches to Teaching Boccaccio's "Decameron."* Ed. James H. S. McGregor. New York: Modern Language Assoc. of America, in press.

_____ . "Bible." *Gay and Lesbian Literary Heritage.* Ed. Claude J. Summers. New York: Holt, 1995. 92-100.

_____ . "'Madame, Spare That Mole!': Comic Responses to Psychosexual

Threats in Sterne's *Tristram Shandy.*" *PAPA: Publications of the Arkansas Philological Assoc.* 16 (spring 1990): 15-30.

Griffin, Dustin H. *Satires Against Man: The Poems of Rochester.* Berkeley: U of California P, 1973.

_____. "Rochester and the 'Holiday Writers.' " *Rochester and Court Poetry.* Ed. Alan Roper. Los Angeles: William Andrews Clark Memorial Library, 1988. 33-66.

Hallam, Paul. *The Book of Sodom.* London: Verso, 1993.

Hocquenghem, Guy. *Homosexual Desire.* Trans. Daniella Dangoor. Pref. by Jeffrey Weeks. 1978. Reissued with new intro. by Michael Moon. Durham, NC: Duke UP, 1993.

Johnson, J. W. "Did Lord Rochester Write *Sodom?*" *Papers of the Bibliographical Society of America* 81 (1987): 119-53.

Lever, Maurice. *Sade: A Biography.* Trans. Arthur Goldhammer. San Diego: Harvest/Harcourt Brace, 1994.

Marcus, Leah S. *The Politics of Mirth.* Chicago: U of Chicago P, 1986.

Miles, Barry. *Ginsberg: A Biography.* New York: Simon and Schuster, 1989.

Orlovsky, Peter. *Clean Asshole Poems & Smiling Vegetable Songs.* Pocket Poets Series #37. San Francisco: City Lights Books, 1978.

Oxford English Dictionary. Compact Edition, 2 vols. New York: Oxford UP, 1971.

Paulson, Ronald. "Rochester: The Body Politic and the Body Private." 1978. Rpt. in *John Wilmot, Earl of Rochester: Critical Essays.* Ed. David M. Vieth. New York: Garland, 1988. 45-67.

Reedy, Gerard. *The Bible and Reason: Anglicans and Scripture in Late Seventeenth-Century England.* Philadelphia: U of Pennsylvania P, 1985.

Righter, Anne. "John Wilmot, Earl of Rochester." Chatterton Lecture on an English Poet, 1967. Rpt. in *John Wilmot, Earl of Rochester: Critical Essays.* Ed. David M. Vieth. New York: Garland, 1988. 1-26.

Rimbaud, Arthur, and Paul Verlaine. *A Lover's Cock and Other Gay Poems.* Trans. J. Murat and W. Gunn. San Francisco: Gay Sunshine P, 1979.

Rochester, John Wilmot, Earl of. *Complete Poems and Plays.* Ed. with an intro. by Paddy Lyons. London: Dent, 1993.

_____. *The Letters of John Wilmot, Earl of Rochester.* Ed. with an intro. by Jeremy Treglown. Chicago: U of Chicago P, 1980.

Roston, Murray. *Biblical Drama in England.* Evanston, IL: Northwestern UP, 1968.

Stallybrass, Peter. "Patriarchal Territories: The Body Enclosed." *Rewriting the Renaissance: The Discourses of Sexual Difference in Early Modern Europe.* Ed. Margaret W. Ferguson et al. Chicago: U of Chicago P, 1986. 123-42.

Stallybrass, Peter, and Allon White. *The Politics and Poetics of Transgression.* Ithaca, NY: Cornell UP, 1986.

Thörmahlen, Marianne. *Rochester: The Poems in Context.* Cambridge: Cambridge UP, 1993.

Turner, James Grantham. *One Flesh: Paradisal Marriage and Sexual Relations in the Age of Milton.* Oxford: Clarendon P, 1987.

Walker, Keith, ed. *The Poems of John Wilmot, Earl of Rochester.* Oxford: Basil Blackwell for The Shakespeare Head P, 1984.

Weber, Harold. "'Drudging in Fair Aurelia's Womb': Constructing Homosexual Economies in Rochester's Poetry." *The Eighteenth Century: Theory and Interpretation* 33 (1992): 99-117.

Simeon Solomon
and the Biblical Construction
of Marginal Identity in Victorian England

Gayle M. Seymour, PhD

University of Central Arkansas

SUMMARY. During the formative stages of his sexual development (1855-1860), the Pre-Raphaelite artist Simeon Solomon (1840-1905) appropriated the authority of the Bible to explore, camouflage, and ultimately, legitimize his own homoerotic yearnings. Using Plummer and Troiden's four-stage constructionist model of Gay Identity Acquisition to provide an interpretive framework for six of the artist's early Old Testament drawings, this paper charts Solomon's development from awareness, to crisis, to acceptance. Solomon's use of biblical subjects to express his inner states reflects his construction of a socially marginal homosexual identity, an act which allowed him to overcome the despair and the isolation engendered by his peripheral standing in Victorian society. *[Article copies available for a fee from The Haworth Document Delivery Service: 1-800-342-9678. E-mail address: getinfo@haworth.com]*

Gayle M. Seymour, an associate professor of Art History at the University of Central Arkansas, has been researching the art and life of Simeon Solomon since 1982 and completed a doctoral dissertation on the artist in 1986 at the University of California, Santa Barbara. Her work on Solomon includes numerous conference papers and an essay in the catalogue of the Solomon Family Exhibition at the Geffrey Museum in London.

Correspondence may be addressed: Department of Art, 117 McAlister Hall, University of Central Arkansas, Conway, AR 72035-5003, or electronically at gayles@cc3.uca.edu.

[Haworth co-indexing entry note]: "Simeon Solomon and the Biblical Construction of Marginal Identity in Victorian England." Seymour, Gayle M. Co-published simultaneously in *Journal of Homosexuality* (The Haworth Press, Inc.) Vol. 33, No. 3/4, 1997, pp. 97-119; and: *Reclaiming the Sacred: The Bible in Gay and Lesbian Culture* (ed: Raymond-Jean Frontain) Harrington Park Press, an imprint of The Haworth Press, Inc., 1997, pp. 97-119. Single or multiple copies of this article are available for a fee from The Haworth Document Delivery Service [1-800-342-9678, 9:00 a.m. - 5:00 p.m. (EST). E-mail address: getinfo@haworth.com].

Paradoxically, Simeon Solomon's arrest for sodomy at age 33 had the immediate effect of erasing him from High Art circles, but of allowing his resurrection as a subject of interest to post-Stonewall gay cultural historians. Thus, in 1987 Neil Bartlett mounted a one-man show based on the life of the artist,[1] and Solomon's paintings and drawings have been used to illustrate such seminal studies as Reade's *Sexual Heretics,* Dellamora's *Masculine Desire,* and Fone's *Road to Stonewall.* Curiously, however, Solomon's understanding of his sexuality–as expressed in his art–has yet to be analyzed. This paper will examine how Solomon attempted to appropriate the authority of the Bible,[2] by adopting certain of its themes, to explore, interpret, and define his own homoerotic yearnings. Through the ancient stories of David, Jonathan, Saul, Nathan, and Esther, Solomon found sanctioned biblical precedent for his feelings and, during the formative stages of his sexual development, used these themes as a way of camouflaging and legitimizing his homosexuality.

No consensus has yet emerged regarding the process of homosexual identity formation. Gay theorists have largely divided themselves along the lines of "essentialist" and "constructionist" positions. While most would agree that homosexual behavior has existed in all cultures and in all times, the essentialist view holds that a distinct gay identity has existed throughout history, relatively unchanged, while the constructionist view focuses instead on the ways in which different societies' values affect the way people conceive of their sexuality (Koponen 139). Yet the concepts of homosexual identity and homosexual lifestyle are relatively recent ones. If, as the constructionists argue, gay identity is a social construction, and a recent one, then it becomes problematic to speak of "gay people" apart from particular social, economic, political, and historical conditions. Jeffrey Weeks has shown that even though the term "homosexual" did not exist until 1869, among men clear signs of a distinct homosexual lifestyle and identity began to emerge in Britain in the late-seventeenth century and were identified and described in the latter part of the nineteenth century (Weeks 2-4). Given this, an artist such as Simeon Solomon is obviously of crucial importance since his lifetime (1840-1905) exactly coincides with the formative period of the modern concept of the homosexual person, and his art and life may shed some light as to how those who engaged in homosexual activity during the nineteenth century attempted to construct their own identity.

In certain of Solomon's Old Testament drawings, executed between 1855 and 1860, when Solomon was aged 15-20, may be read subtexts that suggest that during his adolescence, whether consciously or subliminally, the artist interpreted, defined, and struggled to make sense of his erotic proclivities. Significantly, Solomon appears to have progressed through identifiable stages in this development, from awareness, to crisis, to acceptance. While I acknowledge that great care should be used in applying contemporary gay identity theory to an earlier historical era, especially one that was just beginning to recognize such a concept, I will attempt to use a constructionist model of sexuality first described in 1975 by Kenneth Plummer (135-153) and elaborated upon by Richard Troiden in 1989, which marks four stages of Gay Identity Acquisition: stage one, *sensitization*; stage two, *identity confusion*; stage three, *identity assumption*; and stage four, *commitment*.[3] (Although some of Solomon's work from the late 1860s and early 1870s reflect a *commitment* stage, this last stage will not be described within this paper since I am dealing only with the adolescent and post-adolescent Solomon.) This model, incidentally, is roughly parallel to other theoretical models which describe strikingly similar patterns of growth and change as hallmarks of homosexual identity formation: Elisabeth Kübler-Ross's five-stage model of Individual Reconciliation, Vivienne Cass's six-stage model of Homosexual Identity Formation, and Eli Coleman's model of the five developmental stages of the coming-out process (Koponen 16). It is important to recognize that for any of these models a neat and orderly step-by-step progression from beginning to end is unlikely ever to occur; indeed, stages might be merged, realized simultaneously, or skipped altogether (Troiden 47-48).

A few facts about Simeon Solomon's childhood and adolescence are known. He was born into a wealthy Jewish family in London on 9 October 1840 to Michael, then 51 years old, and Catherine or Kate Solomon (née Levy), age 38 or 39. Simeon's birth certificate lists his father as "embosser," a profession which allowed the family considerable financial security, enough at least, to allow three of his eight children to enter art schools (Geffrey Museum 6). The young Simeon apparently had a real gift for drawing, especially in pen and ink, and in 1850, at the age of ten, he entered his brother Abraham's Gower Street Studio to begin his artistic training (Williamson 158). Simeon was only twelve when he began more formal classes at Carey's Drawing School in Bloomsbury. In the fall of 1855 the aspiring Solomon entered the Royal Academy Schools as a probationer and by January 1856 had successfully passed the necessary tests which made him eligible to begin as a full-fledged student. He was only 15. The memoirs of Henry Holiday (1839-1927) are the chief source of information about the youth of Solomon and record the 20-year friendship shared by these two artists. Holiday remembered that he and Solomon "not unnaturally gravitated to each other, and sat side by side at work" (Holiday 37), since they were the two youngest students at the RA Schools.

During this time Solomon began a detailed *Sketchbook,* now in the Museum of Art at the Ein Harod Kibbutz, Israel,[4] which was referred to in several contemporary accounts by members of the Pre-Raphaelite circle and which contains some of Solomon's earliest Old Testament drawings.

The biblical character who seemed to hold the most fascination for young Solomon was David. Of all the Old Testament figures, it is David who is perhaps the most fully and vividly presented, and as Frontain and Wojcik have pointed out, the complexity of David's story—he was warrior, lover, adulterer, poet, killer, and restorer—allows the writer and the artist wide space for individual interpretations (1).[5] It is perhaps logical that the fifteen-year-old Solomon should identify with David, the young shepherd boy, the youngest of Jesse's eight sons (Solomon himself was the youngest of eight children). Furthermore, David's intimate relationships with men— most notably that with Jonathan—offered Solomon legitimizing models for the love between men. According to the First Book of Samuel, David and Jonathan publicly displayed their love for one another by openly swearing a lifetime pact together: "Then Jonathan and David made a covenant, because he [Jonathan] loved him as his own soul" (1 Sam. 18:3). Later, when Jonathan learned of the imminent threat to David's life, they met in secret, kissed each other and wept in their farewell (1 Sam. 20:41-2). These passages—together with David's powerful lament after Jonathan's death, "thy love to me was wonderful, passing the love of women" (2 Sam. 1:26)—allowed young Solomon to work out issues of sexual identity. One can only imagine the overwhelming sense of relief and liberation for a middle-class Jewish boy to see his own feelings acted out as an exalted, heroic passion. Perhaps drawing the relationship of David and Jonathan allowed him a way to camouflage his own very particular feelings. We know that beginning in 1855 Solomon was developing a strong emotional attachment with a member of the same sex, his chum at the Royal Academy Schools, Henry Holiday. While there is no evidence to suggest any genital activity took place between them, Solomon's choice of the David-Jonathan theme at this time in his life, at the very least, suggests the artist's subconscious interests in the subject of male-male friendship and, perhaps, indicates that he was becoming aware of his feelings. Thus, for Solomon, David might be considered an "object" of fascination which subsequently came to symbolize the artist's "ponderings over potential homosexuality" (Plummer 135).

On 22 July 1856 the fifteen-year-old Solomon completed his first David illustration, *The Story of David* (Tate Gallery, London, Figure 1), a highly finished drawing, in which the artist's imaginative power and precocious technical skill are clearly in evidence. For this work Solomon employed a

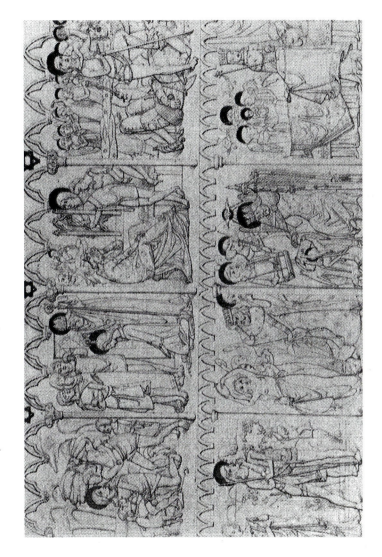

FIGURE 1. Simeon Solomon, *The Story of David*, 22 July 1856. Pencil/buff paper, 25.40 × 36.83 cm. The Tate Gallery, London (Courtesy Tate Gallery, London).

quaint, medieval style suggesting his knowledge of medieval manuscripts, such as those of the Franco-Flemish school of around 1250.[6] Also neo-medieval are Solomon's compartmentalized, trefoil design of the architectural border (much like that of a medieval illuminated manuscript page), his use of continuous outlines on the figures, and the linear treatments of the drapery folds.

Solomon's drawing charts eight episodes in the life of David (left to right and top to bottom): (1) David, the youngest son of Jesse, is summoned to appear before the prophet Samuel (1 Sam. 16:11-12); (2) Samuel anoints David "in the midst of his brethren" (1 Sam. 16:13); (3) David plays the harp to refresh King Saul (1 Sam. 16:23); (4) David is triumphant after his fight with the Philistine Goliath (1 Sam. 17:51); (5) Saul's son Jonathan meets David (1 Sam. 18:1); (6) Saul is jealous when the women greet David after the victory over the Philistines (1 Sam. 18:1-9); (7) David composes the Psalms (2 Sam. 23:1); (8) David dies and is succeeded by his son Solomon (1 Kings 1:11-39). Significantly, Solomon avoided the more outwardly dramatic episodes of David's life–his military campaigns and his passionate affair with Bathsheba–and concentrated, instead, on the hero's intense psychological relationships with Jonathan and Saul.

In our first glimpse of David, both in the Bible and in compartment one of Solomon's drawing (Figure 2, left), the hero's appearance is described: "Now he *was* ruddy, *and* withal of a beautiful countenance, and goodly to look to" (1 Sam. 16:12). Solomon depicted David as a somewhat limp and fragile boy, tenderly cradling a lamb in his arms. The messenger, in contrast, which the artist rendered in a deliberately awkward pose in keeping with early Pre-Raphaelite stylistic conventions,[7] is decidedly more aggressive. With one emphatic gesture of the hand and intense eye contact, this figure makes Solomon's point–David is singled out. The young shepherd boy is suddenly thrust, unsure of his mission, into a situation that makes him separate and different from his peers.

Compartment two (Figure 2, right) continues this theme of partialness, as David is anointed with oil by Samuel at God's command "and the Spirit of the Lord came upon David from that day forward" (1 Sam. 16:13). Here Solomon stressed that David was not only different from the others, but even disapproved of, as registered in the haughty air of his brothers. Thus, it is possible to relate the subtext of these two compartments to a semiconscious moment when Solomon, identifying himself with David, interpreted the biblical narrative to express his own sense of "differentness"–only later to be translated into sexual differentness. According to the four-stage model, this corresponds to the *sensitization* stage of homo-

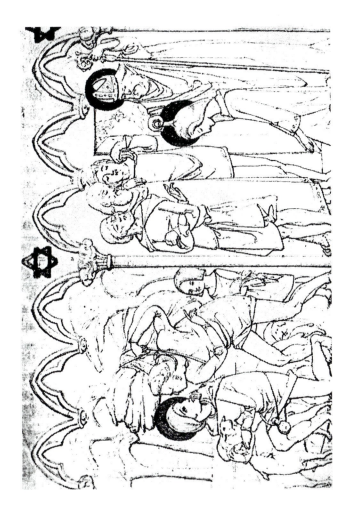

FIGURE 2. Simeon Solomon, *The Story of David, Detail* (left: compartment one, David is summoned to appear before Samuel; right: compartment two, Samuel anoints David).

sexual identity development, which, Plummer and Troiden say, is characterized by generalized feelings of marginality and perceptions of being different from same-sex peers (Troiden 50). As Debra Mancoff has shown, throughout his life, but probably most deeply felt in his early teens when he first associated with his peers in art school in the 1850s, Solomon was keenly aware of his physical appearance: his ethnicity and his diminutive stature (150). In 1857, for instance, in a letter to the sculptor Alexander Munro, Solomon sketched a cartoon of himself in which he compared his small physique to a giant pair of men's Sydenham trousers. This is not to suggest that small males who feel "different" in childhood will necessarily exhibit sexual feelings for other men later in life, but that gender-atypical physiques and feelings of marginalization may provide the "potential basis for subsequent interpretations of self as possibly homosexual" (Troiden 52).

Compartment five (Figure 3, left) openly depicts a tender embrace between David and Jonathan, presumably an illustration of the biblical verse which states that "The soul of Jonathan was knit with the soul of David, and Jonathan loved him as his own soul" (1 Sam. 18:1).[8] Significantly, young Jonathan looks more like a medieval knight than the son of an ancient Hebrew king. The tradition of visualizing Hebrew antiquity in medieval terms goes back to the many commentaries written on the Jewish texts in which Jonathan is described as the flower of medieval knighthood, "The perfect knight, the very essence of chivalry" (Pentateuch and Haftorahs 948). Furthermore, with his upright and stiff profile pose, Jonathan assumes the dignified presence appropriate to the son of a king, which intimates his social superiority in their relationship.

Of the eight compartments in *The Story of David,* two concern themselves with David's relationship with Saul. Compartment three depicts the young David playing on his harp when one of Saul's black moods came upon him "so Saul was refreshed, and was well, and the evil spirit departed from him" (1 Sam. 16:23). In compartment six (Figure 3, right), Solomon stresses how the tables have turned in their once friendly relationship. For Saul, feelings of admiration have turned to ones of increasing jealousy and resentment as David's prestige grows in the kingdom. When the army returns from a successful military campaign, Saul is angered when the women, who come out to greet the heroes, sing that their admiration for David is ten times that of Saul: "Saul has slain his thousands, and David his ten thousands" (1 Sam. 18:7). In this episode Solomon, once again, offers his own unique interpretation. Instead of showing Saul's jealous animosity toward David, Solomon shifts Saul's negative emotion toward the women, depicting in the monarch's body expression the disgust

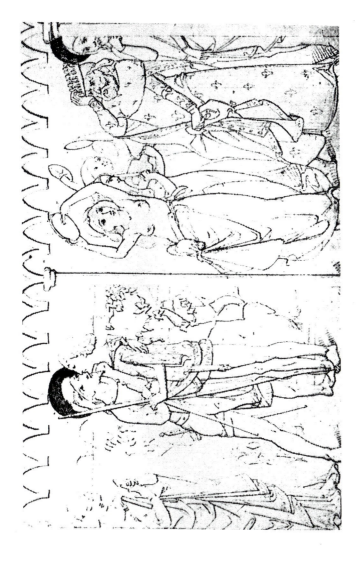

FIGURE 3. Simeon Solomon, *The Story of David, Detail* (left: compartment five, Jonathan meets David; right: compartment six, Saul is jealous of David).

elicited by the seminude females, and in David's recoiling posture confusion and bemusement as he gazes from the sidelines at the active female spectacle. Here again, Solomon's treatment of the theme fits within the sensitization stage of our model. Troiden states that for males, childhood marginality commonly includes feelings of indifference or repulsion toward females (50). Thus, at age 15, Solomon, through this drawing, whether consciously or not, expressed his developing feelings of marginality and his interests in stories of same-sex attraction which indicate a potential for his eventual adoption of homosexual identity.

The relationship between David and Saul continued to occupy Solomon in the late 1850s, but with a difference. As early as 1857, when Solomon was 17, he tackled the subject of Saul and his intense moods: his fits of violence and his aggression toward David. In 1859 the artist exhibited a drawing (#143) of David and Saul at Gambart's *French Gallery* with a passage from 1 Samuel 16:23 quoted in the catalogue: "And it came to pass, when the *evil* spirit from God was upon Saul, that David took an harp, and played with his hand: so Saul was refreshed, and was well, and the evil spirit departed from him." While this work, unfortunately, is yet untraced, it is nevertheless possible to reconstruct a general idea of this drawing through two preparatory sketches, probably executed in 1857[9] and an unpublished engraving of 1862. In these works Solomon explores the psychology of the David-Saul relationship and, in particular, Saul's alternating feelings of love and hate for David. Solomon's sketch of the seated King Saul, inscribed *Saul Under the Influence of David's Song* (Jewish Museum, London, Figure 4)[10] depicts an older man literally crippled by his mental torment, his left shoulder, arm, and hand utterly distorted as if racked by physical pain. In the upper left corner, there is a strangely voyeuristic image, presumably the face of David, who appears to spy on Saul from a small square opening in a wall separating them, much like a guard watching over an isolated prisoner in a jail cell. In exploring the psychology of the relationship between David and Saul, and the concomitant feelings of anxiety, fear, and frustration, Solomon seems to have entered the next stage of sexual identity development: stage two, *identity confusion*. In this stage, which according to Troiden begins on the average at age 17, the neophyte often transforms his homosexuality into a secret. As Plummer explains, "in part the problem that emerges at this stage is one of not being recognized, of not becoming transparent, of keeping the secret" (144). Keeping the secret, of course, requires isolating oneself from others. Thus, Solomon's drawing evokes the anxiety of separation, the solitude and alienation, conditions often experienced by prehomosexuals during their adolescence.

FIGURE 4. Simeon Solomon, *Saul Under the Influence of David's Song*, c. 1857. Pen and ink over pencil, 18.41 × 13.97 cm. Jewish Musuem, London (Courtesy of the Jewish Museum, London).

In another sketch, inscribed *Saul Under the Influence of David's Music* (Jewish Museum, London, Figure 5), circa 1857, Solomon concentrated on Saul's facial features. But beyond the obvious resemblance to Assyrian relief sculpture, in keeping with the artist's striving for archaeological accuracy, the viewer is struck by the element of inner turmoil conveyed by the fixed gaze and the almost total relaxation of the muscles of the mouth, evoking the decontraction of a man who has just had a nightmare. Once again, Solomon's drawing reflects the inner conflict of the *identity confusion* stage. According to Troiden, neophytes find themselves in a kind of sexual limbo, suffering "inner turmoil and uncertainty surrounding their ambiguous sexual status" (53). Troiden goes on to explain that the stigma surrounding homosexuality also contributes to *identity confusion*. Plummer, as well, notes that societal condemnation of same-sex attraction creates situations of guilt, secrecy, and isolation (142). With this in mind, the story of David and Saul may be read as an analogue for Solomon's own feelings of frustration and despair. The deep sense of physical and emotional isolation suggested by Solomon's two sketches offers the viewer insights into his construction of a socially marginal homosexual identity.

Through Solomon's unpublished engraving, *David and Saul* (British Museum, London, Figure 6), one can reconstruct a general idea of the design, though reversed in the engraved version, of the artist's original 1859 drawing. Dated 1862, this engraving was presumably intended as one of twenty illustrated scenes from the Old Testament to be engraved by the Dalziel Brothers. Six of the series were eventually published in *Dalziel's Bible Gallery* in 1880 and a set of twenty were published in *Art Pictures from the Old Testament* in 1897 (Fox). The *David and Saul* engraving, for unknown reasons, was never published. For the nearly symmetrical composition, organized around the central incense burner or lamp which separates David from Saul, Solomon employed a narrative system implying a contrast of opposites: sanity/madness, goodness/evil, innocence/knowledge. One can only speculate whether Solomon was influenced by Robert Browning's poem "Saul" (published 1845, enlarged 1855), and whether the artist intended, as did the poet, to contrast David's superior spirituality to Saul's doubting faith. But in contrast to his 1855 *Story of David,* compartment three, where Saul is put to sleep by David's song, in Solomon's engraving David is unable to refresh the ailing King; on the contrary, his presence seems to intensify Saul's demons. Solomon interprets Saul as an emblem for frustration conveyed through the monarch's uncomfortable pose, his brooding face, and above all the unconscious wringing of his hands as if in mental distress. Significantly, Solo-

FIGURE 5. Simeon Solomon, *Saul Under the Influence of David's Music*, c. 1857. Pen and ink, 18.41 × 15.24 cm. Jewish Museum, London (Courtesy of the Jewish Musuem, London).

FIGURE 6. Simeon Solomon, *David and Saul,* 1862. Engraving (by Dalziel Brothers), 16.20 × 12.50 cm. British Museum, London (Courtesy British Museum).

mon's inclusion of the javelin under Saul's throne reminds the viewer that Saul will attempt to repress his feelings for David by killing their inspiration.

Solomon's point is well illustrated and developed by a later dramatic work, André Gide's *Saül,* written between 1897 and 1898, and published in 1903 (Pollard 328). In Gide's interpretation, Saul's madness revolves around the double theme of political power and sexual attraction. Saul is keeping secrets. One is that because the aging monarch's son Jonathan will not succeed him, Saul's death will lead to political instability; the other is that he has repressed homosexual feelings for David (Lerner 38). David, of course, stands as the nexus of both problems: he is the unknown successor to Saul's throne, as well as the impetus for Saul's acknowledgment of his sexual tendencies. As Lerner has succinctly pointed out, "these two roles are incompatible, as the first endears David to Saul, and the second makes Saul attempt David's murder" (44). Whether Solomon intentionally interpreted the relationship of David and Saul as sexual, one cannot say for certain; however, the intensity of Solomon's image is undeniable.

On New Year's Day 1859, at the age of 18, Solomon completed a pen and ink drawing entitled *Nathan Reproving David* (Victoria and Albert Museum, London, Figure 7). In this work, Solomon casts his hero in a story centered around the themes of knowledge, guilt, and shame. When David allows Uriah the Hittite, the husband of Bathsheba, to be killed in battle so that he might conceal his responsibility for her pregnancy, Nathan uses a parable to reveal the evil of David's actions. Solomon's composition is dominated by the two large figures: Nathan, David's trusted advi-

FIGURE 7. Simeon Solomon, *Nathan Reproving David*, 1 January 1859. Pen and ink over pencil, 14.93 × 17.63 cm. Victoria & Albert Museum, London (Courtesy Victoria & Albert Museum).

sor, who tells his master the parable of the rich man, the poor man, and the ewe lamb; and David, identified by his robe decorated with the star of David, who collapses in shame and repentance, trying to shield his ears as if from frightening thunder. Using a device frequent in medieval art and revived in the 1850s by the artist's Pre-Raphaelite colleagues,[11] Solomon simultaneously depicts the salient episodes of the parable in roundels. The top one shows a man tenderly cradling a lamb which the biblical narrative describes in poignant detail: "But the poor *man* had nothing, save one little lamb, which he had brought and nourished up: and it grew up together with him, and with his children; it did eat of his own meat, and drank of his own cup, and lay in his bosom, and was unto him as a daughter" (2 Sam. 12:3). From a window at the left, the poor man is watched by the rich man who "had exceeding many flocks and herds" (2 Sam. 12:2). In the roundel below the poor man is shown devastated after the rich man has slaughtered the poor man's cherished lamb in hospitality to a traveller.

In spite of the narrative emphasis, however, Solomon focuses on the psychologically climactic moment as David, after hearing the parable and proclaiming that the rich man must die because of his selfish behavior, sinks to his knees as he registers the shocking truth of Nathan's reply, "Thou *art* the man" (2 Sam 12:7). With the utterance of only a few syllables, Nathan suddenly makes audible the secret David was keeping even from himself. It is the moment of cognition which Solomon stresses in this drawing: David's moment of truth, the full weight of which causes him to crumble. The significances of this story for a sexually unsure adolescent of 18 must be understood as more than that of the unjust landlord or of royal arrogance. In Solomon's interpretation, this is a story of secrecy and disclosure, of innocence and knowledge, and one that points to the crisis of acknowledging personal identity. Using an argument originally sketched in the introductory volume of Michel Foucault's *History of Sexuality,* Eve Kosofsky Sedgwick has explained that in the late eighteenth century, " 'knowledge' and 'sex' become conceptually inseparable from one another—so that knowledge means in the first place sexual knowledge; ignorance, sexual ignorance" (73). As a Jew who was bar mitzvahed, Solomon would probably retain the original Hebraic association of sexual intercourse with knowledge established by dual meaning of the verb *yada*—most prominently used in the Genesis "begetting" passages which the King James Version translators offer directly, establishing our still current euphemism of "to know someone in the biblical sense." Solomon himself made the connection between knowledge, sexuality, and transgression by illustrating on the tapestry in the background the expulsion of Adam and Eve after they ate of the fruit of the tree of knowledge.

While Solomon's image of David is loaded with intimations of guilt and shame, it also acknowledges, to a lesser degree, acceptance. If the accusation were not true, why would it cause so much emotional pain? Troiden has articulated that the last phase of the *identity confusion* stage is often marked by a general acceptance and acknowledgement of homosexual behavior, feelings, or fantasies (58). Identity–"Who am I?"–becomes the key issue at this stage. Thus, the theme of David's moment of heightened self-awareness may have for Solomon an autobiographical significance: the agonizing image of David may reflect the artist's own crisis of sexual self-definition.

The themes of guilt, anxiety, and secrecy that Solomon had depicted in many of his Old Testament drawings up to 1859 were gradually replaced in the early 1860s by ones–for which Solomon continued to use biblical subjects to express his inner state–of joy (*David Dancing Before the Ark,* 1860), resolution (*Moses in his Mother's Arms,* 1860), and celebration (*Young Musician in the Temple,* 1860). By 1860, in all probability, Solomon had progressed to the third stage of homosexual identity formation, *identity assumption.* According to Troidon's model, "the earmarks of this stage are self-definition as homosexual, identity tolerance and acceptance, regular association with other homosexuals, sexual experimentation, and exploration of the homosexual subculture" (59). Indeed, gradually over the course of the 1860s, Solomon became a part of the homosexual subculture of London that revolved around the poet Algernon Charles Swinburne and which included such men as Walter Pater, Richard Monckton Milnes (who owned what was then perhaps the largest collection of erotic books in Britain), and Eton don Oscar Browning (with whom Solomon traveled to Italy in 1869 and 1870 and through whom the artist was able to establish numerous friendships with adolescent boys at Eton). Clearly, Solomon was defining himself as homosexual and presenting himself as such, at least when he was safely in the company of other homosexuals.

In all probability, Solomon reached *identity assumption* in 1860, or perhaps slightly earlier (19-20 years old). Solomon was able to resolve the feelings of guilt that had emerged through *identity confusion* by appropriating, once again, the authority of the Bible. But instead of looking to the David theme for his legitimizing precedent, Solomon found his strength in another biblical hero–Esther. A single work in Solomon's oeuvre (a semiconscious commemoration, perhaps) marks the beginning of the *identity assumption* stage. On 16 October 1860, just seven days after his twentieth birthday, Solomon completed a pen and ink drawing entitled

Queen Esther (Robert Isaacson Collection, New York, Figure 8). When this drawing was sold in 1862 upon the death its first owner, Thomas Plint, the Leeds stockbroker and famous Pre-Raphaelite patron, a more descriptive title was given in the Christie's catalogue, "Queen Esther Hearing of the News of the Intended Massacre of the Jews under Artaxerxes."[12] The setting is clearly a sumptuous palace of the Persian Empire, resplendent with a peacock perched on the back wall, at the right. Solomon has included the "hangings," "pillars of marble," and "pavement of . . . marble" that he found vividly described in his reading of Esther 1:6, 7. In keeping with his habitual striving for archaeological precision, Solomon depicted wall reliefs in the background simulating Persian processional reliefs. The harp on the wall to the left of Esther's shoulder and the inlay furniture are based on Egyptian originals in the British Museum.[13] Solomon's anachronistic use of Egyptian objects in this Persian story is per-

FIGURE 8. Simeon Solomon, *Queen Esther,* 16 October 1860. Pen and ink, 28.50 × 35 cm. Robert Isaacson Collection, New York (Courtesy Robert Isaacson).

haps intended to remind the viewer that when this book of the Bible was written, in the third century B.C.E., the Jews were under the domination of Egypt.

The story of Esther, associated with the Feast of Purim, observed by Jews in March, is usually read as one of national triumph, celebrating the heroic Jewess who saved her people from destruction. But instead of thanksgiving and rejoicing, Solomon interpreted this theme as one of anguish which leads to decision-making. In the drawing Solomon depicts the intensely disturbing moment described in Esther 3:6, as Esther's maids come to tell their Queen of the plot of Haman, one of the powerful princes of the entourage of Esther's husband, the Persian king Artaxerxes II (referred to in the Bible as Ahasuerus), to destroy the Jews throughout the kingdom. But rather than just lament, like an emotional oriental woman, Solomon depicts Esther, through the stiff lines of her body strengthened by the angular forms of the elbows, as a woman about to show her capacity for thought under stress, self-control, and determined action.

Sedgwick has shown that the Book of Esther embodies both homosexual and Jewish self-definition (75-83). Esther's agony, which Solomon depicted with such force in his drawing, is caused by the fact that she is keeping a secret. Following the strict instructions of her cousin and guardian Mordecai, a Benjamite official at the palace, Esther concealed her Jewish identity from her Gentile husband. Not only did she deny her faith and her people by marrying "outside," she lived a secret life of nondisclosure, denial, and fear precisely because she did not have a firm sense of her own Jewish identity, of who she was. She is, for a time, able to rationalize her deception since the chief minister of the court, Haman, has repeatedly demonstrated his intense hatred of the Jewish race. Haman declared that the Jews were different from other people and thus unclean and an abomination against nature: "There is a certain people scattered abroad and dispersed among the people in all the provinces of thy kingdom; and their laws *are* diverse from all people; neither keep they the king's laws: therefore it *is* not for the king's profit to suffer them" (Esth. 3:8). Incidentally, Haman is willing to pay money for the privilege of exterminating the Jews. But because one knows how the story will end—that the Jews will not be exterminated, that Esther will not be killed by her husband, and that Haman will die—it is possible to interpret Esther's determination to disclose her secret as a fantasy of "coming out." Perhaps for Solomon, this story provided a meaningful parallel for his own struggle to disclose his identity and a subconscious desire to "come out." Indeed, as Sedgwick has pointed out, Esther's avowal to disclose her secret identity would prove to be a transformative revelation: her disclosure will save her and her people from mass slaughter (76).

For Simeon Solomon the dream of "coming out" was impossible. Living in the homophobic society of Victorian England, he had much to fear. Not only was "the crime against nature" unlawful, even being suspected of it meant risking one's social position and opening oneself to potentially serious injury; it also threatened the security and reputation of one's family. Indeed, in 1860 Solomon still lived at the family home in Gower Street with his mother and some of his unmarried siblings. As Sedgwick has articulated, the fear of an adult child coming out to one's parent is not that they would be killed or wished dead; it is the even more destabilizing fear that the secret would kill the parent (80).

Simeon Solomon was an artist, a Jew, and a homosexual. All three of these identities he had to construct. Since identity can be defined as the perception of self in reference to specific social settings (Troiden 46), in Victorian society all three were considered marginal. Solomon's peripheral standing as a Jew in proper Gentile society is perhaps parallel or analogous to his marginal status as homosexual, but with important differences. Solomon knew he was a Jew and he had a family, a culture, and a history already in place to help him form his Jewish identity and legitimize it. It should be obvious, even in the few examples discussed within the scope of this paper, that Solomon was intensely proud of his Jewish roots. But gay people seldom grow up in gay families, are rarely exposed to a homosexual subculture in childhood, or taught any information about homosexuality. The struggle to form that identity is done alone.

Solomon found within the familiar stories of the Hebrew Bible an avenue to address and to an extent resolve his inner tensions. In the theme of the relationship of David and Jonathan, for instance, Solomon discovered a biblically authorized same-sex relationship and, without explicitly calling attention to his own feelings, he used it as a tool of self-validation. In other Old Testament themes such as that of David and Saul, Solomon imbedded his art with psychologically complex structures–attempting perhaps to identify a narrative of repressed homosexual desire–which reflect the deep emotion of despair and the isolation engendered by marginality. It is even possible, retrospectively, to chart Solomon's gradual acceptance of his feelings–through stages described by sociologist Richard Troiden, for example, such as *sensitization, identity confusion,* and *identity assumption*–in an effort to show how biblical texts were used by a young artist trying to piece together a homosexual identity. There can be no question that Solomon's drawings are loaded with symbolic content and that this symbolism is usually personal, indeed autobiographical. In part, perhaps, because he was young, he was daring in his expressive message: the *Queen Esther* has a heroic cast, her affirming story, a transformative power; the emotional intensity of *Nathan Reproving David* is nothing less than soul-searching; the expression of solitude and alienation in *King Saul* is painfully touching.

NOTES

1. Neil Bartlett (author) and Robin Whitmore (artist and set designer) performed their first version of "A Vision of Love Revealed in Sleep" at the Battersea Arts Centre, London, February 18-21, 1987. It was subsequently revised and performed at a derelict warehouse on Butler's Wharf, Tower Bridge, London, October 20-November 14, 1987. In December 1987 Bartlett performed his solo version at Oxford, Sheffield, Glasgow (The Third Eye Centre), Edinburgh, and Loughborough, and internationally at Copenhagen in April 1988. "A Vision of Love Revealed in Sleep, Part III," was revised and the cast enlarged in 1989, and performed at the Drill Hall Arts Centre, March 1-18.

2. There are three possible versions of the Bible that Solomon could have used for his Old Testament subjects: the King James Version, first published in 1611 and widely used in the Victorian era, even by some anglicized Jews; its comprehensive revision made in 1769, known as the "Authorized Version"; and, the Pentateuch with Haftorah, published in London in its English translation by David Levi in 1787 (and in 1853 Isaac Leeser published a complete Old Testament in English specifically for Jewish educational needs at home). In view of the fact that this essay concerns itself with the output of a Jewish artist, I will use the accepted English translation of the Jewish Bible which is that of the Jewish Publication Society of America, published in 1917, which takes into account nineteenth-century Jewish Bible scholarship and rabbinical commentary. For information on different Bible versions, see *Encyclopedia Judaica* 4: 868-871.

3. While Plummer and Troiden describe the four-stage model in essentially the same manner, they use slightly different terminology for naming the four stages: Plummer refers to them as *sensitization, signification and disorientation, "coming out,"* and *stabilization*; Troiden, as *sensitization, identity confusion, identity assumption,* and *commitment*. I have chosen to use Troiden's more recent categories throughout this essay.

4. Ten drawings from the 79-page Sketchbook have been published; see Lambourne 59-61.

5. For illustrations of the history of David in Western art, although none of Simeon Solomon's work are mentioned, see Landay.

6. For in-depth information concerning Pre-Raphaelite appropriation of illuminated manuscripts, see Treuherz 153-169.

7. Examples of Pre-Raphaelite drawings using similar stylistic conventions are conveniently available in Tate Gallery 245, 247. See in particular William Holman Hunt's *Lorenzo at the Desk of the Warehouse* (1848-1850) and John Everett Millais's *The Disentombment of Queen Matilda* (1849).

8. Upon first glance, the image of David and Jonathan kissing suggests the moment of their parting as described in 1 Samuel 20:41-42; however, since the eight episodes are arranged in chronological order, and since the sixth compartment illustrates an episode (1 Sam. 18:7) which took place before their departure, it stands to reason that compartment five must illustrate the meeting of David and Jonathan.

9. Dating these two drawings is problematic; however, based on comparative stylistic analysis, they most likely date to 1857.

10. This drawing was cut from the last page of the Solomon Sketchbook in the Ein Harod Museum. The odd shape of the drawing corresponds to the shape created by five large glue marks in the Sketchbook. The title for the drawing is taken from Solomon's inscription, written at the bottom of the Sketchbook page.

11. Ford Madox Brown had used such roundels in his 1850 drawing *The Lady of Shalott*; see Tate Gallery 249. The image was even more widely known after it appeared as an engraved illustration in the 1857 Moxon edition of Tennyson's poetry.

12. *Highly Important Collection of English Pictures and Drawings Thomas E. Plint Esq., Leeds,* Christie, Manson & Woods, 7 March 1862, (lot #15) 4. In 1896 this drawing was exhibited at the Goupil Gallery in London (#23) as "Queen Esther Hears of Haman's Plot for the Destruction of her People." This drawing had been previously titled *The Anguish of Miriam* when it was exhibited at the Maas Gallery, London, in 1961 (#108) and subsequently at the Durlacher Brothers Gallery, New York, in 1966 (#12).

13. Solomon probably had access to reproductions of these Egyptian objects through his friend William Holman Hunt which the latter had commissioned by the furniture builders Messrs. Crace of London; see Ormond 55.

WORKS CITED

Dellamora, Richard. *Masculine Desire: The Sexual Politics of Victorian Aestheticism.* Chapel Hill: U of North Carolina P, 1990.

Fone, Byrne. *A Road to Stonewall: Male Homosexuality and Homophobia in English and American Literature.* New York: Twayne, 1995.

Fox, A. *Art Pictures from the Old Testament.* London: SPCK [Society for the Propagation of Christian Knowledge], 1894.

Frontain, Raymond-Jean, and Jan Wojick. "Introduction: Transformations of the Myth of David." *The David Myth in Western Literature.* Ed. Raymond-Jean Frontain and Jan Wojick. West Lafayette, IN: Purdue UP, 1980. 1-10.

Geffrey Museum, London. *Solomon a Family of Painters.* London: Geffrey Museum, 8 November-31 December; Birmingham: 18 January-9 March 1986.

Holiday, Henry. *Reminiscences of my Life.* London: Heinemann, 1914.

Koponen, Wilfrid R. *Embracing a Gay Identity: Gay Novels as Guides.* Westport, CT: Bergin & Garvey, 1993.

Lambourne, Lionel. "A Simeon Solomon Sketchbook." *Apollo* 85 (January 1967): 59-61.

Landay, Jerry M. *The House of David.* New York: Saturday Review P, 1973.

Lerner, Anne Lapidus. *Passing the Love of Women: A Study of Gide's Saül and Its Biblical Roots.* Langham, MD: UP of America, 1980.

Mancoff, Debra N. "As Others Saw Him: A Self-Portrait of Simeon Solomon." *Museum Studies* 18 (1992): 146-155, 187-188.

Ormond, Richard. "Holman Hunt's Egytian Chairs." *Apollo* 82 (July 1965): 55-58.

Pentateuch & Haftorahs Hebrew Text English Translation and Commentary. Ed. J. H. Hertz. London: Soncino P, 1981.

Plummer, Kenneth. *Sexual Stigma: An Interactionist Account.* London: Routledge & Kegan Paul, 1975.

Pollard, Patrick. *André Gide, Homosexual Moralist.* New Haven: Yale UP, 1991.

Reade, Brian, ed. *Sexual Heretics: Male Homosexuality in English Literature from 1850 to 1900.* London: Routledge and Kegan Paul, 1970.

Sedgwick, Eve Kosofsky. *Epistemology of the Closet.* Berkeley: U of California P, 1990.

Treuherz, Julian. "The Pre-Raphaelites and Medieval Illuminated Manuscripts." *Pre-Raphaelite Papers.* Ed. Leslie Parris. London: Tate Gallery, 1984. 153-169.

Tate Gallery, London. *The Pre-Raphaelites.* London, Tate Gallery, 7 March-28 May 1984.

Troiden, Richard R. "The Formation of Homosexual Identities." *Journal of Homosexuality* 17 (1989): 43-73.

Weeks, Jeffrey. *Coming Out: Homosexual Politics in Britain from the Nineteenth Century to the Present.* London: Quartet Books, 1977.

Williamson, G. C. *Murray Marks and His Friends: A Tribute of Regard.* London: John Lane, 1919.

Oscar Wilde and the Scarlet Woman

Ellis Hanson, PhD

Cornell University

SUMMARY. In the late nineteenth century, England was embroiled in a political debate over the importation of Roman Catholic rituals into the Anglican Church, not to mention the re-establishment of the Roman Church itself in Great Britain. Victorian anti-Catholic rhetoric draws upon the figure of the Whore of Babylon to depict the Roman Catholic Church as the Scarlet Woman, a *femme fatale* who perverts Christianity and seduces Englishmen with elaborate rituals and lascivious whisperings in the confessional. In writing *Salomé,* Oscar Wilde played ironically on the hysterical eroticism of the No Popery movement by mining the paradox of biblical sensuality. He invested his play with a biblical wealth of archaic metaphors and gestures that took their cues from The Song of Songs and The Book of Revelation. He became the ecclesiastical dandy that evangelicals feared most, a poet enamored of the Scarlet Woman, a would-be convert who exposed the scandal of Christianity as art. *[Article copies available for a fee from The Haworth Document Delivery Service: 1-800-342-9678. E-mail address: getinfo@haworth.com]*

He had read in the dark annals of the Inquisition, that a victim who had recanted, and was led to believe that he was to be reconciled to

---

Ellis Hanson teaches lesbian and gay studies in the English Department at Cornell University and is the author of *Decadence and Catholicism* (Harvard University Press, forthcoming).

Correspondence may be addressed: English Department, 250 Goldwin Smith Hall, Cornell University, Ithaca, NY 14853; or by e-mail: eh36@cornell.edu.

[Haworth co-indexing entry note]: "Oscar Wilde and the Scarlet Woman." Hanson, Ellis. Co-published simultaneously in *Journal of Homosexuality* (The Haworth Press, Inc.) Vol. 33, No. 3/4, 1997, pp. 121-137; and: *Reclaiming the Sacred: The Bible in Gay and Lesbian Culture* (ed: Raymond-Jean Frontain) Harrington Park Press, an imprint of The Haworth Press, Inc., 1997, pp. 121-137. Single or multiple copies of this article are available for a fee from The Haworth Document Delivery Service [1-800-342-9678, 9:00 a.m. - 5:00 p.m. (EST). E-mail address: getinfo@haworth.com].

the bosom of Mother Church, approached to embrace the image of the Virgin, when suddenly the arms of the figure opened, and receiving him into her embrace, a hundred knives pierced him to the heart.

–Rev. W. Chalmers

Although Rev. Chalmers recounted this tale about a half-century before Wilde wrote "The Sphinx" (1894) and *Salomé* (1892), it is ripe with the sort of violent *horror feminae* that distinguished every phase of *fin de siècle* decadence and Victorian anti-Catholicism. In the wake of the Oxford movement, English politics was rocked by debates over a certain Romeward movement in the Church of England, a renewed interest in Catholic ritual and dogma, and the "Papal Aggression," the panicky Victorian epithet that described the reestablishment of the Roman Catholic Church in Great Britain. The No Popery movement, promulgated by enthusiasts of an Evangelical stripe, produced tens of thousands of pamphlets and sermons warning against the "Scarlet Woman" and the decadence of Rome, as though the Church were itself the Whore of Babylon and the Pope no less a degenerate than Tiberius. British anti-Catholicism had been a rabid literary tradition for at least three hundred years, and so No Popery writers had a wealth of material, from the anecdotal to the apocryphal, with which to paint the Roman Church as itself a scandal, a betrayal of Christianity and the Bible. Priests were regarded as Vatican spies and seducers of innocent English women and children. The confessional was seen as a den of iniquitous whisperings. High Church ritualism was likened to the vulgar entertainments of the musical hall.

It is not difficult to see the appeal of this sort of prejudice for a writer like Oscar Wilde, who made a career of exposing the ironies and hypocrisies of the typical English puritan. Indeed, Roman Catholicism was very much a part of Wilde's characteristic pose as an aesthete and decadent. He was the very Catholic personality that Evangelicals feared, an ecclesiastical dandy whose poetry was redolent with ritualism and spicy biblical references, a pagan who sought the blessings of the Pope no fewer than seven times, a deathbed convert seduced by the wiles of the Scarlet Woman. Wilde was enamored with the rhetoric of Christianity–the poetry of faith no less than the tortured language of sin. The Bible was the one fatal book to which he would return again and again in virtually every text he ever published. From his early Catholic poetry to the exquisite sins of Dorian Gray and Salomé to the meditation on shame and the personality of Christ in *De Profundis,* Wilde rewrote the Bible many times, rediscovering in the symbolist music of The Song of Songs or the gothic horror of the The Book of Revelation the very spirit of romance and imagination. André

Gide was especially astute when he wrote that Wilde did not forgive the Gospel its "miracles" (7). Wilde understood what Evangelicals had long feared: in the hands of the Roman Catholic Church, the language of the Bible had become something decadent, seductive, and gorgeous.[1]

Much has been written about Salomé, not only the nameless daughter of Herodias in the Gospels but also her various *fin de siècle* incarnations as a *femme damnée* in the work of, among others, Gautier, Flaubert, Huysmans, Moreau, Beardsley, Symons, and, of course, Wilde. As Huysmans describes her in *A Rebours,* she is the "Goddess of immortal Hysteria" (66), seducing the voyeuristic gaze of Herod, who is at once her stepfather and her uncle, and lusting after Saint John the Baptist (or, at any rate, his head). In decadent literature she acquires the transhistorical aura of myth. In Wilde's play, Salomé also has a historically particular significance with respect to British anti-Catholicism and the hysterical sensuality of its rhetoric. She is the very figure of the Roman Catholic Church as it was pilloried in Evangelical tracts. Evident in the literature of the No Popery movement is a rampant panic about female sexuality, which often finds expression in bizarre and paranoid images of seduction and betrayal by the Mother Church. The desire for spiritual righteousness goes hand in hand with a concern for national, racial, and sexual purity in this tradition. A supposedly religious threat is articulated as an invasion, a challenge to Queen Victoria and the Constitution, a racial disease or degeneracy, a threat to the bourgeois family, or a threat to the sacredness of married life. The fact that there have been queens, constitutions, families, and faithful wives even in ardently Catholic countries generally escapes the writer's notice. The No Popery movement is an excellent example of the way in which religious and sexual discourses seem inevitably to overlap, the way that religion often presumes a certain discipline or deployment of sexuality. Instead of a rational comparison of doctrinal claims, anti-Catholic literature offers impassioned rhetoric about the Church as the Whore of Babylon, not to mention bizarre and sometimes fabricated stories about monastic satanism, convent brothels, seduction in the confessional, and the sadism of the Inquisition. This preoccupation with the erotic lends to this tradition a peculiar pruriency, which puts me in mind of Richard Hofstader's remark that anti-Catholic literature was the pornography of the Puritans. The Church is seen as vampiric, with all the sexual baggage that term implies. It is represented as seductive, perverse, decadent, often feminine, and certainly deadly. The Victorian deployment of the term "perversion" as virtually synonymous with "conversion" is by no means innocent. Having established the Church as the Scarlet Woman, conversion collapses easily into seduction, and "popery" into sin. Even traditional theorists of conversion to Catholicism were not immune to conceiving the spiritual tug of the Church in erotic terms. G. K. Chesterton, a contemporary of Wilde and the very archetype of the smug and earnest convert, wrote of the Church as a terrifying and magnetic force that, for its initiates, "begins to take on the tragic and menacing grandeur of a great love affair. The man has exactly the same sense of having committed or compromised himself; of having been in a sense entrapped, even if he is glad to be entrapped."[2] In this context, Wilde's recurrent tendency to conversion no longer appears to be at odds with his preoccupation with seduction. Indeed, much of his writing on sexual seduction–for example, *The Picture of Dorian Gray* (1891), "The Sphinx," *Salomé,* and *La Sainte Courtisane* (a fragment, written in 1893)–is also about the seductiveness of Christianity itself, especially in its more voluptuous biblical and ritualistic manifestations.

The most colorful biblical passages that No Popery literature draws on refer to the doom of Babylon. The description of the Whore of Babylon is itself one of those great moments of decadent style in the Bible:

> Come hither, I will shew thee the judgement of the great harlot that sitteth upon many waters; with whom the kings of the earth committed fornication, and they that dwell in the earth were made drunken with the wine of her fornication. And he carried me away in the Spirit into a wilderness: and I saw a woman sitting upon a scarlet-coloured beast, full of names of blasphemy, having seven heads and ten horns. And the woman was arrayed in purple and scarlet, and decked with gold and precious stone and pearls, having in her hand a golden cup full of abominations, even the unclean things of her fornication, and upon her forehead a name written, MYSTERY, BABYLON THE GREAT, THE MOTHER OF THE HARLOTS AND OF THE ABOMINATIONS OF THE EARTH. And I saw the woman drunken with the blood of the saints, and with the blood of the martyrs of Jesus; and when I saw her, I wondered with a great wonder. (Rev. 17:1-6)[3]

This is the moment where Des Esseintes generally fades into a swoon. But these lines had a powerful appeal for puritans as well. They were taken out of context and redeployed by No Popery writers as a condemnation of the Vatican. They juxtaposed the Church with pagan imagery in order to bring to light of day what they saw as a scandalous idolatry, a bloodsucking barbarity, and a veiled eroticism. "Does not Papal Rome, as well as did Pagan Rome, *abound in images?*" one William Bennett writes in a sermon against the "Papal Aggression." "And wherever her influence extends;

wherever temples are erected for her worship, *there* are images, and there are prostrate worshippers. Rome is, in very truth, 'the mother'–the fruitful parent–'of harlots and abominations of the earth.' 'With the wine of her golden cup, this Circe has seduced the kings and intoxicated the inhabitants of the earth.'" Needless to say, the pagan Circe does not appear in the Bible, despite the quotation marks here. Bennett continues along the same lines: "Ignorance is her safeguard: darkness her delight: for then she works unseen, and revels in appropriate deeds. Her name, indeed, is '*Mystery Babylon* the Great, the mother of harlots and abominations of the earth!'" He continues in a decidedly vampiric vein: 'I hasten on to another and a flagrant and most notorious sin; the *cruelty, and intolerance, and persecuting spirit* of the Babylonish woman: her scarlet robes are stained with blood. 'She is *drunken* with the *blood of saints* and with the *blood of the martyrs of Jesus.*' 'In her was found the *blood* of the prophets, and of saints and of all that were slain upon the earth'" (qtd. in Norman 171, 174). This imagery is not unlike that of *Salomé,* with the beheading of Saint John the Baptist and of course the fatal dancer herself, her desire figured in terms of hunger and thirst, blood and wine, and a final necrophilic kiss, spiced with the taste of blood.

Probably the most famous No Popery writer of the time was Patrick Murphy, a former Catholic who traveled the country giving lectures and inciting riots. He was finally beaten unconscious in Cumberland by a mob of irate Irish Catholics and died a year later in 1872. His rhetoric was suitably bombastic and inflammatory, and his impact was enormous. Thousands of No Popery tracts, such as the notorious *The Confessional Unmasked,* were sold in anticipation of his lectures. In his book, *Popery in Ireland,* which went into several editions, he cries out, "Oh, Popery! Popery! thou curse of my country! where once religion, fostered by heavenly influences, flourished with unsullied beauty; how hast thou degraded it in the eyes of every nation in the world! How hast thou dyed the pages of its history with deepest, blackest stains of crime! Alas! . . . Go to, thou mistress of sorcerers; cease from thy superstitious mummeries and abominations." He recounts how he was singled out for the priesthood: "O, miserable infatuation! Not less fascinated was I than the unconscious bird, that is fixed by the eye of the reptile, till it falls a victim to its cunning enemy." With similar melodrama he describes a woman abducted into a convent: "Caught in the gorgeously woven net of Rome, for a time the victim drooped and languished," though later, we discover, "That church which trades in scarlet and crimson draperies, musical exhibitions, and silly mimicries, fascinated her" (73-75, 225-26).

Wilde sometimes uses a similar language of illicit fascination, temptation, and flirtation when describing the Church, although he adopts a tone of self-conscious irony rather than outrage. Obviously, he had little patience with soapbox Christians, nor would they have had much patience with him. In *The Picture of Dorian Gray,* he satirized the type. Lord Henry passes Marble Arch just as some "prophet" is bellowing "what does it profit a man if he gain the whole world and lose his own soul?" With impeccable ironic detachment, Lord Henry remarks, "London is very rich in curious effects of that kind. A wet Sunday, an uncouth Christian in a mackintosh, a ring of sickly white faces under a broken roof of dripping umbrellas, and a wonderful phrase flung into the air by shrill, hysterical lips–it was really very good in its way, quite a suggestion" (161).[4] Nevertheless, those hysterical lips would find their apotheosis in Wilde's Jokanaan, the incensed and somewhat absurd prophet of *Salomé*. But even while a student at Oxford, seriously considering conversion to Rome, Wilde was intrigued by the "hysterical" phrases of the No Popery movement, which were no doubt a frequent cause for annoyance among the numerous converts of his acquaintance. His friend Hunter-Blair was inspired to convert by Cardinal Manning's defense of ritualism; and Wilde was, even as a student, surrounded with other converts, among them his friends Williamson, Dunlop, and MacCall. The language of No Popery tracts, tainted by an ironic tone entirely his own, seeped into Wilde's letters, such as when he wrote, "I now breakfast with Father Parkinson, go to St. Aloysius, talk sentimental religion to Dunlop and altogether am caught in the fowler's snare, in the wiles of the Scarlet Woman–I may go over in the vac," and a couple weeks later he wrote of a friend, "He is awfully caught in the wiles of the Scarlet Woman and wrote to Newman about several things" (*Letters* 30-31, 33).

The very word *fascination* resounds through Wilde's letters and fiction, often in a Roman Catholic context. His Oxford letters to William Ward are especially redolent with the term:

> Still I get so wretched and low and troubled that in some desperate mood I will seek the shelter of a Church which simply enthrals me by its fascination. (31)

Or, somewhat later:

> I won't write to you theology, but I only say that for *you* to feel the fascination of Rome would to me be the greatest of pleasure: I think it would *settle me.* (32)

And on a more Paterian note:

Do be touched by it, *feel* the awful fascination of the Church, its extreme beauty and sentiment, and let every part of your nature have play and room. (31)

We begin to wonder here whether Wilde is the seducer or the seduced, so inviting and effusive are his religious appeals to his friends. Ward himself explained that Wilde's deathbed conversion was not the pathetic and desperate effort of a dying man, but a return to a "first love," one which had "haunted him from early days with a persistent spell" (*Interviews* 1:13). This fascination almost always carried with it a homoerotic nuance, and Wilde delighted in blurring the distinction between inspiration and seduction among men. Usually, the Scarlet Woman was in fact represented by a man. Having been to the Pro-Cathedral to hear Cardinal Manning, Wilde wrote to Ward, "He is more fascinating than ever. I met MacCall and Williamson there who greeted me with much *empressement.* I feel an impostor and traitor on such occasions and must do something decided" (16). Of Bishop Wilberforce, he once said, "I fear he tempted me" (qtd. in Ellman 65). On another occasion, he gave his opinion of the Bible, declaring, "Christ, Paul, and most of the other characters in the book have for me a singular fascination"; and again of Saint Paul, he said, "I fear he tempted me" (*Interviews* 2:337, 381). I am reminded of Dorian's relationship with Lord Henry, when I read Wilde's comment, upon receiving a letter from Newman, "I am awfully keen for an interview, not of course to argue, but merely to be in the presence of that divine man," adding, "I could hardly resist Newman I am afraid" (*Letters* 33).

What is all this fascination? Why this parade of clergymen dancing before Wilde's eyes like the visionary temptations of Saint Antony?

In *The Picture of Dorian Gray,* Wilde expounded upon his conception of seduction as "influence," and this influence is at once textual, sexual, and religious. Lord Henry, like Wilde in his Oxford days, sees the appeal of the Church as a form of seduction: "Religion consumes some. Its mysteries have all the charm of a flirtation, a woman once told me; and I quite understand it" (85). The identity of this woman, this nameless Diotima, is not revealed, but Lord Henry needs no education on the subject of flirtation. The notion of "influence" is, from the beginning of the novel, homoerotic. In the opening scene, which takes place in Basil Hallward's garden, Lord Henry is introduced to Basil's beautiful young model, Dorian. Basil's fascination with Dorian amounts to a highly sublimated flirtation, but it is also strangely mystical. It is articulated in a language of temptation that is hardly more voluptuous than the prose that Wilde used to describe Newman, the Church, and, later, the figure of Christ. "When our eyes met, I felt that I was growing pale. A curious sensation of terror came over me. I knew that I had come face to face with someone whose mere personality was so fascinating that, if I allowed it to do so, it would absorb my whole nature, my whole soul, my very art itself. I did not want any external influence in my life" (22). The word *influence* occurs again when Dorian asks Basil's visitor, "Have you really a very bad influence, Lord Henry? As bad as Basil says?" And Lord Henry replies, "There is no such thing as a good influence, Mr. Gray. All influence is immoral–immoral from the scientific point of view" (28). What he means here by "influence" is something more like "imitation," which Wilde claimed to dislike. One who is thus influenced "becomes an echo of someone else's music, an actor of a part that has not been written for him. The aim of life is self-development" (29). Thus Lord Henry passes on to another sort of influence, seduction as education, which for Dorian is a leading downward, but also a leading out–out of self-ignorance and very nearly out of the closet.

In Lord Henry's presence, through some mystical sympathy between the older man's words and the younger man's consciousness, Dorian senses something strange stirring within himself, a sensation that Wilde likens to the pleasures of music, poetic form, and anamnesis, and at a less explicit level, the pleasures of an as yet unnameable sexual desire:

> Music had stirred him like that. Music had troubled him many times. But music was not articulate. It was not a new world, but rather another chaos, that it created in us. Words! Mere words! How terrible they were! How clear, and vivid, and cruel! One could not escape from them. And yet what a subtle magic there was in them! They seemed to be able to give a plastic form to formless things, and to have a music of their own as sweet as that of viol or of lute. Mere words! Was there anything as real as Words?
>
> Yes; there had been things in his boyhood that he had not understood. He understood them now. Life suddenly became fiery-coloured to him. It seemed to him that he had been walking in fire. Why had he not known it? (30)

This passage is ingenious for the connections it makes between desire and artistic form with regard to a vague mystical knowledge. This is the appeal that Wilde ascribed to Pater's *Renaissance* when, in *De Profundis* (1897), he called it "that book which has had such a strange influence over my life" (471). Pater influenced Wilde the way the literary critics in "The Portrait of Mr. W. H." (1889) influence one another–by seduction, by lies if need be. Influence is not merely the transference of information or facts, but the "transference of personality" (1196). Influence is seduction, but also inspiration, a call to become oneself, an invitation to creative criticism rather than imitation.

The concept surfaces elsewhere in *De Profundis,* this time in a more religious context, when Wilde points out that Christ did not seek to change people, he did not require imitation; rather, Christ was an individualist. Through the beauty of his mere presence, his capacity to say beautiful things, others around him were inspired to realize themselves as well, to be beautiful in their own way. This Christian influence is also celebrated in *Teleny,* an anonymous pornographic novel that, however dubiously, is sometimes attributed in part to Wilde. A homosexual painter named Briancourt compares Christ to a male model who is sitting for him, and he exclaims, "You would be able to fathom the influence He must have had over the crowd. My Syrian need not speak to you, he lifts his eyes upon you and you grasp the meaning of his thoughts. Christ, likewise, never wasted His breath spouting cant to the multitude" (140). Christianity is mesmerizing and dangerous. What Lord Henry is to Dorian, Christ is to Wilde. But it is, once again, a temptation to the antinomian experience of mysticism, a temptation to break rules in the name of the Father, to live by faith rather than by the law. It is also a romantic temptation to allow oneself to be crucified, obliterated, damned, transformed, by the dormant capacities that are awakened within oneself by the presence of beautiful people and beautiful things. Like the Christian, we are born anew at the baptism of mere words and, as Dorian discovers, it is not a "new world, but rather another chaos, that is created in us." It is a temptation to individualism, which, as Wilde defines it, is a "disturbing and disintegrating force" not unlike the workings of grace in a martyr.

The seduction of "mere words" is a temptation of both spirit and flesh. We see this not only in Dorian's eroticized apprehension of "formless things" and "subtle magic" in the voice and presence of Lord Henry, but also in Herod's fatal attraction to both Jokanaan and Salomé. Wilde drew on the ambivalence of Herod, as suggested in Mark–his incestuous delight in Salomé but also his spiritual admiration for Saint John the Baptist: "For Herod feared John, knowing that he was a just man, and holy, and observed; and when he heard him, he did many things, and heard him gladly" (6:20). Wilde's Herod recognizes Jokanaan's holiness: "He is a holy man. The finger of God has touched him. God has put into his mouth terrible words" (571). Herod, of course, knows the importance of "mere words," since Salomé has put some terrible ones into his own mouth. "I am the slave of my word, and my word is the word of a king," he declares, but he is a slave to many words, a confusion of words like the profound confusion that decadent writers like Huysmans and Pater and Gourmont found in the aromatic Latin of the Early Church Fathers and certain Christian mystics. *Salomé* supposedly recreates a moment of cultural conversion, a moment of historical decadence, the death rattle of paganism alongside the birth cries of Christianity. Herod, in his confusion and paranoia, is cast back upon the word, which is now at play, no longer performing its symbolic role as transcendent authority. Wilde has lifted from the Bible a moment in Christian history in which religious instability has obliged a king, under the influence of two lascivious women, a hysterical Christian, and disputatious Jews and Nazarenes, to look to mere words with a new desperation, only to find they mirror his own crisis of meaning. Herod discovers the seduction of mere words, not only in Salomé's dance and her poetic discourse of the body, but also in the hysterical Christian discourse of Jokanaan.

In *Salomé,* Wilde has accomplished an extraordinary feat: he has used a biblical text and biblical language to dramatize the decadent and symbolist fascination with the material word. The biblical word exerts a mystical influence; it fascinates and seduces Herod, no less than Salomé herself. Wilde plays upon a paradox of language, and one of the central paradoxes of Christianity: the word is both symbol and sound, both sense and sensuousness, just as Christ is the Word made flesh, the Son of God and the Son of Man. Like Huysmans, Wilde draws on the popular discourse of hysteria as a mode of the signifier run amok. Just as the Salomé of *A Rebours*—which Wilde had read on his honeymoon, ironically enough–is the "Goddess of immortal Hysteria," so Wilde's Salomé is "monstrous" (574), to use Herod's word. Like the moon that is her virtual familiar, "She is like a madwoman who is seeking everywhere for lovers" (561). Jokanaan, like the disembodied "hysterical voice" of the Christian that Lord Henry hears at Marble Arch, is reduced to his impassioned voice throughout much of the play. Like the hysteric, and like the one who speaks in tongues, Jokanaan speaks in the voice of the Other, "the voice of him who had cried in the waste places and in the houses of kings" (557). Much of his language is drawn from the Bible, and so he represents the pure and divine logos, but carries on like a lunatic or a "drunken man" (566). Herod says, "I cannot understand what it is that he saith, but it may be an omen." Herod has glimmerings of Christian faith–his belief in the prophetic truth of Jokanaan's words–but only in a paranoid fashion, and by the end of the play he is clearly losing his wits. The Jews and Nazarenes, who are yet another reflection of Wilde's distaste for disputatious puritans, are presented as ridiculous rule-bound ideologues whose theological debates are simply babble or the howling of wild beasts. "These men are mad," Herodias finally exclaims. "They have looked too long on the moon" (565).

Herodias herself, though a literalist, claims she is driven mad by the words of Jokanaan, and like her daughter, she partakes of a long tradition of what Foucault has called "the hysterization of women's bodies," the qualification and disqualification of the feminine body as being "thoroughly saturated with sexuality" (104). Madness signifies, in *Salomé,* the peculiarly decadent fate of the Word among "mere words."

Beyond the familiar preoccupation with sexual exoticism and cruelty, all the characters in the play are decadent poets: they are solipsistic, their language militates against meaning, they repeat themselves with the eerie music of a Maeterlinck. Herod lapses into decadent pageantry as he tries to tempt Salomé with all his gems and his peacocks. Jokanaan's speech has an erotic flair, even though it is a panegyric against the sexual transgressions of Herod and Herodias; for example, he dwells with oddly prurient interest on the beauties of the young men of Egypt, their fine linen and purple, their gold shields, their silver helmets, their mighty bodies. Salomé's language constantly veers from its supposed referent, the thing as in itself it really is, into simile after simile, each more absurd than the next. The irony is that Herod's enumeration of his treasures is no more decadent than the biblical account of the New Jerusalem, whose foundations are of jasper, sapphire, chalcedony, emerald, sardonyx, sardius, chrysolite, beryl, topaz, chrysoprase, jacinth, and amethyst. Nor is the vituperation that Jokanaan heaps on Herodias any less decadent than the biblical descriptions of the Whore of Babylon. Nor are Salomé's similes more absurd and sensuous than those of the bride in The Song of Songs, who claims that her breasts are like feeding deer and her lover's teeth are like sheep. In lending to the nameless daughter of Herodias all the poetry of The Song of Songs and The Book of Revelation, Wilde mines the seductive and rebellious power of "mere words" even in the Bible. In drawing his style–at least in the English translation–from the archaic and musical King James Version, he reveals the Bible as the ultimate symbolist tragedy.

In rereading the New Testament alongside *Salomé,* I am struck by the constant tension between spirit and body in biblical metaphors, not to mention the fascination with Christ's body. In *Salomé,* Wilde is not so much attacking Christianity as he is deconstructing the Bible, making it speak over and over a contradiction that is never resolved, namely, that the spirit only makes itself known through the flesh, the Word through mere words. "And the Word became flesh, and dwelt among us," John tells us (1:14). And the Word has a fascinating and beautiful body. As in *Salomé,* the Gospels engage a wonderfully sensual discourse preoccupied with voice, gaze, and touch. It is a discourse of the symbolic word preoccupied with what is eminently presymbolic, with modes of communication and pleasure that precede the child's fall into language. In 1 John we are told, "For all that is in the world, the lust of the flesh, and the lust of the eyes, and the vainglory of life, is not of the Father, but is of the world" (2:16), and yet the epistle opens with the remarkable lines, "That which was from the beginning, which we have heard, which we have seen with our eyes, which we have looked upon, and our hands have handled, of the Word of life," and so on. This wondrous palpability of the Word is apparent in the Gospels as well. The sheep know the shepherd from the stranger by the quality of his voice. Christ cures those who have lost the physical capacity for sight and hearing. He blesses by the touch of his hand, just as the touch of the Baptist elicits the disembodied voice of God. Even beyond the spectacle of his crucifixion, Christ calls attention to his body, especially after his death. "See my hands and my feet, that it is I myself," he says; "handle me, and see; for a spirit hath not flesh and bones, as ye behold me having" (Luke 24:39). This emphasis on the palpability of his body is not without its homoerotic implications, as suggested by his invitation to the doubting Thomas: "Reach hither thy finger, and behold my hands; and reach hither thy hand, and thrust it into my side: and be not faithless, but believing" (John 20:27). The homoeroticism of discipleship was by no means lost on Wilde, who was evidently delighted by Frank Harris's interpretation of Judas's betrayal as the act of a jealous lover who thought himself abandoned for "that sentimental beast John" (*Letters* 756). In *Teleny,* Briancourt proposes that two of his colleagues pose for a portrait of Christ and John as lovers: " 'As I was saying, I shall paint Achmet as the Saviour, and you,' added he to Teleny, 'as John, the disciple He loved; for the Bible clearly says and continually repeats that He loved this favourite disciple' " (140). All romantic speculations aside, to have faith is literally to partake of Christ's body, as established by his oddly Salomesque invitation, "He that eateth my flesh and drinketh my blood hath eternal life" (John 6:54). Indeed, hunger and thirst are repeatedly evoked in the Gospels as metaphors for the yearning after righteousness.

In this biblical manner, Wilde took voice, gaze, touch, and hunger as central tropes through which, in a spectacle of seduction, the senses are placed in dialectical relation to the soul. As Wilde repeatedly proclaimed, "But the Saint and the artistic Hedonist certainly meet–touch in many parts" (*Letters* 265). Wilde's contention that ethics and aesthetics, spiritual belief and sensuous beauty, are by no means mutually exclusive, is represented allegorically by the saint Jokanaan and the hedonist Salomé. In his book on Christian allusions in Wilde, Guy Willoughby has suggested that Salomé is attracted to Jokanaan as a would-be convert. Although the claim is unlikely, it does reflect the experiences of thousands of Victorian ritualists and aesthetes who became faithful converts to the Catholic Church, having first admired its sensual beauty. Salomé and Jokanaan do exercise a peculiar influence over each other. When exposed to each other's presence, their similarity as well as their ideological opposition is revealed. What transpires is not so much a battle of opposites as a dialectical reversal in which the soul and the senses appear to mirror each other. Wilde set the pattern for this reversal in his unfinished play, *La Sainte Courtisane,* which, like "The Sphinx," is another parody of Flaubert's *Tentation.* The dramatic fragment takes place in the Thebaid, where the saintly hermit Honorius is tempted by the voluptuous Myrrhina. In a comic reversal, both succeed in tempting and converting each other, Honorius to the delights of sin and Myrrhina to the delights of Christian love:

> HONORIUS: Myrrhina, the scales have fallen from my eyes and I see now clearly what I did not see before. Take me to Alexandria and let me taste of the seven sins.

> MYRRHINA: Do not mock me, Honorius, nor speak to me with such bitter words. For I have repented of my sin and I am seeking a cavern in this desert where I too may dwell so that my soul may become worthy to see God. (705)

The dialectical reversal of saint and sinner is much more subtle and complicated in *Salomé.* The allegorical positions of various characters in the play give way to a hall of mirrors by which all the characters seem to resemble one another. Similar words are used to describe different characters–especially Salomé and Jokanaan. Even in Aubrey Beardsley's drawings they appear to mirror each other, the black locks and long flowing robe of Jokanaan are like a mirror image of the black locks and long flowing robe of Salomé. Most striking is the structural pattern that both characters share in their relation to the voice. Salomé begins as a body without a voice, admired from afar by the young Syrian, and she is, before her moonlit murder, a voice without a body, literally the "Voice of Salomé," as she celebrates her bloody kisses in the darkness of an unlit stage. Jokanaan is in this sense her inverted mirror image, beginning as the "Voice of Jokanaan," a voice without a body, hidden as he is in the cistern, and ending as a body without a voice, a dismembered head on a silver charger–or as Salomé says, "And thy tongue, that was like a red snake darting poison, it moves no more, it says nothing now, Jokanaan, that scarlet viper that spat its venom upon me" (574).

When Jokanaan and Salomé approach each other on the stage, when indeed they have both voices and bodies, it is not only voice but gaze and touch and taste that define their opposition and their similarity. Their interaction is structured around Salomé's desire to look at Jokanaan, to speak with him, to touch him, and finally to taste his mouth. He responds passionately in the negative to each of her desires: "I will not have her look at me . . . I will not listen to thee . . . Touch me not," he cries, and to her offer of a kiss, "Never, daughter of Babylon! Daughter of Sodom!" (558-59). Apart from the moon, and the evocation of a lunatic gaze, Salomé appears to be the focus of the play's anxiety of the gaze, with its constant refrain, do not look at her, you look too much at her, and so on. But in fact, this pleasure and anxiety of the gaze is dispersed throughout the play, such that Herod has also gazed appreciatively at the young Syrian, though he fears to look on his corpse. The Page has also admired the young Syrian, but must now hide him from the gaze of the moon. In true paranoid fashion, Herod, the perverse subject of the gaze, becomes at last the haunted object of the gaze, a divine gaze from which he hopes to hide himself. Jokanaan is also both the subject and the object of a terrible gaze. As Salomé says, "It is his eyes above all that are terrible. They are like black holes burned by torches in a Tyrian tapestry. They are like black caverns where dragons dwell." He is also, like Salomé, a spectacle for the gaze. "He was very terrible to look upon" (554), says one of the soldiers. But Salomé is seduced by him. His gaze is as thrilling as it is terrible to her, his voice is like wine to her, she longs to touch and admire his pale and wasted body, which is transvalued in her similes into a moonbeam, a shaft of silver, a tower of ivory, white lilies, then execrated in her anger as the body of a leper, a plaster wall where vipers have crawled, a whitened sepulcher. Salomé reveals the sensual body of Jokanaan, the body that his word both denies and confesses, denies in his passionate rejection of her, but confesses, as I have noted, in his passionate enumeration of her mother's splendid sins. The denotation of his words are pious enough in their denegation of the world, but his voice, his gaze, his body, the taste of his blood, are nevertheless a scandal.

While in Jokanaan we find the sensuous body of the saint, in Salomé we find the unexpected spirituality of the hedonist. Whatever her similarities to the Whore of Babylon, Salomé is, like the Madonna, a virgin. The comparison is not a frivolous one, given that the Blessed Virgin was herself suspected by her husband of fornication, as suggested by his momentary desire to "put her away privily" (Matthew 1:19). Salomé also resembles the Blessed Virgin of anti-Catholic discourse and the puritanical diatribes against "Mariolatry" that followed upon the Vatican's recognition of the Immaculate Conception in 1854: despite her virginity, she is the object of considerable idolatry and erotic investment. Salomé makes much of her virginity, as she sees it in the mirror of the moon: "I am sure she is a virgin, she has a virgin's beauty. Yes, she is a virgin. She has never defiled herself" (555). And it is Jokanaan who is the first to scandalize her by the spectacle of his voice, gaze, and body: "I was a virgin, and thou didst take my virginity from me. I was chaste, and thou didst fill my veins with fire" (574). Her final long monologue, spoken to the dismembered head, ends with the line, "Well, I know that thou wouldst have loved me, and the mystery of love is greater than the mystery of death" (574), thus echoing an essentially Christian sentiment, one which she could have quoted almost word for word from the Shulamite bride, who says that "love is as strong as death." Wilde himself said of Salomé that, "Her lust must be an abyss, her corruptness, an ocean. The very pearls must die of love upon her bosom," but, paradoxically, she must also be chaste, a kind of angel: "The curves of her long, pale body . . . are like those of a lily. Her beauty has nothing of this world about it. . . . Thin veils woven by the angels wrap round her slender figure. . . . Her eyes shine and sparkle, and are the very stars of hope and faith" (*Interviews* 1:193). Clearly, Wilde had spiritual aspirations for Salomé that his audiences might understandably have over-looked. Wilde plays upon the paradox that the language of spirit always has a beautiful body, that shame and grace stand ever in close proximity, that the saint is often no more than a perfected hedonist. He strained even to see the lovely figure of Christ in the slim-gilt body of Lord Alfred Douglas. On the eve of his sentencing–his own martyrdom–he wrote a love letter to Douglas, claiming that the boy had Christ's own heart. He lapses into the fragrant biblical language of the Shulamite bride: "I love you, I love you, my heart is a rose which your love has brought to bloom, my life is a desert fanned by your breath, and whose cool springs are your eyes; the imprint of your little feet makes valleys of shade for me, the odour of your hair is like myrrh, and wherever you go you exhale the perfumes of the cassia tree" (*Letters* 398). Clearly, Wilde also had spiritual aspirations for Douglas that his biographers might understandably have overlooked. In this letter, he seems to be playing Salomé to Douglas's Jokanaan, and with about the same degree of success. Perhaps the tragic figure of Wilde should be included in performances of *Salomé,* as he is in the film adaptation directed by Ken Russell. In Aubrey Beardsley's illustrations for the play, Wilde haunts the stage in the guise of the moon or a master of ceremonies. The characters of the play already seem to represent a number of his moods and poses, especially with respect to Christianity. I think it fair to say, rephrasing Wilde's famous comment on *Dorian Gray,* that Jokanaan is what he thought he was, Herod what the world thought him, and Salomé what he wished to be–in other ages, perhaps.

Wilde's Christianity, not to mention his many revisions of biblical narratives, has posed a problem for some of his readers. Modern critics rarely find the religious content of his writings as scandalous or as intriguing as his Victorian critics did. Most contemporary readers–including virtually every gay critic–have all but dismissed his Christianity as a pose entirely without substance, a mere mockery of Christianity. Such readings fail to take into account the fascination with Roman Catholicism that is evident in Wilde's fiction and letters. Nor are they willing to take seriously Wilde's numerous attempts at conversion throughout his life, his early Catholic poetry, or the ingenious religious argument of *De Profundis*. Evident in many of these readings is the homophobic presumption that homosexuals are pure sex from head to foot and therefore incapable of a religious or spiritual life. At the other extreme, some critics have pointed to *De Profundis* as a sign of Wilde's repentance for his homosexuality, and they have discussed his Christian writings as though he were another Cardinal Newman. They commit a very different crime by emphasizing Wilde's religious enthusiasms without acknowledging his ironic distance from Church rhetoric and dogma. As Wilde stated emphatically in his letters, he regarded homosexuality as essentially noble and dogmatic Christians as inevitably tiresome. The Christ he described in his later work was a brilliant personality, an aesthete not unlike himself. Wilde's Christ is also, like his Salomé, a creature of scandal. Wilde revealed not only the Word, but its beautiful body, its fascinating sensuality, its paradoxical eroticism. In the language of the Bible, in the medieval exquisiteness with which the Catholic Church performed its daily miracles, Wilde found the last hope of sensual and spiritual beauty in what he saw as an age of bourgeois philistines and sanctimonious puritans.

NOTES

1. For a more comprehensive reading of Christianity in Wilde's work, see my book, *Decadence and Catholicism*. There are a number of other studies of Wilde's religious opinions. In *Beauty and Belief,* Hilary Fraser analyzes Wilde's beliefs, rather than dismissing them, and positions him within the Victorian tradition of religious aesthetics from the Oxford movement on. Both she and George Woodcock, in *Oscar Wilde: The Double Image,* argue for Wilde's sincerity, though they tend to see his wit and his sexuality as incommensurate with faith. Guy Willoughby has written an entire book, *Art and Christhood: The Aesthetics of Oscar Wilde,* on the religious allusions in Wilde's texts, with especially insightful readings of *Salomé* and "The Ballad of Reading Gaol," but the book is remarkable for its refusal to discuss sex, history, or Wilde's life. Other essays and books which deal specifically with Wilde's religious opinions (Knight, Nassaar, Gordon, Clark, Albert, Gray, Quintus, and Paterson, to name a few) are, by comparison, sketchy.

2. For G. K. Chesterton's anatomy of conversion, see his book, *The Catholic Church and Conversion,* especially 57-64.

3. With respect to Wilde, the question of which Bible to quote is a tricky one, since he was, when he wrote *Salomé,* an Anglo-Irish Protestant writing in French and enamored of the Roman Catholic Church. All biblical references are drawn from a translation that would have been familiar to both Wilde and his Evangelical compatriots in the 1890s: a Revised Version of the English Bible published in Cambridge in 1885.

4. All references to Wilde's fiction, including Lord Alfred Douglas's English translation of *Salomé,* are cited from *The Complete Works of Oscar Wilde.* All references to his letters, including *De Profundis,* are cited from *The Letters of Oscar Wilde.*

WORKS CITED

Anonymous. *Teleny.* London: GMP, 1986.

Chesterton, G. K. *The Catholic Church and Conversion.* London: Burns, Oates, 1926.

Ellmann, Richard. *Oscar Wilde.* New York: Knopf, 1988.

Foucault, Michel. *The History of Sexuality.* Vol. 1. 1976. Trans. Robert Hurley. New York: Vintage, 1990.

Fraser, Hilary. *Beauty and Belief.* Cambridge: Cambridge UP, 1986.

Gide, André. *Oscar Wilde: In Memoriam (Reminiscences).* 1901 & 1905. Trans. Bernard Frechtman. New York: Philosophical Library, 1949.

Hanson, Ellis. *Decadence and Catholicism.* Cambridge: Harvard UP, forthcoming.

The Holy Bible. Revised Version. Cambridge: Cambridge UP, 1885.

Huysmans, J.-K. *Against Nature.* 1884. Trans. Robert Baldick. London: Penguin, 1959.

Murphy, Patrick. *Popery in Ireland; or Confessionals, Abductions, Nunneries, Fenians, and Orangemen.* London: Jarrold, n.d.

Norman, E. R. *Anti-Catholicism in Victorian England.* New York: Barnes & Noble, 1968.

Wilde, Oscar. *The Complete Works of Oscar Wilde.* New York: Harper & Row, 1989.

_____. *Oscar Wilde: Interviews and Recollections.* Ed. E. H. Mikhail. 2 vols. New York: Barnes & Noble, 1979.

_____. *The Letters of Oscar Wilde.* Ed. Rupert Hart-Davis. New York: Harcourt, Brace, & World, 1962.

Willoughby, Guy. *Art and Christhood: The Aesthetics of Oscar Wilde.* Rutherford: Fairleigh Dickinson UP, 1993.

Woodcock, George. *Oscar Wilde: The Double Image.* 1949. Montreal: Black Rose, 1989.

Missionary Positions:
Reading the Bible
in Forster's "The Life to Come"

Gregory W. Bredbeck, PhD

University of California, Riverside

SUMMARY. E. M. Forster's short story "The Life to Come" inter-
sects the concerns of both his colonial fiction (*A Passage to India*)
and his homosexual fiction (*Maurice*). The confrontation in the story
between a native chief and a missionary serves initially to explore
the differences between permissive and prohibitional readings of the
Bible, which reflects Forster's dislike of restrictive English morals.
However, contextualizing the story within the project of translating
Vedic scripture that attended British imperialism near the turn of the
century demonstrates that Forster, like his contemporary and mentor
Edward Carpenter, found within colonialism access to a mode of
thinking that ultimately questioned the validity of either permission
or prohibition as foundations for political argumentation. *[Article
copies available for a fee from The Haworth Document Delivery Service:
1-800-342-9678. E-mail address: getinfo@haworth.com]*

Near the beginning of "The Life to Come," Mr. Paul Pinmay, the
English missionary posted in an undesignated foreign country, plunges

---

Gregory W. Bredbeck teaches gay and lesbian studies in the English Department at the University of California, Riverside, where he is an associate professor.
He is the author of *Sodomy and Interpretation: Marlowe to Milton* (1991).

Correspondence may be addressed: Department of English–40, University of
California, Riverside, Riverside, CA 92521-0323.

[Haworth co-indexing entry note]: "Missionary Positions: Reading the Bible in Forster's 'The Life
to Come'." Bredbeck, Gregory W. Co-published simultaneously in *Journal of Homosexuality* (The
Haworth Press, Inc.) Vol. 33, No. 3/4, 1997, pp. 139-161; and: *Reclaiming the Sacred: The Bible in Gay
and Lesbian Culture* (ed: Raymond-Jean Frontain) Harrington Park Press, an imprint of The Haworth
Press, Inc., 1997, pp. 139-161. Single or multiple copies of this article are available for a fee from The
Haworth Document Delivery Service [1-800-342-9678, 9:00 a.m. - 5:00 p.m. (EST). E-mail address:
getinfo@haworth.com].

139

into despair because he has just had sex with the native chief Vithobai. Sitting inside "a small native hut" in "the roots of an aged tree" which "surged at one place into a natural couch," the missionary reads from "his Holy Bible": "Though I speak with the tongues of men and of angels, and have not–." The reading is interrupted, for

> A scarlet flower hid the next word, flowers were everywhere, even round his own neck. Losing his dignity, he sobbed "Oh, what have I done?" and not daring to answer the question he hurled the flowers through the door of the hut and the Bible after them, then rushed to retrieve the latter in an agony of grotesque remorse. All had fallen into the stream, all were carried away by the song. (65)

Near the end of the story this moment is completed. Vithobai, now christened Barnabas, prepares for a ritual suicide to end the many years of painful denial and repression caused by Pinmay's refusal to have further relations with him. Pinmay, compelled by Vithobai to help him, begins to adorn the chief with blue flowers, but is stopped: "and he refrained, remembering that blue is the colour of despair in that valley, just as red is the colour of love" (78-79). The opening moment of the missionary's angst now becomes a symbolic embodiment of the theme of the story, for the word from the Bible obliterated by the red native flower of love is the Christian word of love: "Though I speak tongues with the of men and of angels, and have not *love,* I am become as a sounding brass, or a tinkling cymbal" (1 Cor. 13: 1, my emphasis).

Moments of opposition such as this–moments in which particular symbols come to support the clash of entire ontologies–are not unusual in Forster's writings. In *Maurice,* for example, the cankered and dying roses surrounding the venerable estate of Penge become juxtaposed to the "bright brown eyes" of Alec Scudder at the precise moment that the protagonist, angered at "[t]he indifference of nature," wonders whether "she couldn't bring it off once" (179)–with the effect of opposing a false, decaying, elite English nature to a natural calamitic and democratic nature. The famous opening of *A Passage to India* achieves a similar effect. The "group of fists and fingers . . . thrust up through the soil" that are the Marabar Hills, the sole interruption in "the sky . . . so strong and so enormous," stand as the metonymy for the interruptive action that transactions with Indian culture will have on British culture (9). The symbolism at the beginning of "The Life to Come" is not especially interesting because of its uniqueness, then, but because of its stereotypicality. It is quintessential Forster, and needs to be treated as such.

Comparing the opening moment of "The Life to Come" to these

moments in *Maurice* and *A Passage to India* is a bit self-serving, for it fortuitously introduces the topic that I intend to explicate in this argument. As both novels together suggest, Forster's trajectory as an artist was vectored by the influence of two dominant topics, homosexuality and British colonialist expansion into India. The two topics split between these novels are fused in the narrative of "The Life to Come," and the ways in which the Bible is read in that short story in many ways comprise Forster's most interesting and successful attempt to come to terms with the imaginative and political powers that these themes could offer up as tools of critique.

FLOWERS OF PERMISSION, WORDS OF PROHIBITION

Sex and exegesis blend within "The Life to Come," for the moment that inaugurates sexual contact between the missionary and the native includes a sermon. Flashing back to the events that prompt Pinmay's guilt, the narrative recounts how Vithobai, while initially publicly rejecting the Christian's teachings, sneaks into Pinmay's hut for some late-night tutelage: " 'I have come secretly,' were his first words, 'I wish to hear more about this god whose name is Love' " (67). Pinmay reacts:

> How his heart had leapt after the despondency of the day! "Come to Christ!" he had cried, and Vithobai had said, "Is that your name?" He explained No, his name was not Christ, although he had the fortune to be called Paul after a great apostle, and of course he was no god but a sinful man, chosen to call all sinners to the Mercy Seat. "What is Mercy? I wish to hear more," said Vithobai, and they sat down together upon the couch that was almost a throne. And he had opened the Bible at I. Cor. 13, and had read and expounded the marvellous chapter, and spoke of the love of Christ and of our love for each other in Christ, very simply, but more eloquently than ever before, while Vithobai said, "This is the first time I have heard such words, I like them," and drew closer, his body aglow and smelling sweetly of flowers. And he saw how intelligent the boy was and how handsome, and determining to win him there and then imprinted a kiss on his forehead and drew him to Abraham's bosom. And Vithobai had lain in it gladly–too gladly and too long–and had extinguished the lamp. And God alone saw them after that. (67-68)

Ironies abound here, but the most important one is the clash between literalism and metaphoricity. Pinmay's exegesis of 1 Corinthians 13 begins with the assumption that the literal word of the Bible requires translation.

In point of fact, 1 Corinthians 13 mentions not a word about Christ, nor about mercy. These are meanings which the missionary adds to the text. Vithobai, on the other hand, is a literal reader. He hears the word love and assumes it means love. Like the flower which sets up two systems of meaning, this passage sets up two styles of reading.

Initially, this clash between the literal and the metaphoric would seem to suggest a hierarchy of sophistication. Vithobai, the naive reader, cannot comprehend the truth which the sophisticated, cultured missionary can reveal. And yet this hierarchization is denied in the text. The moment of seduction begins when Pinmay, not Vithobai, moves from the metaphoric realm of exegesis to the literal realm of human touch. Moreover, the passage associates Vithobai with the text of 1 Corinthians 13 itself. The narrative describes Vithobai's entrance prior to the sermon from Pinmay's point of view:

> And he recalled Vithobai, Vithobai the unapproachable, coming into his hut out of the darkness and smiling at him. Oh how delighted he had been! Oh how surprised! He had scarcely recognized the sardonic chief in this gracious and bare-limbed boy, whose only ornaments were scarlet flowers. (67)

The red flower of love which originally obscured the Christian word in Pinmay's point of view here blends seamlessly with the words of 1 Corinthians 13, for the image of a child emerging from the dark clearly echoes the biblical text:

> When I was a child, I spake as a child, I understood as a child, I thought as a child: but when I became a man, I put away childish things.
>
> For now we see through a glass darkly; but then face to face: now I know in part; but then shall I know even as I am known. (1 Cor. 13: 11-12)

This passage correlates childhood with perfect, unmediated knowledge and adulthood with imperfect, dark, refracted knowledge. Moreover, the curious tense construction of the final line–"but then *shall* I know"–establishes this infantile perfection as both the original state and the deferred goal of human spirituality. When Vithobai leaves the dark and enters the hut as a child in the light, the flowers he wears become associated with this type of perfected wisdom, the goal that 1 Corinthians 13 posits as what was and will be, but what is not now. Pinmay now stands in the present moment as the symbol of spiritual imperfection. Vithobai's "naive" literal reading is authorized as a standard which exposes Pinmay's Christian metaphorics as "that which is in part" and "shall be done away" "when that which is perfect is come" (1 Cor. 13: 10). Vithobai's scarlet flowers are that which *is* the word, not that which *obscures* the word.

The dichotomy drawn between the Christian missionary and the native chief would likely raise the expectation that the text will establish a correlative dichotomy between Christian scripture and some other scripture. But that is not the case. "The Life to Come" does not juxtapose two canons of writing, but rather two modes of reading one canon. And the mode which it most clearly critiques is Pinmay's, a mode dedicated to *adhering* prohibition to Christian teaching. Vithobai "reads" 1 Corinthians 13 as enabling–indeed, as compelling–sexual contact, while Pinmay translates it into a prohibition. This governing dichotomy is subtly suggested by Pinmay's first name, Paul, that "great apostle" (67), for the only discernible prohibitions against homosexuality in the New Testament are in the Pauline Doctrine (1 Cor. 6:9; 1 Tim. 1:10).[1]

This association between Pinmay and prohibition is made even more explicit in the text. Pinmay's anguish over his sexual encounter with Vithobai is repressed by a strident adoption of his role as missionary. He publishes a special pamphlet with his Society, christens Vithobai as Barnabas, and publicizes the chief's love for him as proof of a Christian conversion (69). Yet at the same time Pinmay himself undergoes a scriptural conversion: "He who had been wont to lay such stress on the Gospel teaching, on love, kindness, and personal influence, he who had preached that the Kingdom of Heaven is intimacy and emotion, now reacted with violence and treated the new converts and even Barnabas himself with the gloomy severity of the Old Law" (70). Turning from the New Testament to the Old, Pinmay also turns from a God of Love to a God of Punishment, and from a text of permission to a text of prohibition–for the Old Testament is literally the text of prohibition, the text which, again literally, carves the Law of God–the Law of the Father–in stone. Pinmay's ability to translate the union of lovers into the discrete and acceptable roles of missionary and convert relies entirely on an adoption of prohibition as the central tenet of meaning. The dichotomy between Vithobai and Pinmay, then, does not juxtapose two cultures, but rather uses the figure of two cultures as a way of explicating that both permissive and prohibitional readings are possible and that, in fact, prohibitional readings require much defter maneuvers of exegesis and metaphoricity than do permissive ones.

THE MISSIONARY POSITION

The typicality of Fosterian strategies that I have assigned to "The Life to Come" is not a unique insight. In an uncommonly finessed examination of Forster's posthumously published fiction, June Perry Levine has seized on precisely this idea, claiming that the stories published after Forster's death prove the dominance within his writing of one specific motif. As she sees it,

> The posthumous homosexual fiction of E. M. Forster indicates a marked impulse in all his work: the tame in pursuit of the savage, oscillating within a field of attraction and repulsion. Although the strangeness is repugnant, the tame pursues the savage because conjunction will be completion. (72)

Levine's essay is laudable in that unlike so much work about the posthumous Forster canon it refuses to lapse into easy moralizing or overt homophobia.[2] Moreover, Levine's configuration begins to suggest the strong affinities that exist between Forster and issues of colonial representation, for its centering on an oppositionality between the tame and the savage suggests nothing less than a culture clash. And it is not surprising, in this sense, that "The Life to Come" serves as one of Levine's examples of oppositional confrontation.

What needs to be stressed immediately, however, is that the representation of Vithobai—the depiction of otherness—in point of fact erases any possibility of otherness. There is no space outside of Christian mythology in the text, but only degrees of difference in how to *read* Christian scripture. Indeed, it is this *lack* of difference that forges the strongest link between "The Life to Come" and imperialist strategies of colonization, whose social and psychological configurations Eric Cheyfitz has eloquently and passionately explicated:

> those of us who live within the privilege of Western patriarchy live in an increasingly narrow psychic and social sphere. For we cannot afford to enter most of the social spaces of the world; they have become dangerous to us, filled with the violence of the people we oppress, our own violence in alien form we refuse to recognize. . . . Difference and dialogue are impossible here. We talk to ourselves about ourselves, believing in a grand hallucination that we are talking with others. (xiv)

The dynamics of projection and erasure Cheyfitz explicates are profoundly visible in "The Life to Come," for the story's representation of

Vithobai as a privileged emblem of pure knowledge and unrepressed eroticism bespeaks a certain fetishism, both in a cultural and biographical
sense. Originally written around 1922, "The Life to Come" is roughly
contemporaneous with the composition of *A Passage to India* (1924); the
clash of cultures represented in the story undoubtedly reflects Forster's
experiences with British expansion into India. On October 7, 1912, Forster
commenced his personal passage to India, and four days later landed at
Port Said. The journey paralleled that undertaken by other privileged
British citizens of the time, but for Forster it was tinged with more personal hopes. He planned to separate from his companions and spend time
with Syed Ross Masood, a strapping Indian nationalist Forster had tutored
while at Cambridge and on whom Forster was erotically fixated (Furbank
224-229). While sorting his collected correspondence in 1960, Forster
recalled in his commonplace book the exact types of emotion that he
carried with him on his pilgrimage:

> *Tesserete*, August of 1911, which I spent with S[yed]. R[oss].
> M[asood]. greatly involved. I have just torn up the letters to my
> mother and Aunt Laura. They convey nothing at all. Tesserete, like
> most of everyone's past, is lost. It was in Italian Switzerland, and
> Pino Ithen, a commercial youth known to Masood, got us rooms
> there. I recall no scenery but faintly some scenes, for we were at the
> stage–so familiar to me–where the other person has ceased to be
> interested. It was a honeymoon slightly off colour, and perhaps this
> is why the letters are so dull. (*Commonplace Book* 217)

India represented for Forster not simply the newest expansion of England,
but also an expansion of himself; for his involvement with Masood, as this
entry indicates, stood for him as his earliest grappling with his own homosexual desire. The luxury of time allows the novelist to distance and place
in perspective his emotions in a way the younger man could not, for as he
asks himself in his journal entry, "[b]ut why, having already published 3
novels, did I write such wet letters?" (217). Vithobai in "The Life to
Come" can be seen as just such a "wet letter," for he comes to represent
the erotic freedom and unrepressed expression which Forster yearned
for–for himself, with Masood, and in India.

Forster's intense desire to construct Vithobai as a repository of eroticism and projection shows forth strongly in two letters that he wrote to
Siegfried Sassoon, a fellow British writer and homosexual. Exposing the
sort of coterie environment which he originally envisioned for his homosexual stories, Forster wrote in July of 1923 regarding the story, "Why
can't I always be writing things like this–it is the only freedom. I shouldn't

want any friends or bodily gratifications then." And less than a month later he amplified, "Since you are interested in The Life to Come, its genesis may interest you also. It began with a purely obscene fancy of a Missionary in difficulties" (*Letters* 44-45).[3] Forster, for better or worse, viewed the missionary's position as something a bit queerer than that generally acknowledged by British colonial culture.

Forster's eroticization of Vithobai comes to represent that most pernicious trope of colonial representation, the stereotype. In an influential essay originally published in 1992, Homi K. Bhabha has provided one of the most helpful definitions of this figure:

> An important feature of colonial discourse is its dependence on the concept of 'fixity' in the ideological construction of otherness. Fixity as the sign of cultural/historical/racial difference in the discourse of colonialism, is a paradoxical mode of representation: it connotes rigidity and an unchanging order as well as disorder, degeneracy and daemonic repetition. Likewise the stereotype, which is its major discursive strategy, is a form of knowledge and identification that vacillates between what is always 'in place', already known, and something that must be anxiously repeated . . . as if the essential duplicity of the Asiatic or the bestial sexual license of the African that needs no proof, can never really, in discourse, be proved. It is this process of *ambivalence,* central to the stereotype . . . that gives the colonial stereotype its currency: ensures its repeatability in changing historical and discursive conjunctures . . . for the stereotype must always be in *excess* of what can be empirically proved or logically constructed. (66)

Bhabha's point, to put it more simply and somewhat reductively, is that while stereotypes supposedly designate *that which goes without saying,* they exist only to the extent that they are continually *said.* Because stereotypes derive from the redaction of and extrapolation from broad cultural populations, they cannot stake an authority in referentiality to actual persons. "Reality," from which stereotypes purportedly derive, is consistently that which stereotypes, through their continued iteration, must obliterate. Stereotypes, therefore, create, to use Bhabha's phrase, a "productive ambivalence" (67); they acknowledge cultural otherness but also repress that otherness; they mark a boundary but at the same time create the dynamics which can destroy that boundary. As Bhabha succinctly phrases it, "the recognition and disavowal of 'difference' is always disturbed by the question of its re-presentation or construction" (81).

Forster's deployment of the stereotype is obviously just that, even to the point of perfectly capturing Bhabha's example of "the bestial sexual license of the African" (66). And clearly in the ways in which Vithobai reprocesses Forster's own deferred erotic desires there appear all the processes of "projection and introjection, metaphoric and metonymic strategies, displacement, overdetermination, guilt [and] aggressivity" (81-82) which Bhabha attributes to stereotypes. And yet Forster's representation of Vithobai does not simply couch the proper of English culture within a defensive boundary of ambivalence. Rather, it uses the occasion to activate an ambivalence within the very heart of English culture, within the supposedly direct and natural link between the Christian scripture, prohibition, and sexual repression that are–again supposedly–the creator of and the product of the sexually licentious stereotype of otherness. Within "The Life to Come" the ostensibly *always already* vectored power-relations of colonizer and colonized are both displayed and disrupted. Even as Forster's "stereotype" erases any literal, material space for otherness, it also erases the idea of a fixed, monolithic Christian dogma and a fixed, immutable colonizing ideology. To return to Levine's terminology and to alter it slightly, within the story the tame pursues the savage, but only to the ends of displacing tameness itself. Forster's stereotype is, in other words, ambivalent *with a vengeance.*[4] Historicizing the conditions enabling this representation will be the topic of the remainder of this essay.

TEXTUAL IMPERIALISM

Forster's personal and textual encounter with colonialism was, of course, but one of many that happened in British culture in the late nineteenth and early twentieth centuries. One other one which provides a telling counterpoint to "The Life to Come" is that present in F. Max Müller's translation of the *Upanisads,* the oldest Vedic scriptures of Hindu religion. Published in 1879 and 1884 as the first two volumes in the ambitious Oxford University series "The Sacred Books of the East," Müller's translations comprise the first installment in a twenty-four-volume project designed to make available to English readers reliable, scholarly editions of all the major sacred texts of the Brahmans, Buddha, Zarathustra, Khung-fû-tze, Lâo-tze, and Mohammed (Müller 1:xli). Müller's original notice for the series explains the reason for beginning with the *Upanisads*:

> There is nothing more ancient in India than the Vedas; and, if we except the Vedas and the literature connected with them, there is again no literary work in India which, so far as we know at present,

can with certainty be referred to an earlier date than that of the sacred Canon of Buddhists. . . . This being the case, it was but natural that the attention of the historian should of late have been more strongly attracted by these Sacred Books, as likely to afford most valuable information, not only on religion, but also on the moral sentiments, the social institutions, the legal maxims of some of the most important nations of antiquity. (1:xl)

Müller's recourse to the "natural" curiosity of "historians" and their dispassionate desire for anthropological data reflects his own belief that "the time has come when the study of the ancient religions of mankind must be approached in a different, in a less enthusiastic, and more discriminating, in fact, in a more scholarlike spirit" (1:x). The volume as a whole, however, suggests that this *natural* interest is underpinned by an entirely *political* agenda, for the volume opens with this dedication:

TO
THE RIGHT HONOURABLE THE MARQUIS OF SALISBURY, K.G.
CHANCELLOR OF THE UNIVERSITY OF OXFORD,
LATELY SECRETARY OF STATE FOR INDIA,

SIR HENRY J. S. MAINE, K.C.S.I.
MEMBER OF THE COUNCIL OF INDIA,

AND

THE VERY REV. H. G. LIDDELL, D.D.
DEAN OF CHRIST CHURCH,

TO WHOSE KIND INTEREST AND EXERTIONS
THIS ATTEMPT TO MAKE KNOWN TO THE ENGLISH PEOPLE
THE SACRED BOOKS OF THE EAST
IS SO LARGELY INDEBTED,
I NOW DEDICATE THESE VOLUMES
WITH SINCERE RESPECT AND GRATITUDE
F. MAX MüLLER.

The dedication places the book firmly within the imperialist triumvirate of the church, the university, and the state, and in the process suggests that Müller's work must be read as one of the technologies of colonization.

What is most interesting about Müller's tract as an artifact is the way in which it suggests an inherent bidirectionality to the dynamics of colonialism. Much work on colonialism understandably examines the ways in which it directs issues of power and representation towards the "subject nation" with the intent of implanting systems of governance *within* that nation (Bhabha 70). Müller's tract, however, is intended to construct the *reception* of Indian culture in England–"to make known to the English people" the alien modes of knowledge accessed by the colonial project. As such, the text also suggests that rather than a unidirectional, linear projection, colonialism sets up a polymorphous web of influences with no inherent directionality.[5]

A metaphor is helpful here: colonialist discourse is frequently thought of as an army, a force of power marching across the encountered culture; Müller's text functions as more of a custom house, logging and redeploying the goods of foreign countries for the use of the colonizer. Colonialist discourse is always the negotiation of (at least) two routes of power, one a voyage out, but the other a voyage in; the army and the custom house are the necessary and unavoidable complementary agents of colonialism. The bidirectionality of power lines established by colonialism suggests an even greater ambivalence than that analyzed by Bhabha, one that rests not only in the figure of the other, but that also envelops the entire system of colonizer and colonized. The ambivalence *within* colonial discourse reflects and, sometimes, represses a foundational ambivalence which colonialism embeds within the very conditions of meaning of the colonizing culture.[6]

Müller's translation exposes vividly both the figure of ambivalence within and the foundation of ambivalence implanted by British colonial discourse near the turn of the century. On the one hand, Müller's apparatus enacts perfectly what Bhabha has pinpointed as the "objective of colonial discourse," which "is to construe the colonized as a population of degenerate types on the basis of racial origin in order to justify conquest and to establish systems of administration and instruction" (70). In the general preface to the entire series of translation with which the two volumes of the *Upanisads* begin, Müller says,

> The religions of antiquity must always be approached in a loving spirit, and the dry and cold-blooded scholar is likely to do here as much mischief as the enthusiastic sciolist. But true love does not ignore all faults and failings: on the contrary, it scans them keenly, though only in order to be able to understand, to explain, and thus to excuse them. (xi)

The tone here is paternalistic to the extreme, and the "proper" scholar is established as the responsible parent who loves and yet critiques and guides. This implicit infantilizing is made more explicit as the passage continues:

> To watch in the Sacred Books of the East the dawn of the religious consciousness of man, must always remain one of the most inspiring and hallowing sights in the whole history of the world; and he whose heart cannot quiver with the first quivering rays of human thought and human faith, as revealed in those ancient documents, is, in his own way, as unfit for these studies as, from another side, the man who shrinks from copying and collating ancient MSS. . . . [But] the whole truth must be told, it is that, however radiant the dawn of religious thought, it is not without its dark clouds, its chilling colds, its noxious vapours. (xi)

The metaphor of the passing of a day becomes a veiled version of a human life span, with Eastern religion occupying the position of a not yet socialized infant. The scholar's function, Müller implies, should be the tandem practices of love and discipline, the ability to nurture the desirable and repress the undesirable. What is needed here is, in other words, good parenting skills.

Müller's use of an implicit infantilization foreshadows Forster's infantilization of Vithobai, which immediately suggests that what is at work here is a mode of stereotyping. This idea is substantiated when Müller turns toward the other discourse that so firmly structures the representation of Vithobai, eroticism. Explaining why he has "suppressed nothing, [and] varnished nothing" within the *Upanisads,* Müller states that "There is only one exception":

> There are in ancient books, and particularly in religious books, frequent allusions to the sexual aspects of nature, which, though perfectly harmless and innocent in themselves, cannot be rendered in modern language without the appearance of coarseness. We may regret that it should be so, but tradition is too strong on this point, and I have therefore felt obliged to leave certain passages untranslated, and to give the original, when necessary, in a note. (xx-xxi)

Müller's liberalism ascribes the need for repression to traditions of scholarship, not to anything inherent within the *Upanisads* themselves. Yet this laudable objectivity is quickly cast aside, for Müller himself chooses to "defend" the sexuality of the *Upanisads* through an even stronger type of infantilization:

> [Expurgation] has been done in extreme cases only, and many things which we should feel inclined to suppress have been left in all their

outspoken simplicity, because those who want to study ancient man, must learn to study him as he really was, an animal, with all the strength and weaknesses of an animal, though an animal that was to rise above himself, and in the end discover his true self, after many struggles and many defeats. (xxi)

If Eastern religion stands as the child to the man that is Western religion, Eastern sexual expression stands as the beast to the human of Western sexual repression. Grasping on a Darwinian trope of evolution, Müller "others" the expression of sexuality to the extreme, placing it not as the immaturity that precedes maturation, but as the immaturity that precedes the very species.

Müller's apparatus to the *Upanisads* firmly establishes the object of his scholarly inquiry as the subject of colonial discourse, the degenerate other constructed within and reiterated by the structures of domination and hegemony. And yet there is a different strand of thought that weaves alongside this deployment of stereotyping, and it focuses on an anxiety about the very act of translation itself. In order to explain the difficulties of translating Vedic literature into English, Müller provides a rather long discussion of the word "âtmân, nom. sing. âtmâ," "one of the most important words in the ancient philosophy of the Brahmans" (xxviii). As Müller says,

> It is rendered in our dictionaries by 'breath, soul, the principle of life and sensation, the individual soul, the self, the abstract individual, self, one's self, the reflexive pronoun, the natural temperament or disposition, essence, nature, character, peculiarity, the person or the whole body, the body, the understanding, intellect, the mind, the faculty of thought and reason, the thinking faculty, the highest principle of life, Brahma, the supreme deity or soul of the universe, care, effort, pains, firmness, the sun, fire, wind, air, a son.' (xxviii)

Müller provides this example to demonstrate "the chaotic state from which Sanskrit lexicology is only just emerging" (xxix), but the conclusions he draws are more reaching than this. As he notes, "when âtman occurs in philosophical treatises . . . it has generally been translated by soul, mind or spirit" (xxix). The problem with this is, according again to Müller, "If we translate âtman by soul, mind or spirit, we commit, first of all, that fundamental mistake of using words which may be predicated, in place of a word which is subject only, and can never become a predicate" (xxxi).

What is most interesting about Müller's ruminations on translation is that they do not ascribe the problems he encounters to the Hindu text.

Never is it said that the degenerate nature of Hindu thought makes it unassimilable. Neither is it said that inadequate systems of grammar in Sanskrit fail to account for the difference between subject and object. Nor is it said that Hindu seers, lacking a perfected Western ontology, simply had to approximate the more defined and refined concepts of English in imperfect words. Rather, the problem is assigned to a deep structural flaw within the English language itself: the very rules of grammar that allow English to work disable an accurate importation of the *Upanisads*. Müller's solution to this problem is "to keep as close as possible to the Sanskrit original, and where [he] could not find an adequate term in English, [to retain] the Sanskrit word rather than use a misleading substitute in English" (xxxii). With this solution in place, Müller's text, which displays so strongly the power of British colonial technology, also becomes a vivid display of its impotencies. Every place where Sanskrit enters his translation marks a point where British colonialism fails to penetrate and territorialize Hindu systems of meaning.

Müller, however, is not always content to let the English language display its impotencies, as two examples from the first prapâthaka of the *Khânogya-Upanisad* demonstrate. The first khanda begins with one of the most famous passages of Hindu scripture, a definition of Om:

1. Let a man meditate on the syllable Om, called the udgîtha; for the udgîtha (a portion of the Sâma-veda) is sung, beginning with Om.
   The full account, however, of Om is this:–
2. The essence of all beings is the earth, the essence of the earth is water, the essence of water the plants, the essence of plants man, the essence of man speech, the essence of speech the Rig-veda, the essence of the Rig-veda the Sâma-veda, the essence of the Sâma-veda the udgîtha (which is Om). (1-2)

At the first occurrence of "essence" in verse 2, Müller supplies this footnote:

> Essence, rasa, is explained in different ways, as origin, support, end, cause, and effect. Rasa means originally the sap of trees. That sap may be conceived either as the essence extracted from the tree, or as what gives vigour and life to a tree. In the former case it might be transferred to the conception of effect, in the latter to that of cause. In our sentence it has sometimes the one, sometimes the other meaning. Earth is the support of all beings, water pervades the earth, plants arise from water, man lives by plants, part of speech, the Sâma-veda

the best extract from the *Rik,* udgîtha, or the syllable Om, the crown of the Sâma-veda. (1)

Müller's note, of course, signals a deviation in principle, for it acknowledges that, indeed, essence is a "misleading substitute in English" for *rasa.* This same deviation is present in a briefer example from the ninth khanda,

> 1. 'What is the origin of this world?' 'Ether,' he replied. For all these beings take their rise from the ether, and return into the ether. Ether is older than these, ether is their rest. (17)

To which Müller adds the note: "Ether, or we might translate it by space, both being intended, however, as names or symbols of the Highest Brahman" (17). Like "essence," "ether" is a "misleading substitute in English," for why else would an explanatory note be needed?

These two deviations (and others could be supplied) share a commonality, for both replace moments when the Sanskrit word transgresses English grammatical prohibitions against logical contradiction. Ether and space are, in point of fact, practically antithetical. Ether is a gas which fills space, whereas space is the void which gas would fill. In effect, the Sanskrit version relies on an oxymoron, that the "origin of this world" is both something and nothing simultaneously. Müller's translation effaces this indeterminacy and covers it with a determinant schema: in the beginning there was *definitely* something, even if it was as nebulous as ether. The replacement of *rasa* by essence achieves a similar purpose. "Origin, support, end, cause, and effect" are discrete and antithetical concepts in Western thought, and yet they exjst simultaneously within one Sanskrit word. Müller's note acknowledges a rapid change between these meanings, but it never allows a broaching of the logical prohibition that renders them discrete and different. Hence he says "essence" in the sentence "has sometimes the one, sometimes the other meaning"–but he never allows it to have, as does *rasa,* all at once.

The point to be made here is that while Müller's relative liberalism allows more difference into the English system than do most discourses of colonization, it also guards against a greater difference, a difference not *within* the English system, but *to* the English system. There are two ambivalences here, one which allows an oscillating image of India into the English cultural economy, the other which places England into an oscillating economy of cultural possibilities; one is an ambivalence around different meanings, the other is an ambivalence around different *ways to make* meanings. It is helpful to see this pattern in just such a diacritical way, for it provides a cogent vocabulary for describing the poetics of Forster's "The Life to Come." If both Müller's translation theory and Forster's representation of Vithobai activate the same tropes, they also skew toward different combinations of these two ambivalences: Müller grapples with the emergence of different meanings; Forster's ironically displays the possibility of different ways to make meaning.

TYPES OF PERMISSION

I have suggested that the clash between modes of reading the Bible in "The Life to Come" represents a commentary on the relative merits of permission and prohibition, and these two terms need to be amplified in order to understand precisely the dynamics of Forster's encounters with sexuality, colonialism, and the Bible. Generally speaking, permission and prohibition are typically thought of as aspects of behavioral control, with permission allowing and prohibition disallowing certain actions. This system is clearly visible in "The Life to Come" for Vithobai can be seen as representing permission to engage in homosexual behavior, while Pinmay can be seen as representing a prohibition on homosexual behavior.

There is historical data to support the idea that Forster would read Hindu scripture as containing just such a permission, and this data also suggests that Forster would have been acquainted with Müller's translations. As has been documented by Forster himself and several critics, one primary influence on Forster and his interest in Indian culture was British socialist sexologist Edward Carpenter.[7] *Love's Coming of Age,* which Carpenter published in 1896 and which redacts material printed in three pamphlets by the Labour Press in Manchester in 1894, contains a harsh critique of Müller's translation:

> In one of the Upanishads of the Vedic sacred books (the Brihadaranyaka Upanishad) there is a fine passage in which instruction is given to the man who desires a noble son as to the prayers he shall offer to the gods on the occasion of congress with his wife. In primitive and simple and serene language it directs him how, at such times, he should pray to the various forms of deity who preside over the operations of Nature: to Vishnu to prepare the womb of the future mother, to Prajápati to watch over the influx of the semen, and to the other gods to nourish the foetus, etc. Nothing could be . . . more composed, serene, simple, and religious in feeling, and well might it be if such instructions were preserved and followed, even today; yet such is the pass we have come to that actually Max Müller in his

translations of the Sacred Books of the East appears to have been unable to persuade himself to render these and a few other quite similar passages into English, but gives them in the original Sanskrit! One might have thought that as Professor in the University of Oxford, presumably *sans peur et sans reproche,* and professedly engaged in making a translation of these books for students, it was his duty and it might have been his delight to make intelligible just such passages as these, which give the pure and pious sentiment of the early world in so perfect a form; unless indeed he thought the sentiment impure and impious–in which case we have indeed a measure of degradation of the public opinion which must have swayed his mind. (104)[8]

Carpenter's anger here results from the difference between permission and prohibition in the sense of behavioral regulation. The text instructs in sexual activity (permission) while Müller's texts censor this instruction (prohibition). Yet the rhetoric of this passage also helpfully demonstrates how these notions of permission and prohibition only exist within one level of postcolonial ambivalence, that which exists *within* the colonizing system. For Carpenter here engages his own language of stereotyping, constructing Hindu permissiveness as "primitive, simple and serene," another "dawn," to borrow Müller's metaphor, before the darkness of English repression blots the sun. For Müller, Hindu sexuality is a degraded savage; for Carpenter, it is the noble savage: the *inherent* form of colonial stereotyping remains intact with only its *adherent* value changing.[9]

There is, however, another type of permission which Carpenter finds in Hindu thought, a permission which establishes a diacritical distinction analogous to that between the two types of ambivalence I have discussed, a permission not so much to allow different meanings into a system, but to allow different systems of meaning to limit the manifest totality of the system within which he works. Consider, for example, this quasi-mystical passage from his earliest tract:

Sex-pleasures afford a kind of type of all pleasure. The dissatisfaction which at times follows on them is the same as follows on all pleasure which is *sought,* and which does not come unsought. The dissatisfaction is not in the nature of pleasure itself, but in the nature of *seeking.* In going off in pursuit of things external, the 'I' (since it really has everything and needs nothing) deceives itself, goes out from its true home, tears itself asunder, and admits a gap or rent in its own being. This, it must be supposed, is what is meant by *sin*–the separation or sundering of one's being–and all the pain that goes

therewith. It all consists in *seeking* those external things and pleasures; not (a thousand times be it said) in the external things or
pleasures themselves. (102)

From which he concludes: "To this desertion of one's true self sex tempts
most strongly, and stands as the type of Maya and the world illusion"
(102). Even as Carpenter uses Hindu thought to argue for the "naturalness" of all "sex-pleasures" and chastises Müller's need for prohibition,
he sees all sex-pleasures as equally "unnatural," for all are simply to him
alternative aspects of "Maya," the "world-illusion" of duality, difference,
and perception that marks humans' unenlightened state. And hence it is
not surprising to hear Carpenter say that "what we call asceticism and
what we call libertinism are two sides practically of the same shield"
(101), for what Carpenter found in Hinduism was the permission to see
both permission and prohibition as aspects of prohibition, the ontological
phenomenon of segregation, separation, and reification that maintains the
dualistic state of the unenlightened.[10]

This latter permission marks the "real" other that motivates Forster's
representation of biblical readings in "The Life to Come." Near the end of
the story, when the significance of the red flower is revealed, it is in a
moment of duality: Vithobai lies beside a knife adorned with "blue flowers" and Pinmay recalls that "blue is the colour of despair in the valley,
just as red is the colour of love" (78-79). Vithobai himself changes from a
representative of erotic permission to a character torn in the midst of
antithetical options: "I forgive you, I do not forgive, both are the same. I
am good I am evil I am pure I am foul, I am this or that, I am Barnabas, I
am Vithobai. What difference does it make now?" (79). The answer is, It
makes no difference. The story ends in tragedy, with Vithobai killing both
Pinmay and himself. Finally constructed as the scattered, dualistic subject
of British colonial missionary politics, Vithobai stands as a vivid reminder
of what is *never* in this story: anything *not* English. Both victim and victor
are victimized and victorious; both colonized and colonizer act from the
agency of colonial discourse, but this agency leads to tragedy.[11]

The ending of "The Life to Come," then, ironically suggests that which
it will not say. The dualities of native and missionary, of literal and metaphoric biblical reading patterns, of red flowers of love and blue flowers of
despair, and of sexual permission and sexual prohibition *in the aggregate*
render tragedy unavoidable. Happy endings do not result from proper
choices *within* these dualities; they result quite simply from something
different. In this sense, it is precisely Forster's unwillingness to represent
anything other than a reading of Christian scripture that reveals his awareness of the depths of Hindu thought. Unlike Müller, who professes an

ability to capture "the truth, and the whole truth" (1:xi), Forster's truth is different: that some things remain–and *should* remain–uncapturable.

CODA: ON FORSTER'S ENDS

In the terminal note composed in 1960 to *Maurice* Forster recounts the germinal moment of the novel, which also brings to the fore the importance of his friendship with Carpenter. As he says,

> In its original form, which it still almost retains, *Maurice* dates from 1913. It was the direct result of a visit to Edward Carpenter at Milthorpe. . . . It must have been on my second or third visit to the shrine that the spark was kindled and he and his comrade George Merrill combined to make a profound impression on me and to touch a creative spring. George Merrill also touched my backside–gently and just above the buttocks. I believe he touched most people's. The sensation was unusual and I still remember it, as I remember the position of a long vanished tooth. It was as much psychological as physical. It seemed to go straight through the small of my back into my ideas, without involving my thoughts. If it really did this, it would have acted in strict accordance with Carpenter's mysticism, and would prove that at the precise moment I had conceived. (249)

What he had conceived was *Maurice*: "I then returned to Harrogate, where my mother was taking a cure, and immediately began to write *Maurice*" (250). Forster's end note about his rear end raises an issue about ends in general, and particularly about the ending of stories. In the note Forster also says of *Maurice* that "A happy ending was imperative," and tells of a canceled ending: "I was encouraged to write an epilogue. It took the form of Kitty encountering two woodcutters some years later and gave universal dissatisfaction" (254).

This anecdote recalls one in his correspondence, in which he tells Siegfried Sassoon of a planned but abandoned ending for "The Life to Come":

> I wish the story could have another ending, but however much skill and passion I put into it, it would never have satisfied you. I tried another chapter, it is true, in the forests of the Underworld 'where all the trees that have been cut down on earth take root again and grow forever' and the hut has been rebuilt on an enormous scale. The dead come crashing down through the foliage, in an infernal embrace.

Pinmay prays to his God who appears on high through a rift in the leaves, and pities him but can do nothing. 'It is very unfortunate' says God: 'if he had died first you would have taken him to your heaven, but he has taken you to his instead. I am very sorry, oh good and faithful servant, but I cannot do anything.' The leaves close, and Pinmay enters Eternity as a slave, while Vithobai reigns with his peers.

But Forster saw the ending to be "A gloomy prospect you see–except for Vithobai, who has won the odd trick" (*Letters* 43).

Several things unite these two canceled endings. They both relate to stories of homosexual love; they both bespeak the influence of Carpenter, *Maurice*'s directly, that of "The Life to Come" through the access Carpenter provided to Vedic literature. But most importantly, they both betray an anxiety about coming to an end. The canceled ending of *Maurice* provides a place, an occupation, and an identity for Maurice, whereas the novel as it stands simply ends with the fact that "Maurice had disappeared" (246). The canceled ending to "The Life to Come" supplies a fantastical corroboration of Vithobai's "otherness," inserting into the text the first traces of an alternative religious system, whereas the story as it stands leaves both Vithobai and Pinmay dead within the discourse of colonialism.

In 1929 Forster wrote in his commonplace book, "*Edward Carpenter.* Astonishing how he drains away . . . and he was always finding mystic reasons for doing what he wanted e.g. [homosexuality]. I suppose there was something there, but as soon as one touches it, it's gone" (53).[12] That "something" which cannot be touched is precisely what Forster garnered from his encounter with Carpenter, for what the posthumous fiction inspired by Carpenter reveals is an intense desire to construct narratives that escape the prohibitional and quantifiable knowledges of western religion, of western culture, and of western sex. That this should be emblematized by a touch to Forster's end, and that this should be narratively approximated by missing ends, is only slightly less ironic than the fact that this is my own end.

NOTES

1. Whether or not these passages are actually prohibitions against homosexuality is extremely debatable. John Boswell's refutation of this common reading is, to my mind, entirely convincing (106-07). Yet the point here is not, as it is in Boswell's argument, the *actual* meaning of the passages, but is, rather, the cultural meanings attributed to the passages at the time Forster was writing.

2. For examples of this depressingly frequent mode of commentary, see Ozick and Meyers.

3. In the original letter the word "vision" is supplied and cancelled before the word "fancy." The letters are dated 21 July 1923 and 1 August 1923.

4. I use the term "vengeance" in the same sense as–and with a debt to–Teresa de Lauretis's work on feminist film production: "feminist work in film . . . should be narrative and oedipal *with a vengeance,* working, as it were, with and against narrative in order to represent not just a female desire which Hollywood, in the best tradition of Western literature and iconography, has classically represented as the doomed power of the fetish . . . ; but working, instead, to represent the duplicity of the oedipal scenario itself . . . " (108).

5. My argument will reduce the possibility of polymorphism to a binary image, due entirely to the dynamics of the texts with which I am dealing. But my conceptual framework here is very much indebted to the two dominant innovations of thought pinpointed by Spivak in an analysis of the work of the Subaltern Studies group: "first, that the moment(s) of change be pluralized and plotted as confrontations rather than transition . . . and, secondly, that such changes are signalled or marked by a functional change in sign-systems" (197).

6. In this sense colonial discourse can be seen as a specific historical implantation and activation of the dynamics which Jacques Derrida ascribes to all language in his analysis of metaphor–namely, that the "figure" of metaphor and its secondary, derivative status within Western epistemology both exposes and represses the inherent metaphoricity of epistemology itself (207-271). I examine the applicability of this concept to issues of homosexual identity politics and semiotic in "B/O."

7. The most important work on this topic is Martin, "Double Structure"; but see also Levine and Fletcher. For Forster's own description of his debt to Carpenter, see his essay "Edward Carpenter" (*Two Cheers* 218).

8. The Upanisad to which Carpenter alludes is in *The Upanisads,* 2:73-227.

9. For an excellent discussion of Carpenter's actual travels to India and how it enabled the formation of a mystical form of socialism, see Rowbotham and Weeks.

10. I examine in depth the function of prohibition in Western ontology and in gay and queer activism in "The New Queer Narrative."

11. This embrace of the full philosophical premises of Hindu duality can do much to smooth a constant spur in Forster criticism, that of his attitude toward lower classes. On the one hand, as Martin has argued, "it is clear that for Forster homosexuality can lead to a greater democracy of vision, to a violation of social, racial, and class barriers" ("Forster's Greek" 73). On the other hand, as Stone has argued, there are also instances in which Forster seems to show a contempt toward lower classes. The sort of split consciousness Hindu philosophy implanted in the minds of Forster and Carpenter can account for both of these views: democracy is the best of all possible worlds, but the very conditions that enable democracy are a part of a Western ontology that inhibits true enlightenment.

12. There is a large blank in the original where I have, following the suggestion of the manuscript's editor Philip Gardner, supplied the word "homosexuality."

WORKS CITED

Bhabha, Homi K. "The Other Question: Stereotypes, Discrimination, and the Discourse of Colonialism." *The Location of Culture.* New York: Routledge, 1994. 66-84.

Boswell, John. *Christianity, Social Tolerance, and Homosexuality: Gay People in Western Europe from the Beginning of the Christian Era to the Fourteenth Century.* Chicago: U of Chicago P, 1980.

Bredbeck, Gregory W. "B/O–Barthes's Text/O'Hara's Trick." *PMLA* 108.2 (March 1993): 268-282.

_____ . "The New Queer Narrative: Intervention and Critique." *Textual Practice* 9.3 (1995): 477-502.

Carpenter, Edward. *Selected Writings, Volume 1: Sex.* Ed. Noël Grieg. London: Gay Men's P, 1984.

Cheyfitz, Eric. *The Poetics of Imperialism: Translation and Colonization from the Tempest to Tarzan.* New York: Oxford UP, 1991.

de Lauretis, Teresa. "Strategies of Coherence: Narrative Cinema, Feminist Poetics, and Yvonne Rainer." *Technologies of Gender: Essays on Theory, Film, and Fiction.* Bloomington: Indiana UP, 1987. 107-126.

Derrida, Jacques. "White Mythology: Metaphor in the Text of Philosophy." *Margins of Philosophy.* Trans. Alan Bass. Chicago: U of Chicago P, 1982. 207-272.

Fletcher, John. "Forster's Self-Erasure: *Maurice* and the Scene of Masculine Love." *Sexual Sameness: Textual Differences and Gay Writing.* Ed. Joseph Bristow. London: Routledge, 1992. 64-90.

Forster, E. M. *Commonplace Book.* Ed. Philip Gardner. Stanford: Stanford UP, 1985.

_____ . "The Life to Come." *The Life to Come and Other Stories.* New York: Norton, 1972. 65-82.

_____ . *Maurice.* New York: Norton, 1971.

_____ . *A Passage to India.* New York: Harcourt Brace Jovanovich, 1924.

_____ . *Selected Letters of E. M. Forster. Volume Two: 1921-1970.* Ed. Mary Lago and P. N. Furbank. Cambridge: Harvard UP, 1984.

_____ . "Edward Carpenter." *Two Cheers for Democracy.* London: Edward Arnold, 1951. 218.

Furbank, P. N. *E. M. Forster: A Life.* New York: Harcourt Brace Jovanovich, 1977.

Levine, June Perry. "The Tame in Pursuit of the Savage: The Posthumous Fiction of E. M. Forster." *PMLA* 99.1 (1984): 72-88.

Martin, Robert K. "Edward Carpenter and the Double Structure of *Maurice.*" *Essays on Gay Literature.* Ed. Stuart Kellogg. New York: Harrington Park P, 1985. 35-46.

_____ . "Forster's Greek: From Optative to Present Indicative." *Kansas Quarterly* 9 (1977): 181-92.

Meyers, Jeffrey. *Homosexuality and Literature.* London: Athlone P, 1977.

Müller, F. Max, trans. *The Upanishads.* 2 vols. Oxford: Clarendon P, 1879 and 1884; Rpt. New York: Dover, 1962.

Ozick, Cynthia. "Foster as Homosexual." *Commentary* 52 (1971): 81-85.

Rowbotham, Sheila, and Jeffrey Weeks. *Socialism and the New Life: The Personal and Sexual Politics of Edward Carpenter and Havelock Ellis.* London: Pluto P, 1971.

Spivak, Gayatri Chakravorty. *In Other Worlds: Essays in Cultural Politics.* New York: Routledge, 1988.

Stone, Wilfred. " 'Overleaping Class': Forster's Problem in Connection." *MLQ* 39 (1978): 386-404.

The Well of Loneliness,
or The Gospel According to Radclyffe Hall

Ed Madden, PhD

University of South Carolina

SUMMARY. Radclyffe Hall's 1928 novel, *The Well of Loneliness,* is repeatedly described as a "bible" of lesbian literature. The novel itself repeatedly alludes to biblical stories, especially the story of Christ. Yet there has been little sustained analysis of the biblical language of the novel. Most feminist and lesbian critics have dismissed the biblical allusions and language as unfortunate and politically regressive; religious critics have ignored the novel. This essay reexamines the biblical nature of the novel, especially its portrayal of the lesbian Stephen Gordon as a Christ figure. The study further claims a creative and interventionary power in Hall's use of biblical narratives and tropes, a power traceable in public reception to the novel and in courtroom reactions to the use of spiritual language in a text about lesbianism. By writing the life of a lesbian as a kind of gospel of inversion, Hall turns a language of condemnation into a language

Ed Madden is an assistant professor of English at the University of South Carolina, where he teaches British literature, creative writing, and modernism. His published work includes essays on Charlotte Mew, Paul Monette, and AIDS literature. His poems were featured in the 1994 anthology *Gents, Bad Boys, and Barbarians.* An earlier version of this article was presented in the USC Women's Studies research lecture series, as "The Lesbian Messiah in *The Well of Loneliness,*" in September 1995.

Correspondence may be addressed: Department of English, University of South Carolina, Columbia, SC 29208.

[Haworth co-indexing entry note]: "*The Well of Loneliness*, or The Gospel According to Radclyffe Hall." Madden, Ed. Co-published simultaneously in *Journal of Homosexuality* (The Haworth Press, Inc.) Vol. 33, No. 3/4, 1997, pp. 163-186; and: *Reclaiming the Sacred: The Bible in Gay and Lesbian Culture* (ed: Raymond-Jean Frontain) Harrington Park Press, an imprint of The Haworth Press, Inc., 1997, pp. 163-186. Single or multiple copies of this article are available for a fee from The Haworth Document Delivery Service [1-800-342-9678, 9:00 a.m. - 5:00 p.m. (EST). E-mail address: getinfo@ haworth.com].

163

of validation, making her use of biblical language a kind of Foucauldian "reverse discourse." The novel's power lies in its portrayal of a lesbian messiah, and in its joining of sexological and religious discourses. *[Article copies available for a fee from The Haworth Document Delivery Service: 1-800-342-9678. E-mail address: getinfo@haworth.com]*

The novel offers a uniquely flexible literary vehicle by which the author and therefore the reader can imaginatively enter the hero's persona. If the major protagonist is Jesus Christ and the period is an age of psychoanalytic sophistication, the opportunities for reinterpretation of a legendary story are limited only by the varieties in the human psyche.

–Alice L. Birney, *The Literary Lives of Jesus* (xxv)

In 1972, lesbian critic Del Martin called Radclyffe Hall's 1928 novel *The Well of Loneliness* a "Lesbian Bible" (17). Echoing this term of canonicity, Jane Rule, in her 1975 survey of *Lesbian Images* called the novel the "bible" of lesbian literature. But Rule notes, rather disparagingly, that this "bible" is indebted in too many stereotypical ways to the Bible, stating that Hall "worshipped the very institutions which oppressed her, the Church and the patriarchy" (61). This is a not uncommon criticism of the novel. And yet, in this essay, I would like to look again at the *biblical* nature of *The Well of Loneliness*. I would like to reexamine this novel, the story of a young lesbian writer growing up in early twentieth-century England, as a kind of spiritual narrative–not simply a novel defending lesbianism and homosexuality as naturally occurring aspects of the human condition, but a kind of *gospel* of inversion featuring a lesbian messiah.[1]

Repeatedly, I think, critics fail to examine the power of Hall's use of biblical narrative, especially her striking allusions to the Christ story of the gospels. It is seen as simply another aspect of her overly sentimentalized and melodramatic writing. Or it is critiqued, probably rightly so, as yet another facet of her failure to question the modernist era's stereotypes of lesbianism as a tragic, biological, masculine identity, so that her heroine must inevitably become a suffering Christ figure.[2] But can we reimagine an interventionary rhetorical practice in her use of the Bible? Is this simply a modernist elitist engagement with a great-but-failed text of Western culture, or is it a critical and imaginative attempt at legitimation? What does it mean that one of the first novels about lesbian life is so heavily dependent upon the language and images of the Bible? What is the point of

Hall's literary appropriation of religious texts? How and why does she figure Stephen Gordon, the heroine of this novel, as a lesbian Christ?

In pursuing this line of thought, I will look at the novel in four ways. First, I would like to briefly establish a critical background for reading Hall's use of biblical language, situating my reading of the novel at an intersection between religious and sexological language, and between lesbian/gay and religious literary analysis. Second, I want to examine the text of the novel itself, looking at specific instances of biblical language and their meanings; in particular I want to examine allusions to the life of Christ that suggest that this novel is a kind of refigured gospel, and that Stephen Gordon, the main character, is a messianic figure. Third, I will examine briefly the novel in some of its historical contexts. The novel was successfully prosecuted for obscenity in England in 1928, and in many ways the literary portrait of a lesbian martyr became part of public reception of both the novel *and* the author. Fourth and finally, I will conclude with some thoughts about the impact of Hall's use of biblical language. Since Christian and biblical discourse is and was so often used to condemn homosexuality, this appropriation of biblical language seems to me a quite powerful and critical rhetorical intervention. Raymond-Jean Frontain has described the Bible as both a weapon of condemnation and a tool of validation.[3] I would even suggest that we might read Hall's use of biblical and christological language as a Foucauldian "reverse discourse"–that is, as a reuse of the language of power and condemnation in order to give voice to the powerless. Hall uses biblical language to demand for the love that had dared not speak its name an identity and a spirituality, and to utter a plea for justice and understanding, and she reimagines both the life and parables of Christ to figure a spiritual and a social liberationist narrative of lesbianism.[4]

The Well of Loneliness rests, perhaps uneasily to some readers, at the intersection of two different discourses, both of which influenced Hall's writing. One language is that of the Bible, which provides names, symbols, and resonant syntax, reflecting Hall's own devout faith and her conversion to Catholicism in 1912. Although this may seem odd to some modern believers, Hall's biographers insist that she sensed no dissonance whatsoever between her lesbianism and her religious faith.[5] In fact, she is only one of a number of lesbian writers at the turn of the century who converted to Catholicism–Hall's lover Una Troubridge, Violet Shiletto, Renée Vivien, Tony Atwood, Christopher St. John, and the poets Kathryn Bradley and Edith Cooper, who joined the Catholic Church in order to insure that they might be together in heaven.[6] Radclyffe Hall, in fact, joined the church through the influence of her first lover, Mabel Veronica Batten.

Part of the reason Hall had no conflict might be located in her other primary discourse in the novel, the language of turn-of-the-century sexology, the pseudomedical and pre-Freudian study of sexuality which attempted to formulate a biological and congenital definition of same-sex desire or "inversion." In fact, Hall clung to this language despite the fact that most medical men of the day had dismissed biologistic explanations in favor of psychoanalytic ones, such as childhood suggestion or trauma. (This was an early version of the contemporary *nature* versus *nurture* debate.) Hall was familiar with the work of sexologists Richard von Krafft-Ebing and Havelock Ellis. Their theorizations of the lesbian as a congenital invert provide part of her literary argument: that the lesbian is, in our terms, born that way, and thus is a naturally occurring part of the natural world.[7] As Lillian Faderman explains in her critical 1981 study, *Surpassing the Love of Men*:

> Hall believed that her novel would provide lesbians with a moral and medical defense against a society which viewed same-sex love as immoral or curable. If a female argued that she chose to center her life on another female, she laid herself open to accusations of immorality. . . . If she accepted the psychoanalytic theory that something had happened to her in childhood to cause her aberration, she had no excuse not to seek a cure which would undo the trauma and set her straight. But if she maintained that she was born with her "condition," although some might consider her a freak, she could insist, as Hall actually did, that God created her that way, that she had a purpose in God's scheme of things even if she was a freak. (317-8)

Hall vacillates throughout the novel in her descriptions of inversion, treating it both as a maiming or freakish biological curse–which she describes in biblical language as "the mark of Cain"–or simply as a part of the natural world. Catharine Stimpson criticizes the confluence of sexology and theology, stating that Hall is so bound to theories of sexual inversion that homosexuality can only be read as a sickness that "the politics of heaven, not of earth, must first relieve" (368).[8] Hall always falls back on the language of religious justice and compassion to defend lesbian identity, but it is inevitably grounded in her theoretical understanding of lesbianism as a biological condition. But must we simply dismiss that as an otherworldly politics, or may we not value Hall's attempt to ground social liberation in religious validation?

If Hall's novel can be said to fall uneasily at the intersection of two languages, so can this reading. This paper–like my own critical sympathies–falls between discourses, between the politics and ideas of feminist theory and gay and lesbian studies and an interest in the language and symbolism of the Bible. If we look, briefly, at these two critical perspectives in relation to the criticism of the novel, I think we will find this uneasiness complicated by the failure of feminist critics to address the biblical, and of biblical critics even to address the novel at all. Jane Rule and others have noted the heavy use of biblical allusion in this novel, but invariably they dismiss it. The feminist writer Vera Brittain, in her 1928 review of the novel, described it as "sometimes beautiful and often irritatingly Biblical" (48-9). Although Rule calls the novel the "bible" of lesbian literature, she also calls it alternatively "a horror story for any lesbian who reads it at all" (50). Hall tried to redefine her gender and sexual identity inside the framework of the Bible, the church, and the patriarchy, she explains. Rule concludes of that attempt, "The 'bible' she offered is really no better for women than the Bible she would not reject" (61).[9] More recently, Terry Castle pokes fun at the novel's biblical style, which she characterizes as "hieratic, overwrought, full of melodramatic, dismal pomp" and of "maundering mock religiosity" (51).

Turning to religious critics, we fare even less well. Two works in literary scholarship survey twentieth-century (mostly modernist) adaptations of the life of Jesus–Edwin Moseley's *Pseudonyms of Christ in the Modern Novel* (1962) and Theodore Ziolkowski's *Fictional Transfigurations of Jesus* (1972)–neither of which mentions Hall. The first thirty years of the twentieth century were a fertile period for the reimagining of the life of the historical Jesus and the symbolic value of the Christ. According to Alice Birney's bibliography, *The Literary Lives of Jesus,* in the period 1900-1930 over 100 versions of the life of Jesus appeared in English, ranging from D. H. Lawrence's scandalous *The Man Who Died* to more popular and middlebrow historical fictions. Of those, over half appeared in the 1920s, the decade of Hall's novel. According to Jimmy Dean Smith, many of the more important literary transformations of this cultural text, the story of Jesus, engage the tensions of social class and artistic elitism. Smith claims that the canonical modernists who rewrite this story (W. B. Yeats, D. H. Lawrence, T. S. Eliot, W. H. Auden, Robert Graves), write it in a struggle against middle-class values; he explains, they "reconfigure Jesus as a way to recover myth from both the masses, who cheapen it, and from the elite, who refuse to recognize its vitality" (36).

Hall's novel seems to trouble this modernist tradition by adding the category of sexuality to the analysis. Hall reimagines the myth, but gives it a polemical vitality as a defense of lesbian and gay lives. As we know from Nikos Kazantzakis's *The Last Temptation of Christ* and its subsequent Hollywood adaptation, the mix of sexuality and spirituality in relation to the story of Jesus is a volatile one. Feminist theologian Carter Heyward states that the relation between God and the erotic, or spirituality and sexuality, "is largely one of violent opposition" in the history of Christianity (89).[10] But this already fraught conjunction of the sexual and spiritual in Hall's depiction of a lesbian martyr is more than a rejection of dualism. At stake in the novel is what Thomas Yingling has called "a battle for the scene of persuasion in which the text of homosexuality will be interpreted" (23): what may be said about homosexual or lesbian identity, who is allowed to say it, how it may be interpreted, and what language may be used, are all contestable.

Hall is not without precedent in her use of Christian language in the novel. In the margins of the canon, in more obscure texts of literature and sexology, we find similar explicit appropriations of Christian imagery and language. A. T. Fitzroy's 1918 novel on homosexuality (cited in Faderman 315), for example, is entitled *Despised and Rejected,* a title which invokes Isaiah 53:3: "He is despised and rejected of men; a man of sorrows, and acquainted with grief." This verse, in fact this chapter, is often read as a prophetic image of a Christ acquainted with human suffering, the important christological theme of the suffering servant. Xavier Mayne's enormous 1908 sexological study, *The Intersexes,* includes a very brief section on "Christ and Uranism." ("Uranism" is another turn-of-the-century term for inversion or homosexuality.) He notes not only that Christ never rebuked homosexuality, but that "as we study Gospel narratives . . . , we [have] cause to believe that Christ was an Uranian" (258-9). This reclaiming of Christ as a higher type of homosexual figure not only supports Mayne's vaguely evolutionary reading of the "intermediate sexual type" as a more sensitive type of human being who combines the good qualities of both sexes, but it also reclaims Christ for homosexual believers as a figure of sympathy.

In Havelock Ellis's landmark 1897 study of *Sexual Inversion,* with which Hall was familiar, the appearance of Christian language is more nuanced. Ellis does not invoke specific images or figures, but instead uses the language of one of Christ's parables to support his argument for the congenital nature of homosexuality. Ellis repeatedly alludes to the parable of the sower. He summarizes a number of theories of the etiology of homosexuality, but in each case he dismisses the role of causal events or childhood suggestion. He notes that in each case history examined there seems to be a "well-marked predisposition" (109). Ellis writes, "The seed of suggestion can only develop when it falls on a suitable soil" (110). The person must be constitutively receptive, biologically predisposed, or, in the words of John Addington Symonds, whom Ellis quotes, "previously constituted to receive the suggestion" (109). The body or psyche is soil, the "suggestion" of sexual desire (whether defined by Ellis as seduction by another, the sight of another's genitalia, or other causal events) is a seed, and sexual development is the natural growth of one in the context of the other. Again, Ellis writes, "The same seed of suggestion is sown in various soils; in the many it dies out, in the few it flourishes. The cause can only be a difference in the soil" (131).[11] The congenital invert is like the good soil of the Christian parable, and the gospel of inversion can only find proper ground for development in the biological or psychologically receptive person.

Radclyffe Hall, thirty years later, significantly ups the ante in her appropriation of Christian discourse in the novel *The Well of Loneliness*. Stephen Gordon, the young lesbian in the novel, rejected by her mother, finds her identity in her dead father's locked bookcase of sexological texts. (This uncanny scene of recognition in the library surely rings true for many gay and lesbian readers, who do not grow up in their own cultures, but often find their cultures and identities in the library.) But if Hall is acquainted with the obscure and often locked away texts of sexology and psychology, she is also well acquainted with biblical texts, for the novel is full of biblical imagery, names, and allusions.[12] In the scene of recognition in the patriarchal library, Stephen in fact turns from the sexological tomes to the Bible, demanding a sign from heaven and letting the text fall open. Where the book falls open, Stephen reads, "And the Lord set a mark upon Cain" (205). Stephen reimagines her sexual orientation as the mark of Cain, an image which is later echoed in christological references to the "stigmata of the abnormal" who are "nailed to a cross" (246), and in literal scarring of her face during her service as an ambulance driver in the Great War. Over the course of the narrative, then, Hall metonymically connects lesbianism, the mark of the pariah on Cain, the historical scarring of Stephen Gordon in World War I (a period in which women and lesbians experienced a newfound freedom), and the crucified Christ. Lesbian/Cain/ Christ. This equation–or more specifically the conflation of Cain and Christ in the body of Stephen–suggests a grounding mythology and a liberationist theology for Hall's narrative, that the lesbian author (an evangelist?) is both outcast and messiah, that one is inextricable from the other.

Like the allusion to Cain in the library, Hall's allusions are often reimaginings of biblical narratives or tropes in a contemporary context. For example, Stephen's maidservant Puddle specifically uses the words of Job to lament the hardships of lesbians, who seem to her to have been created the way they are from birth, but born into a world that oppresses and destroys them. "Yes, she must actually argue with God like Job," writes Hall, "and remembering his words in affliction, she must speak those words on behalf of Stephen: 'Thine hands have made me and fashioned me together round about; yet Thou dost destroy me'" (183). Puddle also uses language similar to Ruth's pledge to Naomi when she vows to follow Stephen and help her: "Where you go, I go, Stephen," she says, adding, "All that you're suffering at this moment I've suffered. It was when I was very young like you–but I still remember" (205). I cannot help but be reminded of Paul's (potentially racist) description of the "old law" as a handmaid in Galatians 4, a servant who can only mirror the promise offered by the freewoman. It is as if Puddle represents an Old Testament version of lesbian identity, the unmarried woman, trapped in jobs such as governess or maidservant or tutor, but expecting a better future for women like herself–a future Puddle clearly envisions in the writing of Stephen.

Hall refers to the Old Testament promises of deliverance and freedom in a later scene inscribed by race, sex, and gender. At a party in the novel, in an expatriate artistic community in Paris, a number of gays and lesbians listen to two African-American singers, Henry and Lincoln, sing Negro spirituals. "Didn't my Lord deliver Daniel," they sing; "Then why not every man?" Hall writes that the men singing the song of deliverance "seemed to be shouting a challenge to the world on behalf of themselves and of all the afflicted" (363). Stephen considers their question, but she transforms it. She hears it as an "eternal question, as yet unanswered for those who sat there spellbound." "Why not?" Stephen asks herself, and "Yes, but how long, O Lord, how long?" (364). She makes their song into her own question, but it is no longer a plea based on an Old Testament image of God's protection, the deliverance of the prophet Daniel from the lion's den. It is now an emphatic expectation, almost a demand–no longer *if* but *when.* "How long, O Lord, how long?" she asks in a repetition of the psalmist's cries for solace and deliverance.[13] In Psalm 6:3 the speaker cries, "My soul is sore vexed: but thou, O Lord, how long?" And in 13:1-2: "How long wilt thou forget me, O Lord? for ever? how long wilt thou hide thy face from me? . . . How long shall mine enemy be exalted over me?" Why shouldn't deliverance be offered to all those afflicted, she seems to ask. Why not every man and woman, including the lesbians and gay men?

I do not read this scene blind to its political problems, however. Although Hall describes the members of the party–black, gay, lesbian, Jew, expatriate, artist–as members of a community of the world's "hopeless," much of Hall's depiction of blacks is racist in its emphasis on the primitive, as Hall describes Henry transformed by alcohol in this scene into a "crude animal" and "primitive force" (363). As well, the modernist affection for the primitive extended to African-American artforms such as spirituals just as surely as it did to African masks. But the emphasis of the scene is on how the listeners respond, and in that I find not appropriation of black ethnicity and politics but a recognition of shared goals: their songs tell of a God who will "make vast reparation for every injustice," and one painter listening to their songs imagines "an enormous canvas depicting the wrongs of all mankind" (363). "Not one of them all but was stirred to the depths," writes Hall, "by that queer, half defiant, half suppli-cating music." "Queer," an overdetermined and perhaps overly used word in this novel, has multiple resonances, but here it is surely a marker of both strangeness and social marginality.

Identification with the oppression of others, in fact, is a pivotal point in the novel. When Stephen goes with some friends to a gay bar called Alec's–a kind of epic descent into hell–she is horrified by the degradation she sees, men who have fallen to "the dregs of creation." While there, a young man with a "grey, drug-marred face" calls Stephen, "Ma soeur," my sister. At first repulsed and angry, she suddenly thinks to herself, "It's looking for God who made it," and she responds, "Mon frère," my brother (388-9). Immediately after this familial exchange, Adolphe Blanc, the "gentle and learned Jew," comes to sit beside her. He is "consumed by the flame of some urgent and desperate mission," and he offers a kind of evangelistic calling to Stephen. "Those who have courage have also a duty," he tells her.

> There are happy people who sleep the sleep of the so-called just and righteous. When they wake it will be to persecute those who, through no fault of their own, have been set apart from the day of their birth, deprived of all sympathy, all understanding. They are thoughtless, these happy people who sleep–and who is there to make them think, Miss Gordon? (389)

Instead of responding, in the words of the hymn, "Here am I, send me," Stephen immediately suggests that people can read. Adolphe responds, "They will not read medical books. . . . And what doctor can know the entire truth?" Only "one of ourselves," he says, can bring the "whole truth" to the world. Speaking of the men around them, Blanc says, "From their very degradation that spirit will rise up to demand of the world compassion and justice" (390). Stephen's work, as she is told by the priest-like Blanc, whose very name suggests his goodness, is a work of duty and courage–she is to write in order to awaken awareness, sympathy, and perhaps even justice for "queer" peoples. The scene is then a self-reflexive justification of the novel itself, which is not a medical book which no one will read, but an autobiographically based novel by an author who sees herself as speaking for her people. There is even a suggestion that she may die for them, since, as Blanc tells her, "Many die . . . but they cannot kill the justice of God, even they cannot kill the eternal spirit" (390).

The novel is, in fact, a christological allegory of martyrdom. The protagonist, Stephen, sees herself as, in some way, called to proclaim the existence of her people, and in the end she sacrifices herself for her lover–who is named, significantly, Mary. As Michael Baker, among other critics, has noticed, "the novel contains submerged but pointed parallels to the example of Christ. It is no accident that Stephen is born on Christmas Eve and that her decision to sacrifice herself for Mary's happiness is finally affirmed in front of the supplicant Christ figure above the altar of a little church in Montmartre" (214).[14] Stephen's gift for her lover Mary is a ring, a "pearl of great price" (166), suggesting Christ's parable about the importance of his kingdom, the secret pearl of great price which a man finds in a field and then sells everything he owns in order to purchase. Hall transforms this parable of sacrifice for the kingdom into a token of same-sex love. Stephen also finds herself a "stranger within the gates" when she returns home (212), alluding both to Christ's return to Nazareth (where he receives no honor by his own people) and to his parable of hospitality–of those who refuse to take in the stranger at their own gates (Matt. 25:34-43).[15]

As Stephen embarks on her literary career, her companion Valerie Seymour, mistress of one of Paris's literary salons, tells her, "Remember me when you come into your kingdom" (408), echoing the words of the thief on the cross. Stephen's literary career (if not her life) is figured as a gospel apotheosis, a crucifixion and entry into a kingdom of the blessed. This literary career is also surely a career of evangelism or apologetics, as the passion of Christ is the kerygmatic reason for the gospels, as this novel is self-reflexively about its own inspiration.[16] The protagonist's name, Stephen, is the same as that of the first Christian evangelistic martyr in the Book of Acts. Although the name might allude to James Joyce's Stephen Daedalus, in this portrait of the artist as a young lesbian the emphasis seems more clearly on Stephen's Christ-like qualities. And Stephen's father's name is Philip, the name of the evangelist in Acts who took care of the socially powerless Grecian widows (Acts 6), who planted a church among the racially despised Samaritans (Acts 8), and who baptized the racially and sexually other (the Ethiopian eunuch, also in Acts 8). He was an evangelist to the economically, socially, racially, and sexually disenfranchised.

In the contexts of evangelism, of concern for the disenfranchised, and of a literary project predicated on the exploration of lesbian identity, one might note the brief appearance in *The Well of Loneliness* of Ellis's metaphor of soil and seed. Hall uses the image of seed and soil to refer to Stephen's "deep" ambition to be a writer, an ambition her father wishes to nurture by hoe and water (79). But her writing is ever marked by her sexuality, since from the beginning she creates "queer compositions" (79). Like the "queer" music of the spirituals, Stephen's writing is from the beginning both strange and socially marginal, inscribed by her own "queer" difference. Hall doesn't suggest the parable of the sower in the sense of predisposed receptive soil, but she may more emphatically suggest a gospel calling—to write. Interestingly enough, Stephen's first novel (within the novel) is titled *The Furrow.*

The Well of Loneliness ends with an oft-noted melodramatic prayer to God for "the right to our existence" (437). The novel's action ends with Stephen sending Mary into the arms of a male lover, Martin Hallam, a sacrifice to normative heterosexuality and social sanction that immediately precedes Stephen's final prayer. But to end a reading of the novel with that sacrifice is to see the novel as tragic, perhaps self-loathing, or as Catherine Stimpson describes it, a "narrative of damnation" rather than of escape (244). As a reader I am struck by the emphasis on language in both scenes, a fact which to me suggests an importance of utterance to the conclusion of the novel. At the novel's end, Mary's voice seems "unfamiliar" and it is described as not originating from her own body; Stephen is struck dumb; a disembodied voice comes out of the evening mist (435); even the dog is noted for his powerless "dumbness"; and ghosts fill the room, speaking (436).[17] In a scene that suggests demonic possession, pregnancy, and sexual orgasm, Stephen is taken over by the speaking spirits of gays and lesbians, those who have died, those who are living, and even of those yet to come, "fierce yet helpless children who would clamour in vain for their right to salvation" (437). "Our name is legion," they cry, "You dare not disown us." The use of the name "Legion" alludes to the man possessed by many demons in Luke 8 and Matthew 8, who calls himself "Legion," "because many devils were entered into him" (Luke 8:30). This "legion" of spirits speaks to God and to Stephen, crying out, "We have asked for bread; will you give us a stone?" The reference is to Christ's promises concerning the good father, God. "What man is there of you," Christ asks in Matthew 7, "whom if his son ask bread, will he give him a stone? Or if he ask a fish, will he give him a serpent? If ye then, being evil, know how to give good gifts unto your children, how much more shall your Father which is in heaven give good things to them that ask him?" (Matt. 7:9-11, see also Luke 11:11-13). To not be acknowledged by God, then, is to find oneself without sustenance, without deliverance.

The invocation of the biblical promise–through the repetition of Christ's own parabolic discourse–holds out the possibility of eventual deliverance, of God's "good gifts"–which in this context can only be the acknowledgment, understanding, and justification of homosexual and lesbian lives. The novel ends:

> And now there was only one voice, one demand; her own voice into which those millions had entered. A voice like the awful, deep rolling of thunder; a demand like the gathering together of great waters. A terrifying voice that made her ears throb, that made her brain throb, that shook her very entrails, until she must stagger and all but fall beneath this appalling burden of sound that strangled her in its will to be uttered.
>
> "God," she gasped, "we believe; we have told You we believe. . . . We have not denied You, then rise up and defend us. Acknowledge us, oh God, before the whole world. Give us also the right to our existence!" (437)

In both Matthew and Luke, the promise of bread (not stone) is followed by the healing of the demon-possessed,[18] and in Luke the demon-possessed are specifically the dumb. Christ's healing grants them the power to speak, surely an important intertextual reference to the conclusion of *The Well of Loneliness,* in which Stephen experiences the history and oppression of gays and lesbians not as a will to power or a will to freedom, but as a "will to be uttered" (437). This overwhelming voice of the oppressed speaks through the language of Stephen and of the novel itself. Asking God to rise up and defend the speaker suggests both Job's prayers and the Psalms, a final appropriation of biblical language in the face of both religious disapprobation and social persecution. It also suggests the earlier scene in which the African-American spirituals speak on behalf "of all the afflicted," or even her earliest writing, emphatically "queer." The love that dare not speak its name has found a language, the biblical language of prayer for liberation and the story of a messiah, and the collective "will to be uttered" finds a voice in the story of a lesbian novelist. In Hall's novel, then, the repetition and discursive appropriation of biblical language functions as an interventionary rhetorical strategy, using Christian language to argue for social and religious–indeed, God's–acceptance of lesbians and gay men.

*   *   *

Although Terry Castle's recent reading of the final passage is a rich analysis of the concluding scene, she fails to see the gospel allusion to demon-possession or the use of Christ's parables, and she says of the conclusion: "The less-than-pious reader may well have to suppress a laugh here" because of what she calls the passage's stylistic "infelicities of tone and taste" (51). But what of the pious reader, or of the sympathetic reader, or of the reader moved by the use of the biblical? How are these readers supposed to respond?

At the time of the novel's publication, the pious responded with outrage. The novel was released in July 1928. On Sunday, August 19, James Douglas, the 60-year-old editor of the *Sunday Express,* published a scathing attack of the novel under the headline "A Book That Must Be Suppressed." Calling the novel's theme "utterly inadmissible" and lesbianism an "unutterable putrefaction," he further emphasized the need to silence the novel by pointing out its "undiscussable subject." What Hall had described as a "will to be uttered" he calls "inadmissible," "unutterable," and "undiscussable." It is no wonder he concludes the review by comparing the novel to the Oscar Wilde trial, which made "the love that dare not speak its name" part of public discourse. For Douglas, the very subject must be an absence, a silence. Don't ask and don't tell. He compares homosexuality and lesbianism to a great plague and a leprosy on the body of society, images that suggest both transmittable disease and the possibility of corruption. And he echoes the contemporary fundamentalist emphasis on choice: "These moral derelicts are not cursed from their birth. . . . They are damned because they choose to be damned." In probably the most famous passage from his review, he wrote, "I would rather give a healthy boy or a healthy girl a phial of prussic acid than this novel" (qtd. in Brittain 52-58).

The book was soon prosecuted for obscenity. The Home Secretary and Director of Prosecutions, Sir William Joynson-Hicks (known as "Jix") instructed the English publisher, Jonathan Cape, to cease publishing, then had copies which were printed in France seized when they entered England.[19] In November 1928, the book was tried for obscenity and convicted by the Magistrate Sir Chartres Biron.[20] The book was declared obscene not on the basis of any particular passage or language–there is nothing "unprintable" in it–but on the basis of its overall theme, its argument as a whole. The descriptions of same-sex love in the novel disappear into asterisks rather than explicit descriptions. The closest the novel comes to explicitness is a chapter that ends with a woman kissing her lover's hands "for now she could find no words," followed by the sentence, "And that night they were not divided" (313).[21] The case was appealed in December, but again the book was declared obscene; again the emphasis was not on any particular aspect, but the insistence that the book be taken as a whole argument. Prosecutors also pointed out that it was not a medical book, but available to the general public–ironically underlining the very point that Adolphe Blanc had made about medical books, that the general public would not read them.

A parody of the novel and the obscenity trial soon appeared, *The Sink of Solitude,* illustrated with cartoons by Beresford Egan. One particularly relevant cartoon (see frontispiece) features Radclyffe Hall crucified, her knees bent in the traditional iconographic pose, a cupid making a rude gesture at her, and a naked girl across her thighs (either dancing around the cross, pressed against her, or in some way perhaps emblematic of a spear in her side). Joynson-Hicks appears on the right, like a Roman soldier, halo hovering above him, the book tucked away in his pocket. In the lower-left a strange figure looks on; biographer Michael Baker says it is a woman, "severe and close-cropped" who "gazes stonily at the scene" (257). I think instead that it is Oscar Wilde, looking on this second trial about same-sex love and the literature and lives that would define it. Hall's obscenity trial was, like his trial, a battle for the scene of persuasion and interpretation. Egan's style clearly derives from Aubrey Beardsley, and Beardsley's well-known drawings which accompanied Oscar Wilde's *Salomé* featured just such an ambiguous, sexless observing figure, usually assumed to be a representation of Wilde himself. For example, Wilde was represented as a marginal court jester, or as a large round moon overlooking the scene (see illustrations in Beckson, 196 and 211). That Wilde would be an observer makes sense when we consider the novel's emphasis on "uttering" lesbian and gay identity, and Douglas's comparison of Hall's novel to the Wilde scandal.

Although the poetic parody itself was aimed more viciously at Joynson-Hicks and Douglas, Hall was especially hurt by this cartoon, and she blamed herself for having been used as an insult to God (Baker 257).[22] But the cartoon fed a certain reading of the novel as a figure for Hall's own life; both the novel and the life could be read as narratives of a lesbian martyr, a messiah crucified by the world for her defense of her people. Vera Brittain, for example, concludes her 1968 account of the trials: "If the lesbian of today is regarded, not as a pariah whose eccentricities are a form of depravity, but as a part, if only a small part, of the human pattern, it is largely because Radclyffe Hall accepted crucifixion, and made her own story a factor in the growth of understanding and hence of toleration" (158).

In 1929, Hall began a new novel, originally titled "The Carpenter's Son," but published in 1932 as *The Master of the House* (an allusion to Mark 13:35). The novel is a modern retelling of the story of Christ. The hero is Christophe Bénédit (a pun on "bénédiction" or prayer), a peasant boy born to a carpenter in early twentieth-century Provence, his mother named Marie, his father Jousè. Christophe has visions and healing powers. He is sensitive to all living creatures, even having a dream of Christ tending his childhood pet dog in heaven. He enters World War I, is posted to Palestine, and is killed there while trying to convince his enemies that the war should stop in the name of Christ's "Indestructible Compassion" (485). It may seem another attempt at a more inclusive gospel, a gospel of St. Francis-like compassion and pacificism. But Hall has turned from her daring creative and lesbian reappropriation of the Christ story to a more pedantic and boring version of the story.[23]

There are moments of power and resistance. Christophe tells his tedious cousin Jan of his visions, and says, "These things are all lost–they must have forgotten to write them down, that is why there is something I miss in the gospels." Jan asks, "Who are you to pretend to miss things in the gospels? Are you the four Evangelists perhaps?" (199). But Hall doesn't carry this questioning of the gospel's incompletion further, and Jan simply accuses Christophe of blasphemy for believing that dogs go to heaven (200). The progress of the novel towards "something he must do" (204) seems inexorable, and the novel ends with a heavy-handed crucifixion in Palestine, where Turkish enemy troops capture Christophe, beat and strip him, then nail him to a wooden door. The novel concludes: "presently he became very still and his dying eyes gazed out to the east–to the east where the flaming, majestic dawn rose over the world like a resurrection" (490).

Although this may not seem like the work of an author condemned as a moral poison, it does suggest the centrality of the Christ story to her work, and her life. While she was working on *The Master of the House,* which she treated as an act of penitence, Hall complained of pain in her palms. Gradually, "livid red stains like bruising" appeared in both palms, extending in an ugly red line to her wrist on the right (Baker 273). She sought radiological treatment, but the pain increased, and Hall wrote her new novel, her hands wrapped in bandages. Vera Brittain says Hall was a "bearer of the stigmata," and she suggests that a hysteria resulting from her "martyrdom" in the obscenity trial caused the affliction (81). This incident could only perpetuate the literary myth of Hall as a martyr to her cause.

*   *   *

To conclude, I would like to return, for a moment, to the obscenity trial in an attempt to suggest why I think Hall's biblical language is so powerful, and why it is important that we recognize the disturbing scriptural nature of her lesbian messiah, her gospel of inversion. Although it wasn't a key part of the decision, newspaper reports of the appeal trial repeatedly referred to Attorney-General Thomas Inskip's reference to Romans 1, a chapter repeatedly used as a condemnation of gay and lesbian sexuality and in fact the only reference in the Bible to female same-sex desire (see Brittain 129, 137). It was a critical attempt to reinstitute the prescriptive authority of Saint Paul in the context of a novel more creatively engaged with the promises of the Old Testament and the liberation offered in the story of Christ. Further, newspapers repeatedly quoted his statement of concern about the appearance of the name of God in the novel. "My lord," he said, "some may think this book corrupt because of the way it brings the name of God into the discussion of these passions" (in Brittain 130, 137). At stake is the "battle for the scene of persuasion in which the text of homosexuality will be interpreted" (Yingling 23), and more specifically a battle over who can use rhetorically the word of God, and literally the word "God" in a discussion of lesbianism. It is "corrupt," according to Inskip, to include "the name of God" in a discussion of lesbianism; it is corrupt to use religious discourse in a discussion of same-sex desire–a discussion at the time usually trapped either in the moral language of sin or the psychological language of illness or inversion. To collapse one into another, as Hall emphatically did, was–to mainstream sensibilities of the period–not only offensive, but worth suppressing.

In the trial transcripts it is clear that if the character of Stephen had espoused guilt rather than virtue, or if the novel had been a medical text rather than a public fiction, or if it had not collapsed the languages of sin and sexology, of iniquity and inversion, it would not have had the power the judges saw to "corrupt" an innocent reader. Inskip's concern for the rhetorical insertion of the name of God into a discussion of same-sex sexuality suggests that it is not simply the rhetorical and sexological defense of lesbian sexuality that he and the other men found obscene, though they did find that corrupting; it is additionally the attempt to morally *value* same-sex desire–just as today some religious people find it unacceptable that someone might claim to be both gay or lesbian *and* Christian. Hall reclaimed Jesus for gay and lesbian readers in a way neither the sexologists nor the religious alone could have done. More recently, former Jesuit priest Robert Goss has written of "Jesus, the queer Christ," not a homosexual Christ, but an image of social justice and compassion. He says, "To say Jesus the Christ is queer is to say that God identifies with us and our experience of injustice" (84)–a Christ who is functionally "queer" because he is always outside social norms, resistant to religious and social authority, always on the side of the social outcast, and a model–in Adolphe Blanc's words–of "compassion and justice."[24]

A queer Christ. A lesbian messiah. Is such an image disturbing, desperate? Is it powerful, effective? Perhaps. George Steiner has criticized Sylvia Plath for her use of the Holocaust as a metaphor in her poem "Daddy" because he says she "appropriates an enormity of ready emotion to [her] own private design." She translates private hurt into instantly public and recognizable images. Yet he finally admits that her "tremendous risk" pays off because of her "desperate integrity" (301-2). Are readers willing to accede to Hall a "desperate integrity" for her use of "an enormity of readymade emotion"? I am. Although most feminist critics dismiss her biblical language, and most religious critics ignore her altogether, I would like to reclaim the rhetorical and literary power of her gospel.

How then may we read such texts? As rhetorical appropriations, Hall exploits language and biblical allusion for figural and allegorical potential. The mark of Cain, for example, figures the lesbian as a pariah marked by God–"the men and women who must carry God's mark on their forehead" (352). The references to the story of Christ, however, develop the life story of Stephen Gordon as an allegory of a messiah. Although the metonymical link is the mark written on the body (Cain's mark on the forehead, Christ's stigmata, or the stereotypical gendered markers of inversion in the mannish lesbian), the metaphorical and theological point is that Stephen as lesbian is both a type of pariah and a figure of Christ. Surely it is the heart of a liberation theology project to identify, as Hall has, Christ with an afflicted or oppressed group.

With a liberationist strategy in mind, we might say that texts such as Hall's are epistemological or ontological appropriations rather than simply methodological. Hall appropriates the language of a set of worldviews in an attempt to name and include an experience otherwise unnamed and excluded. If the language of religion is used to condemn homosexuality, as the obscenity trials evidenced all too well, then Hall's use of biblical language suggests both rhetorical strategy and epistemological shift. Stephen even asks, early in the novel, "What am I in God's name–some kind of abomination?" (153), alluding to the texts of Leviticus 18 so frequently invoked against gays and lesbians. Puddle wants to assure her that she is "neither unnatural, nor abominable, nor mad," but a "conspiracy of silence" prevents her from doing so (154). Hence the overwhelming "will to be uttered" at the end, to state, and by stating validate and acknowledge one's identity.

Hall's appropriation of biblical language may suggest what in *The History of Sexuality* Michel Foucault calls a "reverse discourse." Although the languages of law, psychology, and sexology made possible a more extensive social control over homosexuality, he explains, "it also made possible the formation of a 'reverse' discourse: homosexuality began to speak in its own behalf, to demand that its legitimacy or 'naturality' be acknowledged, often in the same vocabulary, using the same categories by which it was medically disqualified" (101). Though not exactly analogous, the use of biblical language to justify homosexuality, to preach–through the parables of Christ–a gospel of inversion, is surely a similar project to what Foucault calls "the insurrection of subjugated knowledges." Hall uses the language of the Bible–its prayers and promises of deliverance and the story of Christ–to legitimate an identity that may be otherwise religiously disqualified by the very texts she uses.

Restating this in other terms–in those of the religious literary scholar rather than a queer theorist–we can say that Hall's epistemological appropriation is a kind of parabolic discourse, marked in her own use of parable to conclude the novel. Describing how a parable works, John Dominic Crossan says that it contains "a radically new vision of world" and "it gives absolutely no information until after the hearer has entered into it and experienced it from inside itself." A hearer's first reaction may be to refuse to enter that metaphorical world, to silence it, to refuse its implications, or to translate it into the comfortable normalcy of his or her own worldview (Crossan 13). Adolphe Blanc had hoped that if a lesbian (a "normal invert") told her story to the world, outside the medical texts and moral pronouncements, the world might understand, and readers might attempt to enter that new world. But as those who claim to be both gay or lesbian *and* Christian know, such uses of language are difficult and contested. To bring "the name of God," as Inskip said, into the discussion of same-sex sexuality may bring accusations of corruption. Those who would try to enter into the intersection of these discourses must always remember that every gospel, every parable, is caught in a hermeneutic or interpretive tension that will indict or bless, condemn or justify its reader. Or as Jesus said, only those with the ears to hear the story can hear it.

In ending with a parable, however, the novel ends not with closure but with crisis. Even if one focuses on the prayer for acknowledgment in order to obviate the reprehensible sacrifice of love (and Mary) that Stephen makes, as I have, one must also note that the prayer is not answered. James Breech says of Jesus' parables that they are often stories without endings, to emphasize the genuine ambiguity of human action, despite spiritual principles (28-29). Hall's use of a parable at the end–if your child asks for bread will you give him or her a stone?–is open-ended: "We have asked for bread; will you give us a stone?" (437). It suggests the validity of a promise of deliverance, but recognizes that the human response might be the stone, not bread. Lincoln and Henry sang, "Didn't my Lord deliver Daniel, / Then why not every man?" And we, with Stephen, might answer, "Why not? . . . Yes, but how long, O Lord, how long?" The question is "as yet unanswered" (364). How long, O Lord, how long?

NOTES

1. Earlier versions of this work were presented at the May 1995 Santa Clara University Conference on Christianity and Literature, "Christianity's Encounters with 'The Other'" and in September 1995 as part of the University of South Carolina's monthly Women's Studies Research Lecture Series. I would like to thank participants at both events for their comments. I would also explicitly like to thank Kim Emery and Margot Backus and the USC gay and lesbian studies reading group for their conversations with me about the novel, and Kevin Lewis and Jimmy Dean Smith for their comments about religious aspects of my analysis.

2. In 1980, Blanche McCrary Boyd noted "it has become fashionable to sneer at *The Well of Loneliness*" (439), and many critics of the novel have dismissed it as a text of outdated stereotypes (the butch/femme), negative attitudes (a heavy emphasis on defensiveness), reprehensible theory (sexology), and a melodramatic ending in which the main character sacrifices her lesbian love so that she may find happiness with a man (an ending attacked for both aesthetic and political reasons). (See Boyd's afterword to the 1981 Doubleday/Avon paperback edition.) More recent analyses of the novel, such as those by Esther Newton, Gillian Whitlock, and Jean Radford, have tended towards more nuanced defenses of what Margot Backus calls Hall's "strategic use of inversion theory."

3. Despite our contemporary cultural context in which the Supreme Court and televangelists (and, indeed, sometimes even our own families) repeatedly invoke the Bible to condemn gays and lesbians and deny them protection and legal rights, in the history of gay and lesbian literature the Bible has been read as both condemnatory and validating. Frontain says of the Bible, "Perhaps no other book has been more influential–for better or worse–in determining the construction of gay and lesbian identity in the modern world, as well as social attitudes toward homosexuality." But, after noting such same-sex models as David and Jonathan, Ruth and Naomi, and Jesus and John, Frontain adds, "Indeed, the Bible has proved to be one of the richest and most creative sources of challenge to the gay and lesbian literary imagination, as well as one of the most powerful tools of self-validation" (92).

4. In this analysis, I will be using the King James Version of the Bible. When Hall cites biblical language in her novel, the language is repeatedly that of the King James. For example, Puddle the maidservant cites Job 10:8, "Thine hands

have made me and fashioned me together round about; yet Thou dost destroy me" (183).

5. For biographical details about Hall, I am indebted to Michael Baker's *Our Three Selves: A Life of Radclyffe Hall* (1985) and Lovat Dickson's *Radclyffe Hall at the Well of Loneliness: A Sapphic Chronicle* (1975). Vera Brittain's *Radclyffe Hall: A Case of Obscenity?* is an incredibly useful resource for both historical details and court documents relevant to the 1928 obscenity trials, which I discuss later in this essay.

6. For a discussion of these lesbian Catholic believers, see Joanne Glasgow's "What's a Nice Lesbian Like You Doing in the Church of Torquemada?" For discussions of Bradley and Cooper, who wrote under the penname "Michael Field," see Mary Sturgeon's *Michael Field* and Chris White's "'Poets and Lovers Evermore': The Poetry and Journals of Michael Field."

7. I will not go into detail into theories of congenital inversion in this essay, but I would note one problem with sexological theory as demonstrated in Hall's novel. Theories of inversion usually equate categories of gender and sexuality. Gay men are represented as feminine, lesbians as masculine. This language, prominent in theories of inversion, collapses biological sexual difference, cultural gender role difference, and the differing desires of sexual orientation and object choice into two easily assimilable (and still all too prevalent) stereotypes. Some feminists criticize Hall's use of the image of the invert as a butch, masculinized lesbian, finding it only a reinscription of stereotypes of gender in a theory of sexuality. But some, such as Esther Newton in "The Mythic Mannish Lesbian," point out that such a representation in its historical context might be read as useful, even progressive, in its cultural contexts, in which the taking on of masculinity was itself a liberating act. In Hall's representation, inversion is quite literally written on the body from birth. Stephen Gordon is born narrow-hipped and wide-shouldered, and she develops into a boyish and tomboyish youth.

8. Similarly, Elizabeth Meese writes, "While acceptance might be sought in heaven since the lesbian, in this reading, is justified or rationalized as a divine creation, it is rarely to be found on earth; such, in any case, Hall claims in *The Well*" (47).

9. I would note here that Rule is an author who has engaged religious traditions in her own work. As Margaret Soenser Breen pointed out at the 1995 National Symposium on Gay Spirituality in Literature and the Media at the University of New Hampshire, Rule's novel *The Desert Heart* might be read as a lesbian revision of John Bunyan's *Pilgrim's Progress*.

10. She further sees this tradition as denying the importance of the incarnation of Christ, and she sees in this spiritualization a "trivialization and denial" of our human, bodily selves (94).

11. Christ's parable of the sower, found in three of the gospels (Matt. 13, Mark 4, and Luke 8), is a parable about reception, and self-reflexively indicts or blesses its own hearers. It is a parable about parables, a gospel about gospels, a metaparable. Christ himself asks his apostles, "Know ye not this parable? and how then will you know all parables?" (Mark 4:13). The seed in the parable falls on a number of types of soil: the wayside, where birds devour it; the stones, where the plants

spring up but are scorched; the thorny ground, where the plants are choked; and the good soil, where the seed yields fruit. Ellis rewrites this parable as a discursive intervention into the arguments about the origins of homosexuality–arguments which are used to ground further arguments about control and acceptance. In this revision, the child who is predisposed biologically to homosexuality (the "congenital invert") is equated with the "good ground" of the parable. Thus, no matter what the social environment, the gospel of inversion can only find good grounds for development in the biologically or psychologically (and, dare one suggest, spiritually) receptive person. Only those with "ears to hear" (Mark 4:9) will be able to hear; only those with the properly receptive organs, the properly constituted psyches and bodies, will be receptive to this particular truth.

12. There are references to Job (183, 218), to Ruth and Naomi (205), to Cain (205, 301, 352), even an obscure allusion to the Old Testament character Agag (240).

13. This psalm is also reinvoked in Chris Glaser's *The Word Is Out,* in a meditation on liberation (the theme of the month of June, the month of the Stonewall Riots) (June 4).

14. Inez Martinez calls many of Hall's heroes "markedly Christian" in their tendency towards self-sacrifice (137, n. 8).

15. This phrase is also invoked by Angela, Stephen's first lover (140, 144). The reference to the stranger at the gates has been more recently used as the title of Mel White's recent autobiography, *Stranger at the Gates: To Be Gay and Christian in America.*

16. Indeed, one might suggest that this gospel has its own kerygma, case history #166 from Krafft-Ebing's *Psychopathia Sexualis.* This historical kernel could be a basis for Hall's extended extrapolation, her gospel.

17. This emphasis on Stephen's (in)ability to speak (or write) is a common one in the novel. For example, when Mary confronts her about Valerie Seymour, Hall writes the emphatically redundant, "And as though she were suddenly smitten dumb, Stephen's lips remained closed and she answered nothing" (431).

18. In Matthew it concludes the Sermon on the Mount, and in both gospels it comes in the context of the threefold promise, "Ask, and it shall be given you; seek, and ye shall find; knock, and it shall be opened unto you" (Matt. 7:7).

19. Joynson-Hicks was an opponent of attempts to reform the Anglican Prayer Book, treasurer of a fundamentalist Bible society, and a rabid enemy of Communists (who were usually found by him in the ranks of the labor unions).

20. Biron appears in Virginia Woolf's *A Room of One's Own,* the series of lectures she gave in October 1928 and expanded in 1929. Before she tells the story of "Chloe liked Olivia," she asks, "Are there no men present? Do you promise me that behind that red curtain over there the figure of Sir Chartres Biron is not concealed?" (82). His appearance there suggests her concern for his censorship of lesbian narratives.

21. Michael Baker cites this sentence as a direct allusion to the story of Saul and Jonathan, in 2 Samuel 1:23: " . . . and in their death they were not divided." The verse describes Saul and his son Jonathan killed together in battle. But per-

haps the more interesting allusion here is the indirect rather than the direct one, for this verse is followed only three verses later by David's lament for Jonathan, that theirs was a love "passing the love of women" (2 Sam. 1:26). Indirectly the allusion points to that famous model of same-sex love in the Bible, the story of David and Jonathan.

22. Hall was also particularly hurt by Douglas's review, which she deemed unchristian. In her first public interview after the review, she asked, "Does the Sunday Express editor's conception of Christianity lead him to think that because God permits certain types to be born into this world they should be thrust aside or ignored?" (in Baker 226).

23. Though modernized, it didn't sell well at all. As one biographer writes, "Unrelieved virtue, across almost 500 pages, makes for dull reading" (Baker 276).

24. Chris Glaser writes, in his collection of biblical meditations for gays and lesbians, "Jesus was queer. Not in our sense, perhaps. But queer enough to be mocked, scorned, despised, shamed, and forsaken" (February 18).

WORKS CITED

Backus, Margot Gayle. "When the Mother Is the Other: Celticism and Inversion Theory in *The Well of Loneliness.*" *Tulsa Studies in Women's Literature* 15.2 (fall 1996): 253-266.

Baker, Michael. *Our Three Selves: A Life of Radclyffe Hall.* London: Gay Men's P, 1985.

Beckson, Karl, ed. *Aesthetes and Decadents of the 1890's: An Anthology of British Poetry and Prose.* Chicago: Academy Chicago Publishers, 1981.

Birney, Alice L. *The Literary Lives of Jesus: An International Bibliography of Poetry, Drama, Fiction, and Criticism.* New York: Garland Publishing Inc., 1989.

Boyd, Blanche McCrary. Afterword. *The Well of Loneliness.* By Radclyffe Hall. New York: Avon Books, 1981. 439-441.

Breech, James. *Jesus and Postmodernism.* Minneapolis: Fortress P, 1989.

Brittain, Vera. *Radclyffe Hall: A Case of Obscenity?* London: Femina Books, 1968.

Castle, Terry. *The Apparitional Lesbian: Female Homosexuality and Modern Culture.* New York: Columbia UP, 1993.

Crossan, John Dominic. *In Parables: The Challenge of the Historical Jesus.* San Francisco: Harper and Row, 1973.

Dickson, Lovat. *Radclyffe Hall at the Well of Loneliness: A Sapphic Chronicle.* New York: Charles Scribner's Sons, 1975.

Ellis, Havelock. *Sexual Inversion.* With appendices by John Addington Symonds. 1897. New York: Arno P, 1975.

Faderman, Lillian. *Surpassing the Love of Men: Romantic Friendships and Love Between Women from the Renaissance to the Present.* New York: William Morrow, 1981.

Foucault, Michel. *The History of Sexuality, Volume 1: An Introduction.* 1976. Trans. Robert Hurley. New York: Vintage Books, 1978.

Frontain, Raymond-Jean. "The Bible." *The Gay and Lesbian Literary Heritage: A Reader's Companion to the Writers and Their Works, from Antiquity to the Present.* Ed. Claude J. Summers. New York: Henry Holt, 1995. 92-100.

Glaser, Chris. *The Word Is Out: The Bible Reclaimed for Lesbians and Gay Men.* New York: HarperSanFrancisco, 1994.

Glasgow, Joanne. "What's a Nice Lesbian Like You Doing in the Church of Torquemada? Radclyffe Hall and Other Catholic Converts." *Lesbian Texts and Contexts: Radical Revisions.* Ed. Karla Jay and Joanne Glasgow. New York: New York UP, 1990. 241-254.

Goss, Robert. *Jesus Acted Up: A Gay and Lesbian Manifesto.* New York: Harper-SanFrancisco, 1993.

Hall, Radclyffe. *The Master of the House.* London: Jonathan Cape, 1932.

———. *The Well of Loneliness.* 1928. New York: Doubleday, 1990.

Heyward, Carter. *Touching Our Strength: The Erotic as Power and the Love of God.* San Francisco: Harper SanFrancisco, 1989.

Kraff-Ebing, Richard von. *Psychopathia Sexualis.* 1886. Trans. Harry E. Wedeck. New York: G. P. Putnam's Sons, 1965.

Martin, Del, and Phyllis Lyon. *Lesbian/Woman.* New York: Bantam Books, 1972.

Martinez, Inez. "The Lesbian Hero Bound: Radclyffe Hall's Portrait of Sapphic Daughters and Their Mothers." *Literary Visions of Homosexuality.* Ed. Stuart Kellogg. New York: The Haworth Press, Inc., 1983. 127-137.

Mayne, Xavier (pseud. Edward Irenaeus Prime Stevenson). *The Intersexes: A History of Similisexualism as a Problem in Social Life.* 1908. New York: Arno P, 1975.

Meese, Elizabeth A. *(Sem)Erotics: Theorizing Lesbian: Writing.* New York: New York UP, 1992.

Moseley, Edwin M. *Pseudonyms of Christ in the Modern Novel: Motifs and Methods.* Pittsburgh: U of Pittsburgh P, 1962.

Newton, Esther. "The Mythic Mannish Lesbian: Radclyffe Hall and the New Woman." *Hidden from History: Reclaiming the Gay and Lesbian Past.* Ed. Martin Duberman, Martha Vicinus, and George Chauncey, Jr. New York: Meridian, 1989. 281-293.

Radford, Jean. "An Inverted Romance: *The Well of Loneliness* and Sexual Ideology." *The Progress of Romance.* Ed. Jean Radford. New York: Routledge and Kegan Paul, 1986. 97-111.

Rule, Jane. *Lesbian Images.* 1975. Trumansburg, NY: Crossing P, 1982.

Smith, Jimmy Dean. "Reconfiguring the Gospel: Jesus in Twentieth-Century British Literature." Diss. U of South Carolina, 1995.

Steiner, George. *Language and Silence: Essays on Language, Literature, and the Inhuman.* New York: Atheneum, 1976.

Stimpson, Catharine R. "Zero Degree Deviancy: The Lesbian Novel in English." *Writing and Sexual Difference.* Ed. Elizabeth Abel. Chicago: U of Chicago P, 1982. 243-259.

Sturgeon, Mary. *Michael Field.* London: George G. Harrap, 1922.

Thompson, Mark. *Gay Soul: Finding the Heart of Gay Spirit and Nature.* New York: HarperSanFrancisco, 1994.

White, Chris. " 'Poets and Lovers Evermore': The Poetry and Journals of Michael Field." *Sexual Sameness: Textual Differences in Lesbian and Gay Writing.* Ed. Joseph Bristow. London: Routledge, 1992. 26-43.

Whitlock, Gillian. " 'Everything Is Out of Place': Radclyffe Hall and the Lesbian Literary Tradition." *Feminist Studies* 13.3 (1987): 555-582.

Woolf, Virginia. *A Room of One's Own.* 1929. New York: Harcourt Brace, 1981.

Yingling, Thomas. *Hart Crane and the Homosexual Text: New Thresholds, New Anatomies.* Chicago: U of Chicago P, 1990.

Ziolkowski, Theodore. *Fictional Transfigurations of Jesus.* Princeton, NJ: Princeton UP, 1972.

Narrative Inversion:
The Biblical Heritage of *The Well of Loneliness* and *Desert of the Heart*

Margaret Soenser Breen, PhD

University of Connecticut

SUMMARY. The Bible acts as an epistemological anchor for the English *Bildungsroman*; however, the biblical narratives are themselves in flux, especially with regard to representations of spiritual development gendered feminine. The extent to which one can consider the traveling/travailling mother a spiritually coherent figure who exists independent of male spiritual authority seems only possible insofar as one adopts the position of the perverse reader, who envisions the envelopment of her stories as narrative inversion. To do so is to believe that accounts of female heroism need not narratively depend on those of male heroism. The term narrative inversion in turn allows the perverse reader to recognize a narrative desire that, because it does not conform to but indeed suggests an alternative narrative possibility for the homosocial plot, remains enfolded within the plot. Inhabiting precisely this paradox of narrative inver-

Margaret Soenser Breen is an assistant professor of English at the University of Connecticut, Groton. She is interested in representations of female *Bildung* in English literature; she has published articles on Charlotte Brontë, John Bunyan, George Eliot, and W. B. Yeats.

Correspondence may be addressed: University of Connecticut, Avery Point Campus, 1084 Shennecossett Road, Groton, CT 06340-6097; or by e-mail: mbreen@ uconnvm.uconn.edu.

[Haworth co-indexing entry note]: "Narrative Inversion: The Biblical Heritage of *The Well of Loneliness* and *Desert of the Heart*." Breen, Margaret Soenser. Co-published simultaneously in *Journal of Homosexuality* (The Haworth Press, Inc.) Vol. 33, No. 3/4, 1997, pp. 187-206; and: *Reclaiming the Sacred: The Bible in Gay and Lesbian Culture* (ed: Raymond-Jean Frontain) Harrington Park Press, an imprint of The Haworth Press, Inc., 1997, pp. 187-206. Single or multiple copies of this article are available for a fee from The Haworth Document Delivery Service [1-800-342-9678, 9:00 a.m. - 5:00 p.m. (EST). E-mail address: getinfo@haworth.com].

187

sion are the lesbian heroines who follow in the Bible's wake. *[Article copies available for a fee from The Haworth Document Delivery Service: 1-800-342-9678. E-mail address: getinfo@haworth.com]*

Lesbian realism is a particularly vexing genre, for its narrative paradigms so often belie the stories being told. (One might also say that the stories belie the paradigms.) At issue in this essay is lesbian realism's perhaps most perplexing aspect, its adherence to the conventions of biblical and, more generally speaking, Christian narratives. By focussing on the realist narrative of pilgrimage, rooted in the Bible and codified by John Bunyan's *The Pilgrim's Progress* (1678; 1684)—a narrative that includes a cluster of figures such as the exile, the martyr, the outcast, and the wanderer—I hope to show that precisely this biblical inheritance provides a key strategy for articulating desire within the conundrum that is lesbian realism.

While the lesbian realist tradition has received increased critical attention within the last ten years, the importance of the narrative of pilgrimage within that tradition has not yet been treated. Terry Castle has noted the "satirical, inverted, or parodic relationship[s]" in which lesbian fiction "may stand to more famous novels of the past" (146); still, lesbian realism's investment in literary continuity has remained largely unexplored.[1] Most criticism has instead considered the destabilizing or volatile bond that exists between lesbian stories and the realist strategies they employ. This perspective underscores the resulting paradox of employing realist conventions: those novels that attempt to represent lesbian desire realistically risk reproducing its overarching plot of male homosociality. So suggests Terry Castle, in her reading of Eve Kosofsky Sedgwick's analysis of realism. Teresa De Lauretis reaches a similar conclusion. Writing of *The Well of Loneliness* (1928), De Lauretis remarks that "the text's inability to articulate a lesbian sexual indifference . . . [results in the] reinscription of lesbianism in hom(m)osexuality or sexual indifference" (211).[2] Realism's plots, in effect, are male-centered; they configure heterosocial and -sexual relations as functions of homosocial and homoerotic exchanges between men.

There are, however, two sides to this paradox. Writers of lesbian fiction face a theoretical disorientation, but disorientation can prove the vitalizing base for a counter literary tradition. For Bonnie Zimmerman, in turn, lesbian fiction depends upon a "perverse" reading strategy: lesbians "resist 'heterotexts' by . . . rewriting and thus reappropriating them as lesbian texts" ("Perverse" 139). By telling a story that employs realist conventions, the lesbian novel "perverts" those conventions and, further, bequeaths this capacity for narrative "dismantling" (Zimmerman, *Safe* 43) to subsequent novels, for which it serves as a model not simply of realism but of lesbian realism. So, much as the lesbian butch conveys her desire via "masculinity," lesbian fiction dons realist drag in order to express narrative desire. Much as the butch inhabits "a cultural tradition pervasively homophobic [in which] masculinity alone conveys a strong connotation of sexual desire for the female body" (De Lauretis 243), so, too, lesbian realism depends upon realism's readily identifiable cultural position as a truth-telling medium, even as the truths that lesbian fiction brings to bear on it remain conventionally untold.

At the crux of lesbian fiction's enveloped relation to realism is this question of truth. Writing of *Desert of the Heart* (1964), Gillian Spraggs observes, realism is "one of the most potent [forms of literature] in presenting images and narratives of human existence . . . that . . . impress with a conviction of 'truth'" (116). Within the tradition of lesbian realism, one such narrative is that of pilgrimage. As articulated by the Bible and Bunyan, the narrative of pilgrimage supplies the archetypal story of truth for the character who is the perpetual outsider to the plots she inhabits. At work in Radclyffe Hall's *The Well of Loneliness* and Jane Rule's *Desert of the Heart,* the pilgrimage narrative proves a key strategy for voicing desire within the lesbian realist tradition.

Styled on the Victorian novel, *The Well of Loneliness* recalls any number of nineteenth-century texts, including *Frankenstein, David Copperfield,* and *Jude the Obscure,* but its commitment to realism is perhaps most discernable in its reliance on biblical allusions, tropes, and narrative patterns to "place" its hero and delineate its plot. Within the tradition of English realism such literary devices are acknowledged vessels of "truth": they convey the values of a predominantly Christian culture,[3] one in which the Bible, *The Pilgrim's Progress,* and *Paradise Lost* "were current, a part of the nation's imaginative and cultural life" (Qualls 12).[4] "Biblical romance" is the predominant narrative pattern in Victorian fiction; desiring that their works be read as "at once secular scripture and sacred scripture" (14), novelists such as Charlotte Brontë, Charles Dickens, George Eliot, and Elizabeth Gaskell wove texts whose characters and plots engaged readers' familiarity with the Bible, as well as Bunyan's and Milton's visions of the Word.[5] In sum, Victorian novelists sought to provide their readership with culturally accessible allusions against which to read their novels and to read them as moral histories.

From this perspective it is hardly surprising that Radclyffe Hall, herself raised in a Victorian household, would adopt biblical language. With *The Well of Loneliness,* Hall aligns herself with Victorian novelists who were drawn to the Bible both because of their conviction of the serious purpose behind their works and because the Bible, together with *The Pilgrim's Progress* and *Paradise Lost,* "seemed to provide the only way towards positing and insuring lasting human values in an age where the pilgrim's query 'Where is truth?' found a hundred answers and none" (Qualls 14).[6] In this manner, Victorians asserted "truth," even as their plots' "complications and variations are Victorian expressions of an age's uncertainties about the very figures it insists upon" (13). How much more uncertain is Hall's relation to the figures in her work. A "Victorian" novel written a decade after World War I, *The Well of Loneliness* charts the progress of sexual invert Stephen Gordon for a readership for whom lesbianism legally did not even exist. The linear structure of the English *Bildungsroman* may owe much to Isaiah 40:3 ("The voice of him that crieth in the wilderness, Prepare ye the way of the Lord, make straight in the desert a highway for our God"), especially to Bunyan's allegorical treatment of the passage in *The Pilgrim's Progress.*[7] Novelist Hall's own position *vis-à-vis* that religious inheritance is, in turn, perhaps best articulated by hero Stephen: "I want you to know that *I'm trying to play straight*" (348; emphasis added). For Radclyffe Hall, embracing a biblical heritage entails writing a realist novel in which lesbian love proves tragically unsustainable.[8]

The Bible acts as a kind of stabilizing text, specifically for a body of writers highly conscious of the instability of its ways of knowing. In and of itself, however, the Bible is hardly a stable text. The narratives of spiritual damnation and salvation are often disturbingly similar. The biblical outcast/ wanderer is at times a figure of abandonment (Cain), spiritual tribulation (Job), ethnic difference (Ishmael), prophecy (John the Baptist), martyrdom (Stephen), and, finally, salvation (Jesus). That one biblical prototype may encompass a range of meanings is at least in part a marker of epistemological limits. Can one really tell the prophet from the pariah? The question looms because, paradoxically, the figure of the outcast remains entirely central to readings in both the Hebrew and Christian Bible.

This difficulty of assessing representations of spiritual placement is augmented in the case of what one might call, somewhat anachronistically, the female pilgrim, the woman who undergoes a spiritual journey. Biblical examples of this figure are complicated if not overshadowed by the gender imbalances that ensure women's socially subordinate positions. Because of this dynamic, women's stories within the Bible highlight sexual difference: spiritual travel becomes aligned with sexual travail.[9] Eve, Ruth, and the Virgin Mary, all of whom stand behind Stephen Gordon's *Bildung,* are key figures of sexualized female spiritual placement, even as the meaning of each placement depends upon the woman's patriarchal connection/disconnection.[10] Eve's sexual transgression precipitates her (and Adam's) departure from Eden. Ruth's widowhood, by comparison, inaugurates her journey to Judah. Despite her status as a doubly marginal figure (widow and ethnic outsider), she remains in Judah with mother-in-law Naomi. And *because* she remains, she ultimately becomes a biblical matriarch, a "Mother in Israel" (Ruth is King David's great-grandmother). Mary's story in turn amplifies Ruth's and reverses Eve's. Like Ruth, Mary is a socially vulnerable figure, but precisely Mary's virginity signals that she is the mother of God. She is "the second Eve," whose virginity answers the sexual transgressiveness of the first. Importantly, Eve, Ruth, and Mary all inhabit narratives that initially insist on the women's patriarchal disconnection even as their narratives' positioning within the Bible insists on the women's patriarchal connection and, indeed, envelopment. Ultimately, Eve's story underscores her subservience to Adam, Ruth's story ends with husband Boaz's patrilineage and connection to David superseding her own, and Mary's story celebrates the birth of human divinity gendered male.

The Bible may act as a kind of epistemological anchor for such key filter texts as *Paradise Lost* and *The Pilgrim's Progress* and for the novels that rework the biblical paradigms, together with those of Milton and Bunyan; however, the biblical narratives are themselves in flux, especially with regard to gendered representations of spiritual development.[11] The extent to which one can consider the traveling/travailing mother a spiritually coherent figure who exists independent of male spiritual authority seems possible only insofar as one adopts the position of the perverse reader, who envisions the envelopment of her stories as narrative inversion. To do so is to believe that accounts of female heroism need not narratively depend on those of male heroism. The term narrative inversion in turn allows the perverse reader to *recognize* a narrative desire that, because it does not conform to but indeed suggests an alternative narrative possibility for the homosocial plot, remains enfolded within the plot. Within the Bible and the realist plots of progress that draw on it, the desire to recount female narratives apart from male mediation is rendered illegible or unspeakable for the conventions of truth-telling.[12] Inhabiting precisely this paradox of narrative inversion are the lesbian heroines who follow in the Bible's wake.

Such is the case with *The Well of Loneliness*'s protagonist Stephen Gordon, whose *Bildung* Hall announces with biblical language:

> She would notice with a sudden pain in her heart that [her father] stooped when he walked. . . . Then the thought would come that perhaps its great kindness had caused [his back] to stoop as though bearing a burden; and the thought would come: "He is bearing a burden, not his own, it's someone else's–but whose?" (94)

Recalling Galatians 6:2 ("Bear ye one another's burdens, and so fulfill the law of Christ"), this passage prefigures Stephen Gordon's sexual and intellectual coming of age, when, in her moment of self-discovery, the mannish lesbian recalls John Bunyan's Christian. Similar to that paradigmatic traveler of English realism, who with a burden on his back and (the good) book in hand begins his spiritual journey, an adult Stephen, alone in her father's study, performs a close reading of herself with the help of two books. The first, *Psychopathia Sexualis,* by nineteenth-century sexologist Krafft-Ebing, answers the question that she had earlier posed: her father's "burden," to which the copious margin notes attest, was the knowledge of her inversion; that burden is now hers. The second book is her father's "old, well-worn Bible" (232); reading it she casts herself as a latter-day Cain. Clearly delineating the trajectories of her revelation (sexuality and Christianity), Stephen frames her *Bildung* (and, indeed, *The Well of Loneliness* as a whole) as a pilgrim's progress of inversion.

Significantly born on Christmas Eve, Stephen recalls a number of biblical figures, including Cain, Ishmael, Job, St. Stephen, the Virgin Mary, and Christ.[13] Like so many readers of the Bible, Stephen wonders if she is damned or saved. The signs of each state are confusingly similar. So the young Stephen prays that she might heal the maid Collins's swollen knees: "I would like to wash Collins in my blood, Lord Jesus" (16). With, however, her passage into adulthood the identification with Christ blurs into one with Cain. Stephen continues to place herself and her inversion on a Christian continuum: "she was seeing before her all the outward stigmata of the abnormal—verily the wounds of One nailed to a cross" (280). At the same time she contemplates telling her lover Mary, "I am one of those whom God marked on the forehead. Like Cain, I am marked and blemished" (344). Exiled from her home, where home is both Morton and the house of Christian propriety, Stephen recalls Hebrews 13:14: for her "there [is] no real abiding city" (84). Like Ishmael in Genesis 16:12, she finds that "every man's hand [is] against [me]" (138); she is the outcast reader who cannot clearly locate herself in the conventional passages of Christian belief, even as she can dream that "in some *queer* way she was Jesus" (16; emphasis added).

This kind of superimposition is consistent throughout the novel and is particularly suggestive of the reading experience of narrative inversion with which the lesbian hero must contend in her attempt to locate herself within the Bible. The textual self-effacement that Stephen undergoes occurs not simply through the epistemological implosions of conventional oppositions of good and evil; Stephen's simultaneous alignment with biblical heroes and heroines, while it helps convey the complexity of her gendered subject position, as well as the queerness of her orientation, ultimately discloses the gender imbalances, specifically the discrediting of female authority, that pervades and indeed directs the narratives of biblical righteousness and Christian progress. Placed side by side, Stephen's first two names, Stephen and Mary, underscore her incapacity to fit neatly into Christian convention, even while they identify her as a Christian hero/ine. Named Stephen by her father "because he admired the pluck of that Saint . . . [who] had gripped his imagination" (4) before she is even born, she is quickly christened Stephen Mary Olivia Gertrude upon birth. As the narrator wryly comments, "Man proposes–God disposes" (5). The full name points to the limitations, the fictitiousness of a single dominant narrative directing one's development and, importantly, the gendered trajectory of that development.

Stephen's first two names do predict her *Bildung,* but it is a *Bildung* shaped by narrative inversion. The importance of Stephen's second name is all but obscured by the narrative (Acts 6-7) that stands behind her first name. Saint Stephen was the first Christian martyr, who was accused of blasphemy and stoned to death.[14] Exiled from the conventions of English life that she nonetheless esteems, *The Well of Loneliness*'s Stephen seems to inhabit a secular version of her namesake's story. By comparison, Stephen's second name holds little narrative sway over her life: Stephen does not, for example, possess the intercessory capacity that is associated with the Virgin Mary within Catholicism, to which Radclyffe Hall converted as an adult. But this impotence is perhaps Hall's point, not only because English realism draws largely on a Protestant biblical tradition but also because Mary is both Stephen's second name and the name of her lover. In sacrificing her lover to the convention of marriage, Stephen comes to resemble her second namesake. Stephen, who believes that her lover Mary's happiness depends upon marriage, precipitates the rupture of their own union. In so doing, she catapults Mary into an alliance with their best friend Hallam, whose name, significantly recalling Tennyson's beloved, suggests that *the* salient homosocial bond is not between Stephen and Mary but between Stephen and Hallam. In "giving" Mary to Hallam, Stephen has become, like the biblical Mary, a vessel for the Christian marriage feast. Paradoxically, Stephen can "be" Mary only insofar as she cannot "have" Mary.[15]

The last page of the novel agonizingly details this inversion of Stephen's desire:

> the room seemed to be thronging with people. . . . she could see their marred reproachful faces with the haunted, melancholy eyes of the invert–eyes that had looked too long on a world that lacked all pity

and all understanding: "Stephen, Stephen, speak with your God and ask Him why He has left us forsaken!" . . .

They possessed her. Her barren womb became fruitful–it ached with its fruitful and sterile burden. It ached with fierce yet helpless children who would clamour in vain for their right to salvation. They would turn first to God, and then to the world, and then to her. . . . "You, God . . . you world . . . you, Stephen . . . we have asked for bread; will you give us stone?"

And now there was only one voice, one demand; her own voice into which those millions had entered. . . .

"God," she gasped, "we believe; we have told You we believe. . . . We had not denied You, then rise up and defend us. Acknowledge us, oh God, before the whole world. Give us also the right to our existence!" (506)

In this highly allusive passage Stephen imagines the marginalized voices of inversion invoking the language not only of Psalm 27:7-9 ("Hear, O Lord, when I cry with my voice. . . . Hide not thy face far from me . . . thou hast been my help; leave me not, neither forsake me, O God of my salvation") but also of the Crucifixion (Matt. 27:46) and the Sermon on the Mount (Matt. 7:9; Luke 11:7): they cry for spiritual sufficiency, for "bread" not "stone." Surrounding and inhabiting Stephen, these voices may "announce" her as a modern-day Mary by making her "barren womb . . . fruitful," but they prove painfully distinct from the conventional annunciatory figures of Christianity. The voices emanate from "reproachful faces with *haunted* eyes" (emphasis added), from the spectres of inversion rather than either the angel Gabriel or the Holy Spirit.

Addressing Stephen as Virgin-invert, the voices pray for her intercession, a Catholic inflection in a passage that all the while sustains the standard biblical trope for the woman's spiritual journey: Stephen finds that her spiritual burden is ultimately her disempowered sex. "Christianity," writes Julia Kristeva, "is doubtless the most refined symbolic construct in which femininity . . . is focused on maternality" (161). Mary's essential femaleness may proclaim her Mother of God, but not before the narratives that circumscribe her (biblical as well as Christian) suspend her textual importance. By comparison, Stephen, who, sexually speaking, stands "between the sexes," finds that sexual inversion exacts narrative inversion. Stephen's desire (for both women and storytelling) is enveloped by the "truths" that anchor realism in male homosocial exchange, the "truths" that simultaneously ironically "allow" invert Stephen to "give" Mary to Hallam and necessarily override the women's lesbianism. The conventional plot of progress reduces to a gasping imprecation Stephen's capacity both to mother and to speak for herself as well as other inverts.

Her burden simultaneously "sterile" and "fruitful," Stephen occupies a narratological paradox. The realist plot does not answer her prayer for the "right to . . . existence"; the prayer itself, though, spiritualizes this predicament and so ultimately questions not Stephen's but realism's authority to tell Stephen's progress. At novel's end, abandoned by convention, Stephen, like the speaker in Ecclesiastes, knows, "there is no new thing under the sun" (Eccles. 1:9). An exile within the very plot of progress that realism engages to represent exiles, Stephen becomes a figure of biblical righteousness, a metapilgrim for whom realism's truth-telling capacity is but a "vanity of vanities" (Eccles. 12:8).

Stephen's silencing is the price of Hall's commitment to a realist tradition anchored in biblical paradigms. So, too, is Hall's own silencing. Remarking on this outcome, Jane Rule observes in *Lesbian Images* (1975):

> [Hall] worshiped the very institution which oppressed her, the Church and the patriarchy. . . . Inside that framework she made and tried to redefine the only proud choice she had. The 'bible' she offered is really no better for women than the Bible she would not reject. (64)

In *The Well,* lesbian desire remains unspeakable.

Given Hall's investment in biblical "truths," the novel's tragic cast seems all but inevitable; so, too, does the public outcry that followed the book's release in 1928. Although it received generally favorable reviews, *The Well* was branded obscene and immoral by some, and by the end of the year the British government had banned it. Appearing that same year, Beresford Egan's cartoon "The Sink of Solitude" provides an interesting commentary on the novel's banning. [See frontispiece.] On the one hand, Egan lampoons Hall's biblical earnestness. The cartoon offers a caricature of a crucified Hall, with serpentine tongue lasciviously extended, while her bent legs serve as the hurdle for a naked woman, labia prominently displayed. On the other hand, the cartoon also underscores the hypocrisy of "crucifying" Hall on the grounds of moral and civil good: to the right stands a government official who has pocketed her book; floating above his head are a halo and heart, a combination which points out the ambiguous relation between the moral and civil narratives present not only in *The Well* but also in the government decision to ban the novel. Does moral goodness sanction sexual desire, or is it that sexual desire legitimizes moral goodness? The Egan cartoon insists on these questions. Despite its sordid depiction of Hall, "The Sink of Solitude" comes very close to condemning the government's narrative surveillance.

Narrative surveillance is, of course, already at work in *The Well*: Hall's is a muted representation of lesbian desire. For the perverse reader of narrative inversion, however, Stephen Gordon's desire remains clearly audible. Accordingly, as in *The Well of Loneliness*, so in Jane Rule's own novel, *Desert of the Heart*: narrative inversion conveys lesbian desire. In the case of *Desert of the Heart*, though, the protagonists are not, as is Stephen, metaleptically overwhelmed by the burden of convention.[16] Rather, like H. D.'s "sea-shell," whose "shell-jaws snap shut / at the invasion of the limitless" ([6]), they prove narratively impenetrable. As the highly allusive titles of both novels suggest, *Desert of the Heart* begins where *The Well of Loneliness* ends. Unlike the Samaritan woman in John 4 who, in drawing water from a well for Christ, discovers the well of life,[17] Stephen, who professes Christianity, stands, at novel's end, alone; like the city of Sodom's spiritual depravity, her narratological abandonment is a "well[] without water" (2 Pet. 2:17). As dry as this well is the "no-man's land of sex" (84) that the invert inhabits. In their emphasis on barrenness, both images resemble Jane Rule's own, the desert. But what is cause for Stephen's sorrow is cause for celebration in *Desert of the Heart*. Realism's narratives of progress cannot detect the inverted love story of cartoonist Ann Childs and literature professor Evelyn Hall, whose name recalls the author of *The Well of Loneliness*.[18] *Desert of the Heart* celebrates the inscrutable foreignness—the illegibility—of Ann and Evelyn's shared pilgrimage.

In a 1976 interview with Geoffrey Hancock, Jane Rule indicated the importance of Protestant spiritual texts for understanding the development of her novel's two heroines, Evelyn and Ann.[19] Rule speaks of Anglo-American literature's (and specifically her own) Protestant inheritance:

> Our literature is full of [that inheritance]. The very cadences of our language are given to us in ritual form. Or were given to me anyway. The first novel I ever wrote was entitled after a phrase in the General Confession. The language is just there and the rhythms are very deep. . . . I think a lot that shocks me about the world we live in is rooted in Christian teaching. . . . And I think embedded in that mythology is what terrifies me most about the values of our culture. So it's very, negatively important. (in Hancock 65)

Fashioning lesbian *Bildung* as a journey, Rule not only calls attention to the ubiquity of biblical and Christian narrative paradigms within the realist novel, but also, like Hall, figures the lesbian as the metapilgrim of those paradigms.[20] The lesbian is a metapilgrim because her narrative of development is inverted within the overarching plot of progress, a plot which Rule in turn renews by figuring Ann's and Evelyn's *Bildung* (and orientation) as a wandering in the desert. "As I walked through the wilderness of this world . . . I dreamed a dream," begins the narrator of John Bunyan's *The Pilgrim's Progress* (39). In *Desert of the Heart* it is a wilderness, geographical as well as epistemological, that Ann and Evelyn inhabit.[21]

Casting her text as a lesbian pilgrim's progress, Rule (much as Hall before her) offers a critique of the conventional Christian formulae for expressing faith, a critique apparent from the novel title itself. "Desert of the heart" echoes a line in the general confession of the *The Book of Common Prayer*, which opens, "Almighty and merciful Father; we have erred, and strayed from thy ways like lost sheep. We have followed too much the *devices* and *desires* of our own hearts" (23; emphasis added). Using the line to inform the meaning of the novel's title, one can argue that "devices" and desires" correspond to a definition of "desert" as spiritual abandonment. Given the line, which implicitly constructs the "heart" as wayward, "desert" becomes the locus of disconnection between God and worshiper.

This reading resonates with the Bible's own frequent coupling of "desert" and "heart,"[22] two of the more evocative combinations of which are as follows:

> Hear my prayer, O Lord, and let my cry come unto thee.
> Hide not thy face from me in the day when I am in trouble; incline thine ear unto me: in the day when I call answer me speedily. . . .
> My *heart* is smitten, and withered like grass. . . .
> I am like an owl of the *desert.* (Ps. 102:1-2, 4, 6)

and

> Thus saith the Lord . . . cursed be the man that trusteth in man and maketh flesh his arm, and whose *heart* departeth from the Lord.
>
> For he shall be like the heath in the *desert,* and shall not see when good cometh; but shall inhabit the parched places in the wilderness, in a salt land and not inhabited. (Jer. 17:5-6)

The psalm, whose caption in the King James Version reads, "A Prayer of the afflicted, when he is overwhelmed, and poureth out his complaint before the Lord," recalls Stephen's prayer at the end of *The Well of Loneliness.* The coupling of "desert" and "heart" in the passage from Jeremiah, which Robert Davidson deems "without parallel in prophetic literature" (in Metzger and Coogan 343-347), in turn voices the prophet's protest against the political and religious platforms that would help lead to the Diaspora. That both passages attempt to answer the absence of any outwardly affirming sign responding to the exercise of belief helps explain their insistence on an antithetical relation between divine and human faith. In a world whose lack of faith is the ultimate sign of godlessness, the heart becomes a desert.

The cultural context for *Desert of the Heart* is, by comparison, not a political diaspora but a capitalist centralization, with its commercialization of spiritual belief.[23] *Desert of the Heart* takes up the conventionalizing of faith, its transformation into a semiotic system whose purpose is, above all, its own circulation. Like the biblical passages, the novel itself insists on a godless world. Set in Reno, Nevada, home to gambling casinos and divorce courts, the novel compares that city to the biblical Sodom, as well as to Bunyan's city of spiritual marketing, Vanity Fair. In Reno, God's "truths" are ironically everywhere.

Juxtaposing this world is the landscape of pilgrimage that the two lovers (Ann, who works in a casino, and Evelyn, who has come to Reno for a divorce) suggest. They retrieve pilgrimage, within Christian and realist texts the conventional narrative for the hero/ine's development, as the narrative for their coming out. Taking place within Reno and its surrounding desert, their love story impels what Marilyn Schuster calls a "strategy of subtle subversion: social and literary conventions are put to the service of their own destruction" (433). With the backdrop to their pilgrimage a modern-day Sodom, Evelyn and Ann's narrative trajectory is not the "enabling escape" that for Catharine Stimpson enacts "lesbian's rebellion against social stigma and self-contempt" (244). Rather they inhabit the inverted narrative of the "desert of the heart," where the impossibility of obtaining spiritual comfort generates for the lesbian exile the desire for emotional self-sufficiency.

Rule's critique of biblical paradigms' hold over the possibilities of novelistic representation directs the opening of the novel:

> Conventions, like cliches, have a way of surviving their own usefulness. They are then excused or defended as the idioms of living. For everyone, foreign by birth or by nature, convention is a mark of fluency. That is why, for any woman, marriage is the idiom of life. And she does not give it up out of scorn or indifference but only when she is forced to admit that she has never been able to pronounce it properly and has committed continually its grossest grammatical errors. For such a woman marriage remains a foreign tongue, an alien landscape, and, since she cannot become naturalized, she finally chooses voluntary exile.

Evelyn Hall had been married for sixteen years before she admitted to herself that she was such a woman. (1)

The definition of marriage as a convention draws attention to both the social plots that constrain women and the patterns of spiritual narrative that help figure the novel as a literary form: conventionally speaking, both the novel's and women's stories are predicated upon and resolved through marriage.

Rule's opening, in other words, invites one to read *Desert of the Heart* as a response to the conventions of gender and genre available to the social and literary texts of female progress. These share a common cultural repository in spiritual narratives, which cast the anticipated union with God as a marriage feast. While this figuration always feminizes the believer, who becomes bride to Christ's bridegroom, marriage, for the female pilgrim, is not simply the endpoint but also the precondition of her travel. But if biblical and, more generally, Christian texts insist that women are at home with marriage, Rule asks whether marriage is at home with the novel heroine. For Evelyn Hall, even though she retains the title "Mrs." and her husband's surname after she has left him, it is not. "Foreign," "alien," and "exile" place her in a biblical tradition that she immediately problematizes. For Evelyn marriage may be "the idiom of life"; yet, because her academic training has insisted on an interpretive capacity denied her spiritual grandmothers, she is able to reenvision marriage as "the long detour" (173), and so inhabit a love story predicated upon divorce.[24] Evelyn's coming out insists on lesbianism's illegibility within the inverted narratives of female development.

Evelyn's flight to Reno initially seems to reverse the direction of biblical exodus, the journey from Egypt, through the desert, to the Promised Land. Evelyn is from the San Francisco Bay area, considered by Reno's inhabitants "a promised land . . . a promised sea" (84). The novel compares Reno itself to Sodom and to Bunyan's reworking of that biblical city, Vanity Fair. Visiting a local casino, Evelyn encounters a man who, dressed as a minister, quotes Faithful, Christian's traveling companion in *The Pilgrim's Progress*:

> There can be no divine faith without the divine revelation of the will of God! Therefore, whatever is thrust into the worship of God that is not agreeable to divine revelation, cannot be done but by human faith, which faith is not profit to eternal life! . . .
>
> This is Vanity Fair. Who judges me but Hate-good? Who are you, all of you, but Malice, Live-loose, Love-lust, Hate-light . . . (195-196)[25]

The passage draws attention to Reno as a manufacturer of convention. Whether the man is mad or, in fact, an overzealous cleric–whether the city is an actual, latter-day Vanity Fair or a glitzy parody of it–is not the point; the ineluctability of such debate is. Reno and the heckler occupy the same imaginative context; both enact a metanarrative of Christian progress, whereby the scene's last line, the well-known Bunyan quote, "I buy the truth," is not a statement of spiritual essentialism but of the conspicuous consumption of Christian paradigms. Reno in effect resembles the biblical Sodom condemned by the prophet Jeremiah: the cultural space where "prophet and priest are profane" (Jer. 23:11). Reno does not simply desecrate convention but rather reproduces it through parody. The city, in fact, occasions Evelyn's discovery that her exile remains circumscribed by convention. Its desert landscape confirms that the Christian conventions to which she still clings have divorced her.

But if Reno maps out Evelyn's spiritual desertion, it also enables her meeting Ann Childs, who is quick to point out that the world of Christian propriety and the moral wasteland of Reno are inextricably linked, the former indeed sanctioning the existence of the latter. Her descriptions of Reno play on the conventional oppositions of "the well-watered plains of the Lord" and Sodom and Gomorrah, and in so doing recall how in Genesis 13:10–"the plain of Jordan . . . was well watered everywhere, before the Lord destroyed Sodom and Gomorrah, even as the garden of the Lord"–those places are one and the same. For Ann, "Every place is a Sodom and a Gomorrah. . . . The faithful say the plain was well watered, even as the Garden of the Lord, before he destroyed the cities. I don't believe it. There never was any water here, not fresh water" (112). Skeptical of the distinction between desert and garden as landscapes of damnation and salvation, Ann sees Reno as an ontological supermarket along the straight and narrow road of narrative possibility. There consumers temporarily indulge themselves in an array of products, even as their best buy remains convention. Its clubs supplying the church with "both the money to be spent and the souls to be saved," Reno is, for Ann, "a perfect kingdom, based on nothing but the flaws in human nature" (200-201). As such it is itself an allegory of religious belief, complete with its own set of conventions that parody those of pilgrimage.

Like Evelyn, Ann is a critical reader of the context she inhabits. Ann works in a casino that offers employees and visitors alike a parodic City of God, dominated by commercial images of femininity, more specifically of female sexuality, that traffic in (and prostitute) representations of the female pilgrim. So one woman *cum* wayfarer treks ninety miles across the desert for her job as a change apron. Strapped to her belly, the fifty pound apron itself reminds Ann of "a fetus in its seventh month" (101). The coin dispenser parodies the ineluctable burden of female sexuality, or again, the childbearing capacity to which women's spiritual placement is biblically linked. Ann recognizes this trope for female pilgrimage and remains aloof, removed even from her former lovers, Silver and Bill, whose names reflect the ubiquity of the marketplace. Tellingly, Ann's nickname is "little fish." "Little fish" inscribes her within a Christian romance, where Evelyn is the fisher of [wo]men who "hook[s] and land[s]" her (148). "Little fish" is also Virginia Woolf's term in *A Room of One's Own* for the woman's thought that, meeting prohibition rather than nurture, darts into hiding. Within the heterosexual marketplace, Ann is a threshold of lesbian consciousness, a thought only acknowledgeable in the cartoons that she refuses to sell. These sketches are designed for Ann's own private instruction, introspection; they constitute the *Bilder* of an alternative *Bildung*.

"English is my second language and I don't have a first" (122), says Dina, the Greek-born protagonist of Rule's third novel, *Against the Season*. The same might be said of Ann and Evelyn, for neither woman lays claim to an essential femininity existing apart from or displaced by the gendered conventions she has experienced. She rather struggles with those conventions. Looking up "evil" in the dictionary, Ann comes across the definition, "That which hinders prosperity and diminishes welfare"; she is left wondering, "Whose prosperity? Whose welfare?" (141). These are the questions of the pilgrim who must negotiate a journey through Sodom and Vanity Fair. They are also the questions that *Desert of the Heart* urges upon the perverse reader of lesbian realism.

In *Desert of the Heart* the most salient metaphors are those of barrenness, which define nourishment not in terms of reproduction but in terms of self-preservation. So the desert and an alkaline lake that provide the backdrop for Evelyn and Ann's romance are part of Rule's "dismantling" of nature (Zimmerman, *Safe* 43). Where fertility demands appropriation, Evelyn and Ann's landscape remains a sterile inviolable one, a wilderness that resists cultivation, that is itself self-sustaining.

So, too, while Evelyn may initially put off Ann's lovemaking by paraphasing the General Confession—"I live in the desert of the heart" (118)—the younger woman directs her attention toward the figurative richness of the actual desert:

> the rain stopped and before them was a valley of brilliant, burning sunlight, arched with rainbows, edged with lightning.
> "This is the desert of the heart," Ann said quietly. (120)

Complete with rainbows reminiscent of the one that seals the covenant between God and man in Genesis 9, the desert momentarily becomes a promised land. With Ann's inversion of the Protestant metaphor for spiritual desolation the desert materializes the "desert of the heart." The desert is the landscape of self-address; it is the objective correlative of Ann and Evelyn's love story, the inverted narrative that remains for exiles from convention after the possibility of defining themselves in terms of an overarching biblical scheme has been swept away.

So realism's modes of truth-telling break down through the women's continual [re]reading of them. Biblical and Christian narratives embed the cryptogram of their union. Much as Bunyan's narrator walks "through the wilderness of this world" (39) in order to dream of pilgrim's progress, Evelyn, near novel's end, walks into the desert in order to struggle with the thought of love. There she is reminded of Christian and Faithful entering Vanity Fair, only to find that she cannot equate their progress through it with her continuous wandering within it:

> Evelyn began to walk slowly back the way she had come, neither Faithful nor Christian. There is no allegory any longer, not even the allegory of love. I do not believe. Even seeing and feeling, in fact, what I do not believe, I do not believe. It's a blind faith, human faith, hybrid faith of jackass and mare. That's the only faith that I have. I cannot die of that. I can only live with it, damned or not. (224)

Where human experience does not lay claim to universality, the link between human and divine faith remains tentatively lodged within "the desert of the heart," the narrative of inversion. And not because of any lack of interpretive capacity on the part of the female pilgrim. Here it is realism's plot of progress that fails, not the female pilgrim. If Evelyn's lesbianism is "blind" and "hybrid" (and, by extension, sterile), it is because there is no possibility for a "straight" correspondence between lesbian experience and realist "truths." She and Ann (much like Stephen Gordon before them) are the metapilgrims of realist fiction. But introspection for Evelyn and Ann consists in a continual reassessing and perversion of the biblical conventions to which Stephen herself resolutely ascribes. The realist tradition that is the novel's narratological Sodom cannot codify Evelyn and Ann's relationship. Together, the two women constitute a "cryptic cartoon" (244) whose narrative desire remains indecipherable for the "truths" of spiritual progress that they themselves read so well.

NOTES

1. Indeed, in a recent essay Marilyn Farwell has defined the lesbian narrative as a transgressor of realist narrative strategies:

> The lesbian narrative . . . can be defined as a disruptive story in which the female is given subjectivity, not as a substitute man, but as an oversized, monstrous woman–as a lesbian. This definition, of course, leaves out some traditionally defined lesbian narratives, because the narrative system, not simply the character images, must be the site of transgression. (167)

2. With "hom(m)osexuality," De Lauretis is invoking Luce Irigaray's pun on sameness ("homo") and man ("homme").

3. Within this context "Christian" proves a general marker that suspends rather than underscores the differences between various Protestant and Catholic beliefs.

4. The biblical citations in this essay refer to the King James Bible, because it is generally speaking the version that has profoundly shaped English realism and, more particularly, because both Jane Rule and Radclyffe Hall (her conversion to Catholicism in adulthood notwithstanding) draw on this version.

5. As Barry Qualls has pointed out in numerous conversations, the imaginative hold that the Bible exercised over Victorian writers can be seen in the frequent biblical "typing" of novel heroines. Charlotte Brontë, Charles Dickens, George Eliot, and Elizabeth Gaskell, for example, all make use of the Book of Esther in their novels. The self-effacing heroines of *Bleak House* and *Felix Holt* are both aptly named Esther. Gaskell, in turn, uses the name ironically: in *Mary Barton,* Esther is a fallen woman, a cautionary figure incapable of "saving" her niece. In *Villette,* whose metanarrative condemns realism's incapacity to offer stories that celebrate female independence, the one female character who insists on self-expression is tellingly named Vashti.

6. While this essay primarily explores the biblical figures that help organize Hall's and Rule's novels, I have also extended my analysis to include *The Pilgrim's Progress,* a metatext of the English novel, which has received very little feminist and, to my knowledge, no lesbian attention.

7. For example, a passage in *The Pilgrim's Progress* reads,

> Look before thee; dost thou see this narrow way? That is the way thou must go. It was cast up by the patriarchs, prophets, Christ, and his apostles, and it is as straight as a rule can make it. This is the way thou must go. . . . there are many ways butt down upon this; and they are crooked, and wide; but thus thou may'st distinguish the right from the wrong, that only being straight and narrow. (59)

8. It is important to note that Hall's embracing of a biblical heritage sustains a eugenic vision within *The Well of Loneliness.* The spectre of miscegenation hovers above Stephen's experience of cultural exile: she increasingly depends upon a motley group of social outcasts for companionship, among them the brothers

Henry and Lincoln, who are African-American musicians. Chapter 45's detailing of Lincoln's rendition of a spiritual does not serve to suggest a connection between the oppressive experiences of racism and heterosexism but rather to foreground Stephen's loss of her cultural birthright. While Lincoln sings and Stephen listens, the narrator describes Lincoln as having "the patient, questioning expression common to the eyes of most animals and those of all slowly evolving races" (416). Hall's point seems to be that the stigmatizing of inversion exacts Stephen's forfeiture of her social privilege, which has been buttressed by class- and race-based insulation.

9. In his article on *The Pilgrim's Progress,* Dayton Haskin distinguishes between Christian's burden of interpretation and Christiana's burden of sex or childbearing. Particularly interesting is his discussion of the etymological link between "travel" and "travail."

10. While the parallels between Stephen and the Virgin Mary are perhaps the most obvious, Stephen also recalls Eve and Ruth. Like Eve, Stephen is banished from her paradise, Morton, the family estate, because of her sexuality. Governess-companion Puddle responds to this news of exile by identifying herself as a latter-day Naomi, who will follow Stephen/Ruth. The comparison to Ruth is particularly resonant for lesbian heroes. See, for example, Isabel Miller's *Patience and Sarah* and Jeanette Winterson's *Oranges Are Not the Only Fruit.*

11. For a discussion of the gendered patterns of spiritual *Bildung* in Bunyan's *The Pilgrim's Progress* see my essay.

12. In splicing together scenes from Parts 1 and 2 of John Bunyan's *The Pilgrim's Progress* in order to underscore the heroine's struggle to define herself apart from male mediation, both *Jane Eyre* and *Villette* disclose one of Charlotte Brontë's own novelistic strategies to offset the conventions of truth-telling, the patterns of progress, available to the realist writer. Brontë's reworkings of Bunyan produce widely different effects. While both Jane Eyre and Lucy Snowe narrate their own stories, only Jane Eyre can claim an autonomous voice; Lucy Snowe's history remains obscured by the plot's interest in the fortunes of her two love interests, Dr. John and M. Paul.

13. The novel contains numerous biblical allusions which help place Stephen as a persecuted hero. One key comparison, which I do not explore in this essay, is to Job. At various times, Stephen is aligned with that paradigmatic figure of suffering righteousness. See, for example, Chapter 24, in which governess/companion Puddle quotes Job 10:8 in order to describe Stephen's torment: "Thine hands have made me and fashioned me together round about; yet Thou dost destroy me."

14. See F. F. Bruce's entry on Stephen in *The Oxford Companion to the Bible* 714. Acts' description of Stephen's persecution provides an explicit reworking of Luke's account of Jesus.

15. Esther Newton closes her key essay by observing that Mary's story–in some sense, the story of the lesbian, as distinct from that of the invert–has yet to be told. I hope to complicate Newton's argument by exploring how the name Mary points not only to Mary Llewellyn but also to Stephen Gordon. Narrative inversion prevents both women's stories from being told.

16. For my use of the term *metalepsis* I am indebted to Ed Madden.

17. I am indebted to Mena Mitrano for this allusion.

18. Bonnie Zimmerman observes as much in *The Safe Sea of Women* 46.

19. In her interview with Geoffrey Hancock, Rule observes the following of her writing style:

> Probably the most influential period for me was seventeenth-century English literature, and that had to do with the long rhythmic control of prose. I don't suppose anybody reading my prose would think it sounds like a John Donne sermon. But that's where I learned how a sentence was made. (69)

20. That *The Pilgrim's Progress* is a metatext for the English (as well as North-American) novel is a commonplace in literary criticism. For Victorian novels especially, one need only consider the titles *Oliver Twist: A Parish Boy's Progress, Vanity Fair* (whose name derives from Bunyan's revisioning of the biblical Sodom), and *Middlemarch* to recognize Bunyan's immediate relevance. His presence is also apparent in nineteenth-century American fiction. The most notable example is Alcott's *Little Women,* whose chapter titles refer explicitly to *The Pilgrim's Progress.*

21. It is interesting to note that the Hebrew word "midbar" has been translated into English as both "wilderness" and "desert."

22. I have counted some 24 times.

23. In her interview Rule observes of the novel, "Those values that we get in Western culture. The claim, or justification is, what you do is productive. You marry and you have children. . . . I wanted to write about activities, ways to life that had no justification inside our value system" (94-95).

24. With regard to Evelyn's divorce, the parallel between *Desert of the Heart* and that key transitional text for the Bible and the English novel, Bunyan's *The Pilgrim's Progress,* is particularly worth pursuing. Evelyn both reenacts the break from family and community that marks the beginning of Christian's progress and rejects the endpoint of that progress, the arrival in the Celestial City, whose symmetric counterpointing of Christian's initial rupture with marriage in turn propels Christiana on her travel. Evelyn's coming out frees her from the interpretive zealotry of male guides, who in Christiana's case resist her attempts to direct her own progress and insist that her development be circumscribed by patriarchally structured marriage.

25. The Bunyan quotations that Rule incorporates here may be found on pages 132 and 126 of *The Pilgrim's Progress.*

WORKS CITED

The Book of Common Prayer. New York: Thomas Nelson and Sons, 1944.

Breen, Margaret. "The Sexed Pilgrim's Progress." *SEL* 32.3 (1992): 443-460.

Bunyan, John. *The Pilgrim's Progress.* Harmondsworth: Penguin, 1984.

Castle, Terry. "Sylvia Townsend Warner and the Counterplot of Lesbian Fiction." *Sexual Sameness: Textual Differences in Lesbian and Gay Writing.* Ed. Joseph Bristow. London: Routledge, 1992. 128-147.

De Lauretis, Teresa. *The Practice of Love: Lesbian Sexuality and Perverse Desire.* Bloomington: Indiana UP, 1994.

Farwell, Marilyn R. "The Lesbian Narrative." *Professions of Desire.* Ed. George E. Haggerty and Bonnie Zimmerman. New York: Modern Language Association, 1995. 156-168.

Hall, Radclyffe. *The Well of Loneliness.* New York: Covici Friede, 1928.

Hancock, Geoffrey. "An Interview with Jane Rule." *Canadian Fiction Magazine* 23 (August 1976): 57-112.

H. D. [Hilda Doolittle]. "The Walls Do Not Fall." *Trilogy.* New York: New Directions, 1973.

Haskin, Dayton. "The Burden of Interpretation in *The Pilgrim's Progress.*" *Studies in Philology* 79.3 (1982): 256-278.

Irigaray, Luce. *This Sex Which Is Not One.* Trans. Catherine Porter and Carolyn Burke. Ithaca, NY: Cornell UP, 1985.

Kristeva, Julia. "Stabat Mater." Trans. Leon S. Roudiez. *The Kristeva Reader.* Ed. Toril Moi. New York: Columbia UP, 1986. 160-186.

Madden, Ed. "Narrative Assumptions: Metalepsis, Conversion, and Coming Out." Symposium on Gay Spirituality and the Media. Durham, NH. 29 April 1995.

Metzger, Bruce M., and Michael D. Coogan, eds. *The Oxford Companion to the Bible.* New York: Oxford UP, 1993.

Miller, Isabel. *Patience and Sarah.* New York: McGraw-Hill, 1969.

Newton, Esther. "The Mythic Mannish Lesbian: Radclyffe Hall and the New Woman." *Signs* 9.4 (1984): 557-75.

Qualls, Barry V. *The Secular Pilgrims of Victorian Fiction.* New York: Cambridge UP, 1983.

Rule, Jane. *Against the Season.* Tallahassee, FL: Naiad, 1984.

———. *Desert of the Heart.* London: Pandora, 1986.

———. *Lesbian Images.* New York: Pocket Books, 1976.

Schuster, Marilyn R. "Strategies for Survival: The Subtle Subversion of Jane Rule." *Feminist Studies* 7.3 (1981): 431-450.

Sedgwick, Eve Kosofsky. *Between Men: English Literature and Male Homosocial Desire.* New York: Columbia UP, 1985.

Spraggs, Gillian. "Hell and the Mirror: A Reading of *Desert of the Heart.*" *New Lesbian Criticism: Literary and Cultural Readings.* Ed. Sally Munt. New York: Columbia UP, 1992. 115-131.

Stimpson, Catharine. "Zero Degree Deviancy: The Lesbian Novel in English." *Writing and Sexual Difference.* Ed. Elizabeth Abel. Chicago: U of Chicago P, 1982. 243-60.

Winterson, Jeanette. *Oranges Are Not the Only Fruit.* London: Pandora, 1985.

Woolf, Virginia. *A Room of One's Own.* New York: Harcourt Brace Jovanovich, 1929.

Zimmerman, Bonnie. "Perverse Reading: The Lesbian Appropriation of Literature." *Sexual Practice, Textual Theory.* Ed. Susan J. Wolfe and Julia Penelope. Oxford: Blackwell, 1993. 135-149.

———. *The Safe Sea of Women: Lesbian Fiction, 1969-1989.* Boston: Beacon P, 1990.

Piety and the Agnostic Gay Poet: Thom Gunn's Biblical Homoerotics

George Klawitter, PhD

St. Edward's University

SUMMARY. Thom Gunn has relied on biblical stories throughout his writing career to carry gay-themed poems. Although he characterizes himself agnostic, it is difficult to reconcile this self-definition with the tenderness evident in his biblical poems, a tenderness that many would identify with a kind of piety. Two of these poems reflect Gunn's reaction to paintings by Caravaggio, "The Sacrifice of Isaac" and "The Conversion of St. Paul." For the former, Gunn seems to have intuited Caravaggio's fascination with the naked figure of Isaac who appears about to be sodomized by Abraham. For the Paul poem, Gunn chooses one of two Caravaggio paintings on the subject, the one which emphasizes Paul in a recumbent and vulnerable sexual position. Gunn has also written tenderly of the Virgin Mary and Christ. His poem "Lazarus Not Raised" is an unusual look at the New Testament Lazarus story from Lazarus's point of view as a dead man who is not particularly interested in coming back to life even though he is encouraged to do so by a bevy of male friends. In recent years Gunn has continued to use biblical flavors in his verse,

George Klawitter is an associate professor of English at St. Edward's University in Austin, Texas. He has edited the complete poetry of Richard Barnfield (1990) and written *The Enigmatic Narrator* (1995), a study of homoeroticism in John Donne's poetry.

Correspondence may be addressed: English Department, St. Edward's University, Austin, TX, 78704; or by e-mail: georgek@ admin.stedwards.edu.

[Haworth co-indexing entry note]: "Piety and the Agnostic Gay Poet: Thom Gunn's Biblical Homoerotics." Klawitter, George. Co-published simultaneously in *Journal of Homosexuality* (The Haworth Press, Inc.) Vol. 33, No. 3/4, 1997, pp. 207-232; and: *Reclaiming the Sacred: The Bible in Gay and Lesbian Culture* (ed: Raymond-Jean Frontain) Harrington Park Press, an imprint of The Haworth Press, Inc., 1997, pp. 207-232. Single or multiple copies of this article are available for a fee from The Haworth Document Delivery Service [1-800-342-9678, 9:00 a.m. - 5:00 p.m. (EST). E-mail address: getinfo@haworth.com].

maintaining all the time his agnosticism. *[Article copies available for a fee from The Haworth Document Delivery Service: 1-800-342-9678. E-mail address: getinfo@haworth.com]*

When writers find their creative freedom constrained by a society intent on decorum, they can go underground with their unseemly art or try to best their critics above ground by burrowing under language through metaphor and allegory. In a recent interview Thom Gunn confesses: "You couldn't have written openly gay poetry in the early 50's, when I came here [to America], because it wouldn't have been published" (Gallagher 58). Gunn thus ingenuously explains his introduction to editorial prudery and his own need to find a way around it. Joining the ranks of outsiders who use subterfuge to advance their art, Gunn employed delicate levels of metaphor early in his craft, like others forced into similar tactics–for example, D. H. Lawrence. When society has its standards set, writers find alternate routes to circumvent censors so that, under cover, gay writers can pass off as mainstream what is actually radical revisioning. Over the years no better cover has served them than the images and stories of the Bible: David and Jonathan, Jesus and John have served their turn as vehicles for homoerotic texts. Even for writers who profess no formal religion, the Bible has been a convenience to link them to a readership quite innocent of homoerotic intention.

Thom Gunn fancies himself an agnostic, but his biblical poetry has always demonstrated a warmth that makes a reader wonder just how solid his agnosticism really is. When we survey the poetry Gunn published and republished over the past forty years, it is evident that he is not embarrassed to rely on biblical figures to carry his gay themes. He is comfortable with both Old Testament and New Testament stories, a figure like the sacrificial Isaac catching his imagination no less than a fanciful Madonna fussing over her enigmatic child. Through all the biblical images, the linking thread is piety. Although a person can nurture piety without ever yoking it to a religion or to "religion," in Gunn's "religious" poems, there is a tenderness for the figures that goes beyond reverence for historical personages. In the Bible Gunn has found suitable vehicles to carry his sexual ideas, both early in his career when he was closeted, and now in his mature years when he has become one of the finest gay craftsmen in the poetry business. He traverses a range of characters, from the shadows of the semihistorical Abraham to the midrash of Mary and Jesus. He handles the miracle stories of Lazarus and St. Paul with grace and finesse. He tackles Adamic myth and sentimental Christology with a kind of awe that leaves a reader wondering how Gunn escapes censure in an age of skeptical cynicism. But, of course, that is what a hierophant is all about, even if he cannot explain his own magic. And Gunn cannot.

When Thom Gunn assesses his early motivation for writing poetry, he is, though candid, less than helpful:

> Something was in the way; there was some kind of material that I wasn't able to face up to. I'm not certain what it was: it wasn't simply that I couldn't yet acknowledge my homosexuality, though that was part of it. It was more that my imagination retreated too easily into the world before my mother's death [when he was 15], a world that in practice excluded most of the twentieth century. (*Occasions* 173)

We get the impression from interviews here and there that Gunn is not very good at explaining himself. As late as 1985 he says, "Maybe it would help if I told you now that I'm gay, but don't have any clear image of myself" (Nuwer 68). Similarly, in response to a metrical question he has surely fielded a hundred times in the past thirty years, he says that he wrote in tight stanzaic forms in the 1960s and 1970s as a way of unconsciously balancing the freedom and liberation he experienced using LSD. This insight ignores the fact that he had been using meter and rhyme since day one, making a comment by Alvarez seem more to the point: "The more outrageous the experience–LSD trips, sexual orgies, group gropes–the more fastidious the verse becomes" (80). Thus when we comb Gunn for poetry influenced by the Bible, we are left to our own insights because Gunn has never been aligned with the Bible, most critics preferring to see him as a rebellious, hedonistic poet with a "direct appeal not for angry, but for fierce, young men" (Fraser 367). Most fierce young men do not read the Bible, nor, we suspect, does Gunn much, but between 1952 and 1958, when Thom Gunn was in his twenties, he published in various journals a half dozen poems that rely on Bible stories or images. Thereafter, in the forty years following these early pieces, the Bible surfaces in another handful of poems, albeit without the telling presence it enjoyed in the youthful Gunn. Gunn's biblically influenced poems fall into three categories: early poems with sexual innuendo, later poems that touch biblical personages (for example, angels) only peripherally, and recent poems that pull Gunn into the agonies of crucifixion. Although Gunn's career has not been segmented by any personal catastrophes, no reader can deny that the AIDS epidemic has drawn Gunn into an angst that his early and middle poetry did not evince. In the earliest pieces, the Bible was his cover, in middle pieces his estranged friend, in recent work his nemesis. No poet, even a professed agnostic, can avoid for very long the rich possibilities that the Bible affords a writer to telegraph concerns to the world.

"Lazarus Not Raised" first appeared in *Trinity Magazine* in 1952 and was reprinted in Gunn's second book, *Fighting Terms* (1954). We presume Gunn wrote it in his first years at Trinity College, Cambridge, which he entered in 1950. The poem is ardently religious, capturing the time period just before Jesus raises Lazarus from the dead and pictures a Lazarus not much interested in coming back to life. Gunn readers who know of his agnosticism may be uncomfortable with the strange fervor in this poem. After all, Gunn himself revels in his lack of religion, remarking in a 1977 interview, "I'm eternally grateful to have been brought up in no religion whatsoever" (Scobie 7). There is in "Lazarus Not Raised" a tension between faith and skepticism that begins in the opening lines:

> He was not changed. His friends around the grave
> Stared down upon his greasy placid face
> Bobbing in shadows; nothing it seemed could save
> His body now from the sand below their wave,
> The scheduled miracle not taking place.

The finality of this particular death rides uneasily on the shock of disbelief expressed in the final line in which the miracle of Lazarus's resurrection is "scheduled," not in some future apocalyptic resurgence of all souls, but imminently, expressive of the expectation in the onlookers that, had Jesus been present, Lazarus would not have died (John 11:32). Fact comes up against faith: the dead man mocks the miracle workers who surround him: "He lay inert beneath those outstretched hands / Which beckoned him to life." As the would-be miracle-workers ply their craft, Lazarus makes a halfhearted attempt to animate, but he gives up, preferring "to amble at an easy pace" in the fields of the dead. He chooses to ignore "the nag of offered grace," blinking once and shaking his head. In the final line of each stanza, the pounding repetition of "the scheduled miracle" sneers at the very notion of miracle and melts into a kind of relief as the narrator finally beams:

> I saw somebody peer,
> Stooping into the oblong box of space.
> His friends had done their best: without such fear,
> Without that terrified awakening glare,
> The scheduled miracle would have taken place.

The implication of the final lines is that nothing the friends do can convince the dead man that it is worth his effort to reenter this life: he much prefers his new habitat. The irony of the whole thing is, of course, that the great spoiler is on his way and will eventually force Lazarus back to life with a miracle that is very much "scheduled," Jesus having told his disciples that the delay in going to Bethany was for the sole purpose of letting Lazarus die so Jesus could prove his powers (John 11:15). The joke is on Lazarus. Michelis reads this poem as existential, given Lazarus's choice not to return to life (34), and links it to Kierkegaard's introduction for *The Sickness Unto Death*. Kierkegaard, however, raises a slightly different aspect of the case as he questions the good of raising Lazarus if the man were just going to die later and concludes that no sickness is ever fatal as long as Christ exists (7). Gunn's Lazarus does indeed seem very much alive in the poem, as much a living presence as the friends who try to "revive" him.

For this poem Gunn wanders from his biblical text in several ways. First of all, there is no indication in the gospel that anyone tried to raise Lazarus before Jesus arrives at Bethany two days late, and secondly, Lazarus was not buried in a casket. Bodies at the time were wrapped in cloth and laid on a shelf in a cave. John 11:38 specifically mentions a cave. These variants in the story lead a reader to believe that Gunn had some other purpose in mind than simply having fun with a Bible story by imagining how a dead man might resist resurrection, but the poem is too finely crafted to dismiss as a young man's mockery of the Bible. Gunn was possibly reflecting at the time on death in general or perhaps even a Cambridge death that elicited the usual wishes that the deceased were still around. Swinden has suggested of Gunn's 1950s poetry that the poet "was preoccupied with the contrivances erected by the poet's will and intelligence to cope with what would otherwise have been the intolerable pressure of self-consciousness" (44), which is another way of saying Gunn had to write about himself or he would self-detonate. Gunn's motive is everywhere evident in this early poem as a comment on futile attempts to reverse nature or history: if one does not have the proper credentials, it is worthless to attempt the heroic. The biblical Lazarus, dead beyond recall in this poem, is a perfect vehicle to carry the message of an agnostic poet. The irony, however, lies in the ensuing miracle which remains the most lasting aspect of the Bible story. Listeners are more interested in the spectacular than in the predictable. Although Gunn has the final word on Lazarus's determination to stay dead, every reader knows what is going to happen once the real miracle-worker arrives. Poor Lazarus is going to be commanded back to life. It is the prerogative of the poet to select the moment he wishes to emphasize, and for Gunn the dead-as-a-doornail

Lazarus is infinitely more fascinating than the mummy who emerges from the cave at Jesus' order.

If, then, the poem is not about Lazarus, what is it about? We are tempted to read into the poem some gay-themed material, given the man wrapped in bandage-bondage, the circle of male friends surrounding him with their entreaties wasted on deaf ears, the references to "frozen glands" (l. 9) and "distended body laid" (l. 10), to say nothing of the erotic pun on "raised" in the title, but the poem was written in the early 1950s, much before Gunn came out. The chronology of his sexual awakening, however, does not preclude the Lazarus poem from being gay-themed. We are free to read the Lazarus poem on a level other than biblical. The "greasy placid face" of the first stanza is at the center of friends who stare down at it as it is "bobbing on shadows" in a kind of circle fellatio, ritualistic and possibly an initiation or an invitation extended by "those outstretched hands / Which beckoned him to life." The initiate is cold, his glands "frozen," and he is counselled to "rise now before you sink." Lazarus, however, does not respond to their pleading, although he had earlier been "aroused" (l. 16) when "he chose to amble at an easy pace / In childhood fields imaginary and safe." The man resists the rite that is pulling him from solitary, childish pleasures; he does not want to enter the realm of communal pleasures, of sharing, of giving and taking. Therefore his punishment is "to take slime on the deepest bed of vacancy," a terrible indictment of one who is afraid to make a commitment to sexual maturation: semen as slime and the masturbator's bed the "deepest bed of vacancy." This is not to imply, however, that the poem disdains masturbation; on the contrary, the hero relishes the pastime. If anything, the poem says that what is good for the live geese is not necessarily good for the dead gander, majority rule or not. Lazarus's problem, of course, is not that he fears his friends. His strength is that he does *not* fear them:

> Without such fear,
> Without that terrified awakening glare,
> The scheduled miracle would have taken place.

Thus left to his solitary pleasure, the man remains unregenerate. A reader may say, "Lazarus is just waiting for Mr. Right to come along (in two days)," but the poem stops short of that part of the story.

If Gunn wanted to make a point about the community of sexual maturation, why did he select the Lazarus story? The Bible gives Gunn a curiously unspecific figure. Lazarus is not married. He lives with his two maiden sisters, one of whom is often confused with the Magdalene. His best friend is a messiah macho-man. He is a perfect persona for a sexually ambiguous poem. The homoerotic tensions within the poem are interesting in that they are extrapolations from the canonical text itself, which is quite devoid of homoerotic flavor save for the "love" reference (John 11:35), antiseptic enough as it is. There exists, however, within an early apocryphal gospel, "The Secret Gospel of Mark," a story similar to the Lazarus story and rich in homoeroticism that can help us understand Gunn's affinity for Lazarus. Scholars believe that this particular "secret" fragment predates the canonical gospel of Mark in the following way: an Ur text composed around 70CE no longer exists; sometime later, probably around 100CE, "The Secret Gospel of Mark" was written, and from it derives our present gospel, purged of the "secrets" (Barnstone 340). The text of the "Secret Gospel" contains the story of a young man's resurrection by Jesus, a story that elicited commentary by the early church father Clement (c. 300CE), who maintains in a letter that Mark wrote two gospels (one designed for catechumens, one for the faithful) and was privy to arcane material which would lead believers into the "innermost sanctuary of that truth hidden by seven veils" (Barnstone 341). The latter composition, says Clement, "is most carefully guarded, being read only to those who are being initiated into the great mysteries." Clement reproduces the revitalizing of the young man as the following story:

> And they come into Bethany. And a certain woman whose brother had died was there. And, coming, she prostrated herself before Jesus and says to him, "Son of David, have mercy on me." But the disciples rebuked her. And Jesus, being angered, went off with her into the garden where the tomb was, and straightway a great cry was heard from the tomb. And going near Jesus rolled away the stone from the door of the tomb. And straightway, going in where the youth was, he stretched forth his hand and raised him, seizing his hand. But the youth, looking upon him, loved him and began to beseech him that he might be with him. And going out of the tomb they came into the house of the youth, for he was rich. And after six days Jesus told him what to do and in the evening the youth comes to him, wearing a linen cloth over his naked body. And he remained with him that night, for Jesus taught him the mystery of the Kingdom of God. (Barnstone 342)

The story stresses the integration of Jesus into the family before he spends the night with the young man, but a reader must notice that the emphasis then shifts to the naked body under the linen cloth, details prescribed by Jesus as elements of the nocturnal initiation. Clement goes out of his way to censure the Carpocratian Christians who adulterated the text with added words like "naked man with naked man" that do not exist in the "Secret Gospel." But the text, of course, is enough to stimulate the imagination just as it is, and Clement seals the flavor by accepting the words "and the sister of the youth whom Jesus loved." Clement was determined to return the text to its purity before the Carpocratians sullied it as they wandered "from the narrow road of the commandments into a boundless abyss of the carnal and bodily sins" (341), rhetoric typical of clerical watchdogs, but Clement is sufficiently impressed with the validity of the story to leave the homoerotic subtext intact. I am not saying that Gunn knew this apocryphal story before he wrote "Lazarus Not Raised," but it seems a striking similarity that a gay poet resonates to the same kind of resurrection scene that was used in the second century as a pattern for the homoerotic young man story.

Just as Gunn played freely with the Lazarus story, he exercises license in "Apocryphal," a poem published in 1954 in *Botteghe Oscure* (Rome). It retells the Abraham and Isaac sacrifice story but fancifies the intervening angel to such a point that the creature becomes an extension of Abraham's imagination, "a creature of your will." The angel does not call out from heaven to stay Abraham's knife as Genesis would have it; no, Gunn's angel strides up the hill and confronts Abraham with a mystical riddle concerning a nearby river:

> The stranger pointed, his hand lay upon the valleys:
> 'Observe,' he said, 'the wild unquestioning course
> Of that river, which knows in its rushing not men nor angels;
> My frown, your wonder, as light as bouncing stones.
> What is your greatest faith concerning that river?'

It is another test, as if the man did not have enough on his mind with the required sacrifice of his own son, and Abraham responds by asking the angel to consider the river a whirlpool turned to swirl upon itself by faith. It is a status quo answer, framed by a man who assumes that control is his to use to manipulate all creation into "a cloud of vapour" that floats to the horizon as a prayer-offering to the Creator. This is the fumbling of an old man who sees power as the vehicle for living life righteously. It is, of course, a dogmatic, stifling answer that is not what the angel is looking for. Isaac then awakes from his swoon and when the angel asks the boy for his interpretation of the river, the boy gives a Heraclitan answer:

> It will flow, I suppose, for ever,
> For it is in the nature of rivers to flow.
> It is strong as itself. What force could be more strong?

Isaac thus sees the river as something to be understood and accepted, not forced to do another's will. It is a response the angel likes, partly because it is the same way the angel apprehends the river. But then the angel informs Abraham that although it seems the old man has lost because there are two lined up against him, he has really won because the riddle has been internal to Abraham all along:

> Do not be angry, as he is of your begetting.
> So I am too, and a creation of your will.
> His answer is mine, the strength of our two answers
> Is yours against your own.

What has happened, therefore, is a struggle within the brain of Abraham himself over freedom of the will. His tradition forced him to see life as a given fated by the god(s) above, but the projection of himself into his son and reflected back into himself sees the human being as controlling his own destiny, much as the river flows according to its own rule, unhampered by regulations imposed by dams and dikes.

Since Gunn titles this poem "Apocryphal," we assume that he is aware of having changed the details of the Genesis story to suit his own purpose. The word "apocryphal" suggests that a story is not so much "false" as that it enjoys details that have washed it out of the canon. The *Gospel of St. Thomas,* for example, with all of its fanciful stories of the boy Jesus, was thought too charming to remain in the received Bible. The rigorists who determined what would remain as biblical text and what would not considered its intent inimical to the serious matter of redemption. Gunn finds the Abraham and Isaac story "apocryphal" not so much because of what remains in it but rather because of what may have been lost from it. So as with Gunn's Lazarus poem, we are free to wonder if there is a gay subcurrent to the surface meaning in "Apocryphal." First of all, we are again in a totally male milieu, and the scene is bondage and sacrifice. It would be interesting to read the angel as solely interested in rescuing the bound boy, but his primary focus seems to be on rescuing old Abraham from himself. This is a curious twist in the story, but it is substantiated early in the poem, in fact within the first stanza, in two ways. The angel is first seen by Abraham as a reflection in the knife's blade: "He saw in its shining a shining stranger walk." Secondly, the poem states this is "not God's but Abraham's angel." So what Abraham sees reflected in the blade is himself, or rather an alter ego who will question the ritual sacrifice. What we have in this scenario is the brave realization within the father that his son is valuable alive and respected: the final line of the poem notes "Abraham walked with Isaac down the hill." Unlike the Lazarus poem, the Abraham poem does not exploit phallic language. There is the blade, of course, lifted over the swooning victim who lies with his "neck self-offered to the sun," but these two images do not draw much attention to themselves. There is also in the riddle's answers the swirling whirlpool of self-interest as opposed to free-flowing water, but neither image is sexual in this poem.

Essentially "Apocryphal" is very spiritual. It presumes a kind of faith in the story and an acceptance of myth as an explanation for self-discovery and self-knowledge. It is not the sort of thing a self-respecting agnostic writes much of. Curiously, "Apocryphal" is paired in its first and only printing with a very gay-themed poem titled "Excursion" which Gunn reprinted in *The Missed Beat* (1976). He has chosen, on the other hand, to let "Apocryphal" slip from his mainstream corpus. Garrett, however, reprinted the poem in *Botteghe Oscure Reader* (1974), a reprinting unacknowledged by Gunn's bibliographers Hagstrom and Bixby.

A famous Renaissance painting, "The Sacrifice of Isaac," by Caravaggio, a painter whom Gunn appreciated early on, as we shall see shortly, is reflected strongly in the Abraham poem (see Figure 1). Dating to the first years of the seventeenth century, the painting now hangs in the Uffizi. Looking at the picture, one is immediately struck by the positioning of the three bodies. The nude Isaac is pinioned to the rock by his father who has tied the boy's hands behind his back. Why is the boy nude? Abraham's one hand forces Isaac's head down while the other readies the knife near the boy's body. The nude angel restrains the knife arm with one hand while he points across Abraham's beard to a convenient sheep. Halfway between angel and boy, the shining knife could very well have just reflected the approach of the angel, just as Gunn describes the reflection in his poem. The angel's face is commanding, while Abraham's seems interrupted, shocked and hostile. The boy's face is contorted with unspeakable horror. Isaac, of course, is at this point aware what the sacrifice will be, a question he had earlier raised (Gen. 22:7), but I believe there is more in this picture than ritual sacrifice. Behind the prone body of the naked boy, the father is hunched ominously over the twisted buttocks, and the knife is held in the threatening position of a rapist. The contortions in the boy's face are unlike anything Caravaggio ever painted in the pretty-boy pictures of his early career (Gregori, "Sacrifice" 284) and may very well mirror the agony of forced sexual entry or the anticipation of it. At this point in his career, Caravaggio was already involved with street boys, and at the time of this painting he spent most of September 1603 in jail for a libel suit based on defaming poems distributed by one of the street urchins. Isaac's face may be an outgrowth of Caravaggio's bad experiences with a boy prostitute. Then too, there is that angel pointing out the sheep to Abraham,

FIGURE 1. Caravaggio. *The Sacrifice of Isaac.* Uffizi, Florence, Italy. Used with permission.

a sheep that will be a surrogate sacrifice and might be as well a sexual substitute for Isaac.

Caravaggio's painting, the Genesis story, and Gunn's poem may have more in common than we have ever dared suspect in the past. Ancient rites of passage, by which boys were inseminated by the ranking village elder to fill the youths with good seed insuring fertile stock for the future by proven stock from the past, could have been the basis for the Abraham story to begin with. The custom persists in New Guinea (Lidz 194) although Herdt stresses the predominance of only oral sex in some people, like the Sambia, who believe that "men begot humanity through homosexual fellatio" (*Guardians* 255). The custom of anal intercourse is, however, often a secret kept from anthropologists until such time as they win the confidence of the tribe: "It is actually regarded as essential to the growing boy to be sodomized. More than one informant being asked if he had ever been subjected to unnatural practice, answered, 'Why, yes! Otherwise how should I have grown?'" (Herdt, "Ritualized" 21). The intervention by the Caravaggio angel in a rape scenario furthers the tradition of ritual sodomy, and Gunn's poem brings the story vividly into a modern gay-themed focus. Then too, the Bible story stresses procreation without women:

> The near sacrifice of Isaac restores him to patriliny. . . . By this act, Isaac, on the edge of death, received his life not by birth from his mother but from the hand of his father as directed by God (Elohim); and the granting of life was a deliberate, purposeful act rather than a mere natural process, a spiritual "birth" accomplished without female assistance. (Jay 102)

The Caravaggio painting–and by extension the Gunn poem, of course–retain the absence of women but emphasize a more physical and visual fulfillment of the masculine transfer of heritage, father to son. Just how prevalent homosexual initiation was among ancient Jews we do not know, but scholars continue to raise the issue: "Were those biblical homosexuals–mysteriously tolerated and persecuted in turn, so that they had to be driven out again and again–Jews who worshiped non-Jewish gods or were they enclaves of non-Jews in Jewish settlements?" (Karlen 10). As ancient peoples turned from the worship of an Earth-Mother, they may have dropped homosexual practices that were associated with matriarchy (Karlen 10). That the patriarchal Jews did or did not practice homosexual initiation rites is, however, unimportant to my argument. That Caravaggio (and probably Gunn, the aficionado of Caravaggio) so perceived them is important.

Caravaggio's influence on Gunn's use of another Bible story is evident in "In Santa Maria del Popolo," first published in 1958. The basis for the poem is the conversion of Saul into Paul (Acts 9:1-19), specifically that moment at which Saul is knocked to the ground and blinded as he is en route to Damascus to persecute Christians (Acts 9:3-4). Caravaggio painted two pictures on the conversion of St. Paul: the Odescalchi and the Santa Maria del Popolo. The former is elegant, with Christ in the upper right reaching down to the nearly naked Saul who clutches his hands over his blinded eyes while a groom restrains a horse (see Figure 2). The picture is crowded and gives the marvelous impression that a single second has been captured in paint, like a snapshot: Saul has not yet totally reached the ground, and a branch is cracking off a poplar tree (Hibbard 121). The details are quite finished, and the tension among the three major figures is dramatic. This is not, however, the painting that prompted Gunn to write his poem. A second painting by Caravaggio of Saul's conversion dates to the same years as the first but is radically different in its composition. Saul lies, head to the viewer, in the same little clothing as in the Odescalchi painting, but not nearly as nude (see Figure 3). There is no Christ figure in the painting, and the groom seems passive. What is most strange about the scene, however, is the overpowering figure of the horse, which takes up most of the painting and is positioned with hindquarters to the viewer. The painting is very simple, almost drab, when compared to the Odescalchi painting, and the details, particularly in the horse, a horse not original with Caravaggio but copied from an earlier engraving by Dürer (Gregori, "Age" 42), are not strong. Only the figure of Saul has drama, and this aspect of the picture, plus the absence of Christ, may have been intentional: Caravaggio "wished to convey that the presence of Divine Grace is apprehended not through external signs but in the heart of Man" (Gregori, "Age" 42). Perhaps.

But why would a gay poet respond to the Santa Maria del Popolo painting when it hardly reaches the elegance of other Caravaggio works— for example, the Odescalchi Saul that shows mastery in every inch of the picture? I think the answer is obvious to anyone who looks at the Saul figure in the Santa Maria del Popolo painting. He lies on his back with eyes closed and arms reaching up to embrace something or somebody. There is no pain in his face; it is quite passive. "His helplessness before the will of God is expressed by Paul's recumbent body. . . . Paul is vulnerable to God . . . wounded by a physical blindness that symbolizes his former spiritual blindness" (Hibbard 128). His legs are spread and bent at the knees. The thongs of his centurion skirt are buckled like pursed labia. One foot of the horse is lifted and points at the fallen man's crotch,

FIGURE 2. Caravaggio. *Conversion of St. Paul.* Coll. Odescalchi Balbi di Piovera, Rome, Italy. Used with permission.

FIGURE 3. Caravaggio. *Conversion of St. Paul.* S. Maria del Popolo, Rome, Italy. Used with permission.

and the hoof resembles a glans penis with distinct meatus, while Saul's own phallic sword lies useless at his side. The painting rests above eye level on the right wall of the Cerasi Chapel in the church of Santa Maria del Popolo, so a viewer is forced to look up at it, becoming, as it were, under Saul and gazing straight into that horse's hoof. For Parini, this moment in Saul's life is existential because "Saul *limits* himself in becoming Paul" (139), the moment being the focal point for a choice.

In the afternoon, sunlight bathes the painting from the transept over the altar, but Gunn's poem is not an afternoon poem, although his poem begins by noting that one must wait for the picture to become visible:

> Waiting for when the sun an hour or less
> Conveniently oblique makes visible
> The painting on one wall of this recess.

The shadows and the play of light make sense of the art at this time, but the light does not last long:

> But evening gives the art, beneath the horse
> And one indifferent groom, I see him sprawl . . .
> O wily painter, limiting the scene
> From a cacophony of dusty forms
> To the one convulsion, what is it you mean
> In that wide gesture of the lifting arms?

The poet is intrigued by the uplifted arms, does not understand the meaning, or pretends not to, and suspects that the painter had purpose in the arrangement. What that purpose is he only hints at in the next lines:

> No Ananias croons a mystery yet,
> Casting the pain out under name of sin.
> The painter saw what was, an alternate
> Candour and secrecy inside the skin.
> He painted, elsewhere, that firm insolent
> Young whore in Venus' clothes, those pudgy cheats,
> Those sharpers; and was strangled, as things went,
> For money, by one such picked off the streets.

This remarkable stanza does not invoke the most famous New Testament liar, Ananias, but rather the Ananias of Damascus who is commanded by God to cure Saul of his blindness (Acts 9:11). Ananias demurs, but eventually heals Saul in spite of the fact that he does not understand his mission and "croons a mystery." Thus Gunn attaches sin to both Caravaggio and Saul, the painter recognizing the sin inside the fallen equestrian and daring to brazen it to the viewing world. In the Odescalchi painting, Saul resists the outstretched arms of Christ, but in Santa Maria del Popolo, Saul invites the ecstasy of the moment. The arms are the first thing one sees in the picture (after that obtrusive back of the horse). Unfortunately for Caravaggio, who dabbled in sinners not just in paint but also in the real life of the streets, his own finale was executed by one of the very catamites he picked up as a trick. From the revelation in the painting of the confluence of Saul and Caravaggio, both open to the terror and lure of the unknown, Gunn turns into the church itself, "hardly enlightened," with a pun on his own ignorance and the fading sunlight. Old women kneel there:

> each head closeted
> In tiny fists holds comfort as it can.
> Their poor arms are too tired for more than this
> —For the large gesture of solitary man,
> Resisting, by embracing, nothingness.

They, too, reach into the darkness like the blind Saul and the unilluminated poet who, still closeted in 1958 by his own admission (Gallagher 58), is unable to confront the lie of his own sin and can only reach in the dark to resist nothingness by embracing it. The paradox of this final line is deliciously Donnean, and points back to the Caravaggio Saul who awaits his own lover, unable to see him but grateful for the experience of incipient rapture. The Santa Maria del Popolo painting is essentially a solo portrait because the only other human in it is that quite indifferent groom. There is not even the intrusion of an angel, as appears with Christ in the Odescalchi picture, to soften the effect of the protagonist's solitary trauma. Thus Saul suffers alone. Isaac, it should be remembered, was saved by an intruding angel, and the Odescalchi angel holds Christ back from whatever he thinks Christ is going to do to Saul, so for Caravaggio angels are not simply messengers, but they intervene with both men and gods. In Santa Maria del Popolo, however, angel-saviors do not figure.

Gunn uses angels in several late poems, but they are used in allusions and do not serve the central purpose the angel serves in the Abraham poem. The 1976 poem "Wrestling," for example, alludes to Jacob's wrestling with an angel (Gen. 33:25-31), a wonderfully homoerotic image for any gay poet:

> a tale of wrestling with a stranger
> a stranger, like
> a man.

The poem is an account of a conversation (possibly with Robert Duncan as the poem is dedicated to him) about angels and "sons of angels." The angel metaphor is timeless for its reference to beautiful men and fantasies of "wrestling" with them, and this poem is sexually charged in spite of its Duncanesque obscurity. Duncan did make reference to Jacob's wrestling in a 1960 poem, "The Structure of Rime I," and this poem was undoubtedly known to Gunn who grew close to Duncan in the 1960s.

> Jacob wrestled with Sleep–you who fall into Nothingness and dread
>   sleep.
> He wrestled with Sleep like a man reading a strong sentence.

Like so much of Duncan, the images lack immediacy, but it is evident from the lines that Jacob is not wrestling with a real angel. So Duncan gives us a nightmare where Gunn, the half-hearted agnostic, gives us a real angel. A few years later, in *The Passages of Joy* (1982) two Gunn poems mention angels, "The Menace" and "Another All-Night Party," but in both poems "angel" refers to a trick and has nothing to do with an extraterrestrial spirit at all. "The Menace" exploits "angel" first as an "angel of death" who haunts the sleeper and takes shape only when the narrator challenges him:

> He leaps from the night
> fully armed, a djinn
> of human stature.

The ominous figure turns out to be a store mannequin so that "the-one-who-wants-to-get-me" is actually the narrator himself. Then the nightmare takes the narrator to a street thick with smells and settles him in a porno theater with an adjacent trysting room where "we play / with light and dark." Finally, the narrator gives in:

> and we sleep at the end
> as a couple, I cup
> the fine warm back,
> broad flecked shoulder blades.

The trick turns out to be a working man who has to leave in the morning to get to work, but as he goes, he reminds the narrator that the transformation is complete: "the-one-who-wants-to-get-me," a repeated phrase that now lacks the terror of its earlier use, is a guardian angel, a protector. The poem is a classic "take somebody home" poem, but the use of the angel as a metaphor at beginning and end, with the slightest flavor of Jacob's wrestling, makes it an important reflection of Gunn's pre-AIDS period. So, too, for "Another All-Night Party" with an allusion to Jacob's ladder (Gen. 28:12), but the ladder for Gunn in this poem is nothing more than a stairway to a drug party for "another night of passages."

These angel pictures all vibrate to a gay reader, of course, because their environment is exclusively male, but Gunn has not totally avoided the female from Bible stories. Of the poems that show Gunn's use of the Bible, only two concern women, and these two concern the same woman. Written and published some thirty years apart, the pair have distinctly different appreciations of Mary as the Mother of God. The first, which appeared in August 1954 in *The Times Literary Supplement,* is titled "Jesus and His Mother." Tender and religious to the point of piety, it is not the sort of poem one is likely to find today in the *Times.* Curiously, Gunn does not consider the poem "religious" and rather apologizes that it is a "secular" look at Mary and Jesus (Nuwer 75), but to my mind it is not "secular" at all and can hold its own for piety with the most sugary verses of Richard Crashaw. Some critics, however, do take Gunn at his word. Wasserburg, for example, finds Gunn and Thomas Hardy to be birds of a feather, both "great nonbelieving writers . . . who make their secular values clear in every line, and whose resolutions are all the more powerful for that" (377). For Wasserburg, "the poem of a clearly secular imagination, such as Thom Gunn's, may more effectively disclose spiritual conditions than others that make frequent and overt use of sacred terminology" (389). Occasional or not, Gunn's approach to Mary seems to me anything but "secular." The poem makes Mary seem very maternal, very human, but those qualities do not make the poem "secular." They rather enhance its religiosity because they make the person of Mary wonderfully accessible. Using Mary as narrator, the poem is a plea from a mother who does not understand to a son who all too well understands his place in the world. She wants him to stay home, "in this garden ripe with pears." But she concludes every stanza with a variation on the line and sentiment "I am my own and not my own." It is a touching acknowledgement of Mary's acceptance of Divine Providence, Mary of the Magnificat. She recalls Joseph in stanza two and the twelve apostles in stanza three. She reminisces about Jesus' childhood when "I taught you speech, we named the birds." But the man wants to go. He is sullen. She grows desperate, points out the carpentry tools waiting for his touch, and oversteps maternal decorum when she cries, "I will teach you like a wife / To be my own and all my own." Mary, of course, is in a ticklish position: like all Christians, she is mother to the spouse of all devoted Christians, and thus she is spouse to her own son. Other poets have toyed with this same conundrum (for example, John Donne in "La Corona"), but readers today may find such theological foreplay in bad taste. The scene switches in the penultimate stanza to the Via Dolorosa where Mary hears an outcry. She follows it to a green place where she stares "at a strange shadow thrown." At Golgotha barely recognizing "the boy I bore alone / No doctor near to cut the cord," she ends the poem with the same dank resolution she entertains throughout: "I am my own and not my own."

It is difficult to understand why Gunn has not distanced himself from this rather saccharine poem. It has been reprinted three times: in *The Sense of Movement* (1957), *The Explorers* (1969), and *Collected Poems* (1994). One can only surmise that Gunn is proud of its tight form, written as it is in seven-line stanzas of iambic tetrameter, rhyming *a b b a a b c,* with the final stanza tightened to *a b b a a b b,* a form similar to the stanzaic forms of other poems written in the same period: "Carnal Knowledge" and "The Silver Age" (poems that also use refrain lines), "Julian the Apostate," "Lazarus Not Raised," and that enduring metaphor for coming-out teens, "The Allegory of the Wolf Boy." There remain, however, unnerving anachronisms in "Jesus and his Mother." The scholars in the temple, for example, who quiz Jesus at age twelve, wear "furred" gowns (more typical for a Cambridge don than a rabbinic teacher in Herod's Jerusalem), and when birthing Jesus, Mary is unassisted, "no doctor near to cut the cord." The evoked birth scene is modern. In ancient times, a woman was lucky to have a midwife or neighbor lady, if anyone, handy for the event. But in spite of these time warps, the poem is interesting, coming as it does from Thom Gunn, the San Francisco poet who book after book is pictured in leather, the man who at age nine objected to kneeling at his boarding-school bedside for night prayers, telling the matron, as Gunn recalls, "I don't want to do this. Could I just sit on my bed while they're doing this because I don't believe in God" (Nuwer 75). She was horrified and he was punished, maybe punished enough to convince him to keep a little piety for future use in a poem like "Jesus and his Mother." For whatever cause, the poem is as gently pious as any by Jessica Powers or Thomas Merton, as embarrassing an insight as that may be to a poet who has an agnostic reputation to maintain in an age when it is chichi to be areligious.

A contrastive use of Mary is found in Gunn's poem "Expression," published in 1982, some thirty years after his first Marian poem. Structurally quite unlike the earlier poem, "Excursion" has twenty-eight lines of free verse, with a break after line 9. The first part is a bewildered condemnation of confessional poetry:

Mother doesn't understand,
and they hate Daddy, the noted alcoholic.
They write with black irony
of breakdown, mental institution,
and suicide attempt.

The hallowed subject matters of Plath, Sexton, and Sharon Olds are here
reduced to a pitiful lump of self-serving poetics. Gunn even questions the
sincerity of and motivation for such writing: "the experience / does not
always seem first-hand." So he goes out to the Art Museum looking for
something, something he cannot articulate, and when he stops in front of a
madonna-and-child, he knows this is it. What a strange salvific experience: the altarpiece is cold, expressionless, the virgin stolid and the child
in no-man's-land, neither childish nor mature. Somehow this presence
brings him peace:

The sight quenches, like water
after too much birthday cake.

The woman who had been all too human in "Jesus and his Mother" has
become a piece of static art in the poet's golden years, yet this new version
of the virgin comforts him because the eyes of mother and child have one
thing going for them that confessional poets lack: mystery. Mary and Jesus
in their mutual sorrows and joys have lasted through the centuries, and this
realization seems to resonate in the gay poet who finds identification with
the heavenly pair rewarding after his desiccated experience with confessional poetry. The altarpiece does not whine. It is a tribute to pluck and
patience, the virtues that a modern gay man most needs to survive the
homophobic chaos of modern life. While confessional poets pull the
reader into the maelstrom of unspeakable angst and abuse, misery loving
company, the madonna-and-child could not care less if you empathize or
not, their struggles having already merited history's plaudits. The Virgin
soothes in Gunn what the whiners rubbed sore.

Just as there are evident contrasts between Gunn's early and late uses of
Mary, there are contrasts between his youthful vision of the Garden of
Eden and his later vision of the same. The 1953 poem "Looking Glass"
portrays an itinerant groundskeeper who does not follow the ordinary rules
of gardening and thus is mostly unemployed:

What little watering I do is pleasure,
I let the birds on pear and apple sup,
I do not use my clippers or my rake,

> I do not tie the fallen branches up,
> I leave the weeding and employ my leisure
> In idling on the lawns or by the lake.

He is not the sort of man one would hire to tidy the property, spurning as he does the traditional role of Adam in Eden, a role made vivid by Milton's first man who daily had "to tend plant, herb and flower" (*Paradise Lost* 9.206) even though Milton's Adam realizes that a night or two "with wanton growth derides" anything he prunes or binds. For some reason, Gunn's Adam is uninterested in taming the foliage in spite of his observation that "I still hold Eden in my garden wall." He is a bon vivant who ends this poem a Narcissus figure, looking in a mirror:

> I take it from my pocket and gaze long,
> Forgetting in my pleasure how I pass
> From town to town, damp-booted, unemployed.

This is the kind of rebellious material we expect, of course, from an undergraduate at Cambridge in the early 1950s, a young man whose vision of the good does not extend much beyond himself. Community needs do not interest him—he is Lazarus of the rusting hoe, intent on self-gratification.

Gunn's later Adam pays for this adolescent nonchalance. "Misanthropos" (1965), a long poem in seventeen parts, follows the dark survival of the last man to inhabit earth. He is not "heroic," as Parini has noted (144), but a very ordinary man: he sleeps on stones, fashions clothes out of fur, builds a fire, contemplates the dust, and meditates on the hard lot of being the only human to live after whatever wiped out the rest of the race. Suddenly, in the final segments of the poem (titled "The First Man"), he sees a group of forty men and women appearing on the rim of a rock ridge. He agonizes to join them but frightens the first one he approaches. The creature stumbles back, and the narrator offers him his arm. The others file by:

> They turn and look at me full,
> and as they pass they name me.

It is a reversal of the Eden ritual in which Adam names all the creatures as they parade in front of him (Gen. 2:19-20), but it contains the same problem after the naming:

> What is the name Adam speaks
> after the schedule of beasts?

In Genesis, Adam is disappointed to find no mate among the catalogue of animals, and in Gunn's poem the narrator experiences a similar loneliness, until he turns to the "first man" he originally frightened and reacts to him with a "bitter dizziness." It is, of course, love at second sight:

> I stretch out the word to him
> from which conversations start,
> naming him, also, by name.

If this linkage of man to man were the end of the poem, it would be an interesting enough twist on the Adam-Eve pairing by transmutation of the biblical duo into a gay partnering, but the poem continues with four more quatrains to demonstrate that the narrator gets more than a partner:

> Turn out toward others, meeting their look at full,
>   Until you have completely stared
> On all there is to see. Immeasurable,
>   The dust yet to be shared.

The eye contact all around leaves no end of joy in the narrator's heart as he calculates the futurity of boundless promiscuous coupling. It is difficult to understand how Falck cannot find in Gunn "the kind of experience which must be the ultimate justification of any belief in, and acceptance of, human relationships" (39). "Misanthropos" is full of the search for human contact. But Falck is blinded, it seems to me, by homophobia:

> The special importance of Gunn's poetry . . . is that it touches on those buried areas of the human spirit where various kinds of fetishism, auto-eroticism, narcissism, homosexuality or fascism may have their common sources. (40)

How uncommonly sage to lump all these undesirable "isms" in one heinous group. Moreover, Falck stumbles over his own Americaphobia:

> If Gunn could put away the vacant counter-cultural slovenliness of his California ethic . . . he might be able to recover the faith which once tied him in with English poetry's finest traditions; he might at the same time be able to get himself clear of today's fashionably neo-primitive dissolution of the moral and social human being into his constituent compulsions and energies and become a much-needed recruit to the battered ranks of humanism. (41)

In other words, Gunn should renounce his expatriation and return to England where he could write uplifting verses and join the ranks of moral giants (like Ted Hughes). Ten years later, Paul Giles joins in the California-bashing:

> Gunn has indeed assimilated Falck's caution against poetic hedonism, but instead of regressing into older forms of humanism or English moral seriousness he has advanced into a postmodern, Americanized sensibility. (97)

One wonders how much of this nastiness is intended to get Gunn back to his birthplace, away from the immoral hellhole that is America. Such critics fail to see that "Misanthropos" is an important poem because it is moral, is not narcissistic; it is a wonderful understanding of man's struggle against the dark side of himself. Since Gunn was deep into Camus at the time, particularly *La Chute* (Haffenden 44), we should expect heaviness in the lines, and of course we do get that heaviness, but what begins as a very down poem ends with the euphoria that Gunn loved in the 1960s and 1970s as some gay men prowled endlessly, night after night, for new sexual contacts, without fear of a deadly disease.

That all changed, of course, in the 1980s, and Gunn, ever responsive to his gay community's permutations, produced one of the most sensitive collections of AIDS poetry yet to be published, *The Man With Night Sweats* (1992). The only Bible poem in the set is "Sacred Heart," appropriately a crucifixion poem. It comes to us in iambic pentameter and rime embrasée.

> You dreamt your dying friend hung crucified
> In his front room, against the mantelpiece.
> Yet it was Christmas, when you went outside
> The shoppers bustled, bells rang without cease.

The dream is offset by the Christmas season with bustling shoppers and the smell of evergreens. Outside, festivity; inside, the shock of the dying man. Then after the death come insomnia for the narrator, because sleep might "mislay the wound of feeling," and a vision of "the heart, His Heart, broken with love." At this point the biblical crucifixion wanders into a single image, the one exaggerated by St. Margaret Mary into a devotion. The narrator examines his own side and hallucinates his own heart "losing rich purple drops with every beat," but the vision passes as the narrator discovers he is merely looking at a religious card (the Sacred Heart picture is a favorite on funeral cards distributed at wakes and contains a prayer and the deceased's date of birth and death on the reverse side of the picture) which he drops into the trash. This act of metaphorical deposition is not a rejection of his own pain and suffering, but rather represents his understanding that eventually grief cannot be codified in the Sacred Heart but must be internalized in one's own "sacred heart." The agnostic disposes of the tasteless holy card, while the suffering servant gets on with the business of living in order to make sense out of the plague for a community still in shock from the onslaught.

Throughout his career Gunn has used the Bible for his own purposes. Sticking close to Bible stories and figures in his early poems, he has worked his way into a personal mythology that can cull biblical references when he needs them to settle a point, but his poetry no longer depends on the Bible to carry meaning. Allusions surely enhance meaning, but for Gunn creativity has come to include fewer and fewer references to the Bible. One cannot predict the future of Gunn's themes and images, of course, but he gives no indication of returning to tight biblical material such as he used in early pieces. We no more expect him to write another "Jesus and His Mother" today than we are surprised to learn how he mined the Bible in the 1950s for such a piece. In those early days the gay agnostic wrote veiled verses under the aura of Duncan and Hart Crane, but with the gradual erosion of internalized homophobia, Gunn stands colossal on his own sense of gay poetics, acknowledging his own debt to Duncan in particular, who blazed the trail not just for gays but also for modern American poets generally to write openly (Gunn, *Occasions* 134). Gunn is a totally out poet, and he sifts from Bible lore as he needs to for an occasional image. Meanwhile he reprints without shame the early biblical poems that still cause readers to admire his craft and wonder how much of an agnostic he really is. Piety, of course, can exist separate from religion, but they share many of the same vehicles: a reverence for the unknown, an acceptance of a greater power, a need for enlightenment and redemption. Even as an avowed pagan, Gunn resonates to biblical material, both mythical and historical. It informs his work. Indeed, no poet can ignore what has riddled the ages and what millions champion. Gunn does not accept the religious panorama, but he does use individual biblical brushstrokes without apology to carry meaning in his verses.

WORKS CITED

Alvarez, A. "Marvell and Motorcycles." *The New Yorker* (August 1, 1994): 77-80.

Barnstone, Willis, ed. *The Other Bible*. San Francisco: Harper & Row, 1984.

Duncan, Robert. *The Opening of the Field*. New York: New Directions, 1960.

Falck, Colin. "Uncertain Violence." *New Review* 3.32 (November 1976): 37-41.

Fraser, G. S. "The Poetry of Thom Gunn." *Critical Quarterly* 3.4 (1961): 359-367.

Gallagher, John. "Top Gunn." *The Advocate* 635 (August 10, 1993): 57-59.

Garrett, George, ed. *Botteghe Oscure Reader.* Middleton, CT: Wesleyan UP, 1974.

Giles, Paul. "Landscapes of Repetition: The Self-Parodic Nature of Thom Gunn's Later Poetry." *Critical Quarterly* 29.2 (1987): 85-99.

Gregori, Mina. "Caravaggio Today." *The Age of Caravaggio.* Ed. John P. O'Neill. New York: The Metropolitan Museum of Art, 1985. 28-47.

_____ . "The Sacrifice of Isaac." *The Age of Caravaggio.* Ed. John P. O'Neill. New York: The Metropolitan Museum of Art, 1985. 282-288.

Gunn, Thom. *Collected Poems.* New York: Farrar, Straus & Giroux, 1994.

_____ . *The Occasions of Poetry: Essays in Criticism and Autobiography.* Ed. Clive Wilmer. London: Faber & Faber, 1982.

Haffenden, John. "Thom Gunn." *Viewpoints: Poets in Conversation with John Haffenden.* London: Faber & Faber, 1981. 35-56.

Hagstrom, Jack, and George Bixby. *Thom Gunn: A Bibliography 1940-1978.* London: Bertram Rota, 1979.

Herdt, Gilbert H. *Guardians of the Flutes.* New York: McGraw-Hill, 1981.

_____ . ed. *Ritualized Homosexuality in Melanesia.* Berkeley: U of California P, 1984.

Hibbard, Howard. *Caravaggio.* New York: Harper & Row, 1983.

Jay, Nancy. *Throughout Your Generations Forever.* Chicago: U of Chicago P, 1992.

Karlen, Arno. *Sexuality and Homosexuality.* New York: Norton, 1971.

Kierkegaard, Søren. *The Sickness Unto Death.* Ed. Howard V. Hong and Edna H. Hong. Princeton: Princeton UP, 1980.

Lidz, Theodore, and Ruth W. Lidz. *Oedipus in the Stone Age.* Madison, CT: International Universities P, 1989.

Michelis, Lidia de. *La Poesia di Thom Gunn.* Firenze: La Nuova Italia Editrice, 1978.

Nuwer, Hank. "Thom Gunn: Britain's Expatriate Poet." *Rendezvous* 21.1 (fall, 1985): 68-78.

Parini, Jay. "Rule and Energy: The Poetry of Thom Gunn." *Massachusetts Review* 23.1 (1982): 134-151.

Scobie, W. T. "Gunn in America." *London Magazine* (December 1977): 5-16.

Swinden, Patrick. "Thom Gunn's Castle." *Critical Quarterly* 19.3 (1977): 43-61.

Wasserburg, Charles. "Angels, Atheists, and Evangelists." *Southern Review* n.s. 28 (1992): 371-389.

Inverted Conversions:
Reading the Bible
and Writing the Lesbian Subject
in *Oranges Are Not the Only Fruit*

Amy Benson Brown, PhD

Emory University

SUMMARY. The prominence of the Bible as intertext in *Oranges Are Not the Only Fruit,* both a coming-of-age and a coming-out story, has puzzled readers. This paper argues that Winterson's articulation of a lesbian subject is actually inseparable from her revisionary engagement of the Bible. By repeatedly turning and re-turning several types of narrative about the origins of identity and story-making, Winterson reconstructs both some biblical texts and a hallmark of the gay and lesbian literary tradition as precursors for the prophetic voice of the main character. *[Article copies available for a fee from The Haworth Document Delivery Service: 1-800-342-9678. E-mail address: getinfo @haworth.com]*

What constitutes a problem is not the thing, or the environment where we find the thing, but the conjunction of the two; something

---

Amy Benson Brown is working on a book about women writers' dialogues with the Bible.

Correspondence may be addressed: Department of English and Philosophy, State University of West Georgia, Carrollton, GA 30118-2200; or by e-mail: abbrn@aol.com.

[Haworth co-indexing entry note]: "Inverted Conversions: Reading the Bible and Writing the Lesbian Subject in *Oranges Are Not the Only Fruit*." Brown, Amy Benson. Co-published simultaneously in *Journal of Homosexuality* (The Haworth Press, Inc.) Vol. 33, No. 3/4, 1997, pp. 233-252; and: *Reclaiming the Sacred: The Bible in Gay and Lesbian Culture* (ed: Raymond-Jean Frontain) Harrington Park Press, an imprint of The Haworth Press, Inc., 1997, pp. 233-252. Single or multiple copies of this article are available for a fee from The Haworth Document Delivery Service [1-800-342-9678, 9:00 a.m. - 5:00 p.m. (EST). E-mail address: getinfo@haworth.com].

unexpected in a usual place (our favourite aunt in our favourite poker parlour) or something usual in an unexpected place (our favourite poker parlour in our favourite aunt).

–Winterson, *Oranges* (45)

The heroine of Jeanette Winterson's *Oranges Are Not the Only Fruit* (1985) discovers this fact about the significance of context to interpretation when her grade-school art projects are repeatedly misread, yet this passage also describes a "problem" experienced by many readers of Jeanette Winterson's first and semiautobiographic novel. The structure of this parodic tale of a young girl's recognition and acceptance of her lesbianism within a British evangelical community is patterned on the first eight books of the Bible. For some feminist readers, finding the Bible in a favorite coming-out story "constitutes a problem" because of the traditional association of the Bible with heterosexism; for others, finding a coming-out story in a favorite *Bildungsroman* plot is equally disorienting.

Laurel Bollinger's assertion that while Winterson's larger engagement of the Bible is complex, her "overt references" draw upon only "the most general and conventional sense of each text" (365), indicates that the critical "problem" here is not merely the intertextuality of each chapter with the Bible but the broader process of resignification through which the Bible becomes a vehicle in the representation of a lesbian subject.[1] Because this novel is not only a *Bildungsroman,* but also a *Künstlerroman,* a chronicle of a writer's development, this resignification process is actually inscribed in the plot and narrative strategies of the text.[2] By the final chapter, "Ruth," Winterson has broken the sentence of traditional interpretations of the Bible and remade some biblical texts into precursors for the articulation of a lesbian authority.[3] This process of resignification is accomplished through a revisionist weaving of four basic types of narrative. After briefly defining them, I will examine their function in the figuration of a lesbian subjectivity against the ground of the Bible in *Oranges.*

The most obvious narrative type complicating the basically autobiographical plot is the fable. This seemingly bizarre feature of the text is actually a common strategy of works of feminist biblical revision which frequently either collapse or contextualize biblical stories with other myths.[4] In *Oranges* collages of fairy tale, folklore, biblical symbols, and Arthurian romance interrupt the "straight" or mainly chronological narrative in every chapter and grow in length from the brief fragment in "Genesis" to the extended tale of Winnet Stonejar and the sorcerer in "Ruth."[5] These fable interludes symbolically rehearse the anxieties driving the plot.

As in other works of biblical revision, the fables' parallels with biblical themes and imagery effectively deny the biblical narrative a position of supreme or sole authority and foreground the malleable textuality of the Bible.[6]

A less obvious, but even more crucial type of recurring narrative is the ontological tale, which generally functions to establish identity.[7] This novel not only begins with the story of Jeanette's origins but returns to it at key junctures and complicates its significance with other stories of begetting. In *Oranges,* the ontological narratives center around the issues of sexuality and creativity, the protagonist's identity as a lesbian and as a producer of texts. But that subject, that identity, is not immediately readable, and the resulting difficulties of interpretation and representation fuel a third recurrent type of narrative in *Oranges*: the hermeneutical tale, or story about language and story-making. Episodes throughout the book return to the question of how to "interpret the signs and wonders" (17) of the material world, including the sign and wonder of her own sexual being. The Bible in these narratives often functions both as subject and trope because the disjunction between her church's interpretive practices and those of the larger society sparks Jeanette's interpretive inquiry. Furthermore, the rigorous biblical training of this child who learned to read from Deuteronomy ensures that she will couch her meditations in biblical language and figures.

The fourth and final type of recurrent narrative within the autobiographical fiction, the conversion story, contains the structure on which the larger plot turns. The miniature stories of the " 'converted sweep' " and the " 'Hallelujah Giant' " (7-8) introduce the formulaic structure of the conversion narrative which describes an individual's progress from doubt and questioning through crisis and epiphany to salvation and grace. Almost everyone in *Oranges* has a conversion story. Dedicated to the Lord from birth, Jeanette needs no conventional conversion story, though she is the agent of many others' conversions through her persuasive preaching. All four of these narrative types within the autobiographic fiction (fable, ontological, hermeneutic, and conversion) unfold concurrently, an ontological story told during a fable, or a lesson on hermeneutics explicated during a conversion.[8] The conversion narrative, however, occupies a key position. Just as the Book of Ruth, with its focus on love and loyalty between women, offers a paradigmatic biblical intertext for the novel's themes, the structure of the conversion narrative is paradigmatic for the process of biblical revision, for the crucial achievement of resignification.[9] Examining the development of these stories from "Genesis" to "Ruth" reveals that all of these narrative types coalesce to collectively bear witness to an inverted conversion that becomes Jeanette's own unconventional conversion story and enables the final representation of a lesbian subject who is not divinely damned but saved by her own authorial grace.

"Genesis," the opening chapter of *Oranges,* borrows its biblical counterpart's central themes as well as its title. The key word of the ancient text, "toledot" or begettings, actually marks a genre of ontological narratives including the biblical creation stories and lists of lineages.[10] Winterson's "Genesis" similarly represents the scene of Jeanette's begetting and thus initiates the novel's concerns with both origins and with story-making and interpretation.

The first page informs us that Jeanette's earliest memories are inextricable from a sense of personal difference and destiny: "I cannot recall a time when I did not know that I was special" (3). The repetition of her individual creation story—which opens the novel and is retold in a heightened, poetic passage in the chapter's middle—suggests that the key to Jeanette's specialness lies in her origins, particularly in her mother.

> She had a mysterious attitude toward the begetting of children; it wasn't that she couldn't do it, more that she didn't want to. She was very bitter about the Virgin Mary getting there first. So she did the next best thing and arranged for a foundling. That was me. (3)

The mother's desire for her own virginal conception not only parodicly pairs her with the Virgin Mary, it also implicitly positions Jeanette as Christ, an analogy which becomes more obvious in later chapters as Jeanette recounts her betrayal and sacrifice by the "servants of God" (170).

The gendered reversal underlying the designation of the divine infant as female reflects the unusually matriarchal character of Jeanette's family and church, both institutions founded on patrilineage and patriarchy. Sheep surround the nativity scenes of Jeanette's childhood but "no Wise Men" because her mother "didn't believe there were any" (3). This literal lack of figurines of the magi that attended Christ's birth foreshadows the lack of wise male figures in Jeanette's community. Her father, referred to sometimes only as her mother's "husband" (5), lumbers ineffectually along the periphery of Jeanette's childhood, while the vigorous participation of women in her church even includes female lay preaching until the religious hierarchy represses it in the novel's central crisis in "Judges."

The novel's initial, comic account of Jeanette's origins, however, proves to be only a prosaic backdrop for a second rendition. The abrupt lyricism of the second ontological story, set off from what precedes and follows it by episode markers, imitates a stylistic technique of the Book of

Genesis which suddenly switches genre from prose to poetry to underscore significant passages (Fokkelman 36-40). In the following excerpt,
the use of biblical echoes and poetic devices creates a manic intensity that
is at once parodic and serious, very different from the opening story's tone
of bemused mockery. Jeanette glosses her arrival,

> My mother, walking out that night, dreamed a dream and sustained it
> in daylight. She would get a child, train it, build it, dedicate it to the
> Lord:
>
> a missionary child
> a servant of God,
> a blessing.

Following a star to an orphanage, she discovers a child and declares it hers
"from the Lord." Turmoil, however, displaces the ordinarily serene time
of bonding as the mother "for seven days and seven nights . . . sang to the
child, and stabbed the demons" because she "understood how jealous the
Spirit is of flesh." The mother emerges victorious from this struggle, and
the episode concludes by solidifying her claim as maker of the child.

> Her flesh now, sprung from her head.
> Her vision.
> Not the jolt beneath the hip bone, but water
> and the word. (10)

Understanding this striking episode is crucial to an understanding of all
the ontological stories that follow it. Like the first account of Jeanette's
origins, it emphasizes a fleshless, sexless, even intellectual begetting. But
the perspective on that generative act and its actor has shifted. Previously
the point of ironic comparison for the mother was the figure of Mary. Now,
and equally ironically, it is Milton's Satan. The flesh that springs from the
rebelling angel's head in *Paradise Lost* is the female child, Sin, who is
fated to bear demons eternally. Thus, this passage both introduces the
symbol of the demon (which later appears as the "orange demon," the
individual genius or spirit of Jeannette's sexuality) and underscores the
issue of inheritance.

One value of ontological myths is their ability to explain personal traits
and identity. The rebelling spirit that later enables Jeanette's refusal of
heterosexual expectations is prefigured here in her mother's rejection of
bodily procreation for a begetting by mind and will instead. Yet the episode's final line which asserts that this begetting gave her mother a "way

out" for "years and years" suggests the end point of the resemblance of Jeanette to her maker/mother. While both are rebellious angels, the climax of the novel–its chief divergence from this plot offering spirituality as an escape from the flesh–is the contrast between Jeanette's claiming of her demon and her mother's denial and betrayal.

The framing episodes for this poetic interlude also intertwine the themes of sexual identity with creative vocation or mission. The depiction of the mother's (pro)creative act is preceded by the brief fable of a beautiful princess, so intelligent and sensitive that she was in danger of perishing "by her own flame." An old, hunchbacked woman, well versed in "the secrets of magic," recognizes the princess's gifts and bequeaths her role to the princess. Besides milking the goats, her job as community wisewoman includes the composition of ritual songs and education of the people (9). Vocation and destiny again appear intertwined in the very short episode following, almost as a musical coda, the poetic interlude:

> We stood on the hill and my mother said, "This world is full of sin."
> We stood on the hill and my mother said, "You can change the world." (10)

Although the narrative mode here is no longer that of the fable, the strong use of ritualistic repetition connects this passage to both the fable episode and poetic interlude preceding it. By implication, the revisionist mission suggested here includes the wisewoman's vocation of composing new rituals.

For Jeanette's mother, having a mission means having a map with continents clearly marked and legible, but Jeanette never finds the meaning of the "world" or "change" so immediately readable. Since, like the Book of Genesis, this first chapter inaugurates all the key themes of the rest of the work, the hermeneutical questions that most concern the middle of the novel first appear here as well. Reading young Jeanette's palm, a gypsy woman declares that she will "never marry" or "be still." This apparently random memory actually raises several related interpretive issues at the heart of the later meditations on hermeneutics. The first issue is the body's ability to function as a sign; the gypsy reads the future in the lines of Jeanette's palm. In the next chapter, her family and community misread Jeanette's body, interpreting a spell of deafness as a sign of rapture. Significantly, the only adult capable of reading this bodily symptom correctly, Miss Jewsbury, is a closeted lesbian in the church family. Jeanette herself elicits this correct reading by writing, on a post-office form no less, her condition (25). These episodes imply a linkage between sexuality and textuality that continues throughout the book, but what is it about Jeanette's "hand" that speaks of her sexuality?

Oranges is, after all, also a *Künstlerroman*, a portrait of a writer's development: these links between sexuality and textuality suggest that here the emergence of a lesbian subject is inseparable from the emergence of a writer. Significantly, Jeanette's first encounter with a potential lesbian community is at a "paper shop," later referred to as "the forbidden paper shop" (77). By some symbolic slippage, paper itself carries the connotation of forbidden fruit. But, as a reader familiar only with the literal interpretations of her fundamentalist community, young Jeanette misinterprets "unnatural passions," her mother's euphemism for the paper-shop owners' homosexuality: "I thought she meant they put chemicals in their sweets" (7). A brief examination of the development of these hermeneutical quandaries and ontological narratives in the middle four chapters—"Exodus," "Leviticus," "Numbers," and "Deuteronomy"—will show how Jeanette's growing interpretive sophistication pressures the explanatory power of the old story of origins.

Most of "Exodus" explores the disjunction between the ways Jeanette's church and the larger society read the world. Unlike God's pillar of smoke that leads the Hebrews through the wilderness, the interpretive guidelines given her by her evangelical community leave Jeanette in a fog bank as she enters the school system (48). The failure of the secular world, represented by her needlework teacher, Mrs. Virtue, to award a prize to Jeanette's imaginative recreations of biblical scenes teaches Jeanette about the significance of context to interpretation and the possibility of relative value. These needlework samplers, which evoke the historically feminine craft of textiles, are inadequate mediums for Jeanette's self-expression. Furthermore, Jeanette's analysis of the failure of her sampler to win an award offers a hermeneutical lesson that marks the progress of the writer's education in the larger text: like the doomed sampler, this novel has "everything, adventure, pathos, mystery" (44) but, unlike the unreadable textile, this text actually won the prestigious Whitbread prize for first novels.

This happy outcome likely is attributable to the existence of one audience capable of correctly interpreting Jeanette's childhood representations. While the context and audience of Mrs. Virtue's classroom render the meaning of her biblical sampler "all wrong," it was "absolutely right" in the living room of her best friend and church mentor, "Testifying Elsie" (45). Analyzing the criteria for judgement by these two different audiences leads Jeannette to a hermeneutical epiphany about the role of the perceiver in shaping the perceived. It is this lesson that later opens some of her biblical intertexts, like Ruth, to function as lesbian texts.[11] Not incidentally, Jeanette's "first theological disagreement" (60) arises at this point.

Jeanette's allegorical explication of this "disagreement" through the long fable in "Leviticus" returns to the ontological issue first presented in "Genesis" of fleshless begetting or creation by mind and will alone. In the opening episode, Jeanette's mother and a church friend scream hymns to drown out the sounds of fornication drifting over from the heathens "Next Door." After an account of dreary pamphleteering, Jeanette announces her misgivings about the preacher's sermon, which insists that the essence of perfection is a "flawlessness" unattainable in the mortal realm (60). The remaining half of the chapter offers a fable of a beautiful and reputedly "perfect" wisewoman (reminiscent of the heroine of the opening fable) who is first courted, then beheaded by a prince on a quest for a "flawless" woman (61). While this narrative's leap into fable may seem unrelated to the opening depiction of fornication, its allegorical meditation on the meaning of perfection implicitly links the mother's orthodox despisal of the flesh with a fascistic and traditionally masculine quest for perfect control over creation and generativity.

Disappointed by his failure to find a perfect woman, the prince creates a tome instead, titled *The Holy Mystery of Perfection.* When at last the perfect woman appears but refuses to marry him, he insists, "you must, I've written all about you" (64). The focus on purity and the related drive toward the production of a "perfect race" in the prince's treatise (62) offer a parodic nod toward the purity codes at the heart of the Book of Leviticus.[12] For three days and nights, the wisewoman attempts to disabuse the prince of his conviction that perfection is flawlessness, arguing that perfection truly means "the search for balance, for harmony." For illustration, she offers her own perfect balance of qualities that render her "symmetrical in every respect" (64). Devilish advisors, however, remind the Prince that he cannot retract his book's thesis and maintain his authority. The blood from the subsequential execution of the wisewoman drowns all but the Prince, who escapes up a tree and, like so many leaders, begins to believe his own propaganda, consoling himself that "at least" he has "stamped out a very great evil" (67). Just as he wonders who will replace the drowned advisors, an orange seller–which in the language of this novel translates as a demon vendor–comes by and offers the prince some reading for the road. This book, about "some geezer" who "gets a bolt through the neck" draws a clear parallel between *Frankenstein* and the prince's fantasy of flawless creation: " 'it tells you how to build a perfect person, it's all about the man who does it, but it's no good if you ain't got the equipment' " (67).

This fable's concluding reference to *Frankenstein* suggests that the mother's fantasy of sexless creation, the child sprung from her head in the poetic interlude in "Genesis," can be seen as variation of the fantasy which substitutes intellectual for bodily reproduction. Yet I would suggest that in the structure and alternation of genres within this chapter Winterson attempts to insert a woman's body back into this traditionally masculine ontology. Winterson's narrative here performs the definition it endorses of perfection as balance and symmetry, rather than flawlessness, by building the chapter around an obvious flaw—the rupture between the autobiographical narrative and the fable. Roughly equal in length (eight pages of autobiography followed by seven of fable), the two types of narrative both feature three sections. Thus, the chapter's composition provides a symmetrical, balanced whole that celebrates the hole at its center—the abrupt gap between narrative modes. By quite literally breaking the narrative sequence, this chapter ruptures the sentence of purist patriarchal ontologies with its own performance of narrative creation through order and balance.[13]

In the larger balancing act of the novel's structure, this highly metaphoric, antilinear chapter is followed by "Numbers," a chapter principally devoted to the progress of the autobiographical plot: now an adolescent, Jeanette, "quite by mistake," falls in love with the equally innocent Melanie (77). As the purity codes of the Book of Leviticus inform Winterson's "Leviticus," so two themes from the Book of Numbers inform this chapter: the difficulty of counting the faithful and the wandering of the chosen in the wilderness. Distinguishing the faithful here becomes a classification problem as categories of faithful and unfaithful, natural and unnatural, collide. Jeannette's interrogation of the meaning of the term "unnatural passions" (at once so despised and relished by her church) is related to her growing mistrust of the ontological story provided by her mother.

Jeannette explicitly compares her discovery of her adoption papers "while searching for a pack of playing cards" with her discovery that her mother had "rewritten the ending of *Jane Eyre*" (74-75).[14] When Jeannette was small, her missionary-minded mother read the novel to her "over and over," apparently forever coupling Jane with St. John and the church. One "dreadful day in the back corner of the library," Jeannette finds that Jane actually forgoes a missionary life to return to Rochester, and she vows never more to play cards or read *Jane Eyre*. Both of the texts linked here, the adoption papers and *Jane Eyre*, represent the mother's dishonesty and her denial of sexuality. Jeanette no more came expressly from God than Jane went on to do missionary work. Furthermore, Jane's choice of independence and a sexual life places Jeanette's own calling in question.[15]

The conclusion of "Numbers" expressly presents this matrix of issues and effectively sets the stage for the coming crisis. As their intimacy intensifies, Jeanette and Melanie ask each other: "Do you think this is Unnatural Passion?" (89). While they read their relationship as a natural passion and feel safe in the bosom of their church "family," a brief fable offers the last word, predicting the coming conflict when the church interprets their relationship otherwise. Here, the comfort of the old English mead hall and the warm festive gathering of the "elect" is shown to depend upon the ontological myth of masculine primogeniture.

> Father and Son. Father and Son.
> It has always been this way, nothing can intrude.
> Father Son and Holy Ghost
> Outside, the rebels storm the Winter Palace. (89)

This concluding image, contrasting inside and out, casts Christian myth within a spatial metaphor embodying the dichotomous terms Jeanette is coming to question: faithful (inside) versus unfaithful (outside), and natural (inside) versus unnatural (outside).

Jeanette's growing inability to sort these categories into eternally opposed camps, as her mother would, raises epistemolgical and hermeneutical questions that necessitate the brief discourse on interpretation that interrupts the narrative at this point. Like the biblical Deuteronomy, Winterson's "Deuteronomy" lays down a few commandments, but these tell us less how to live than how to read. More pointedly, they insist that reading is vital to both personal survival and the shaping of a larger history. By protesting the strict distinction between storytelling and fact, Winterson suggests that the "given" reality or circumstances of life are not natural and immutable. Nor is the received wisdom of a culture unsullied by political and economic considerations: "Knowing what to believe had its advantages. It built an empire and kept people where they belonged, in the bright realm of the wallet" (93). To combat the normalizing and policing function of historical narrative, Winterson recommends a steady diet of individually made stories, which offer a sustaining "order and balance" and echo the definition of perfection offered by the "Leviticus" fable. The emergence of the critical reader and crafter of story here, just past the novel's midpoint, summarizes the hermeneutical lessons offered thus far and signals the climax to come in "Joshua," "Judges," and "Ruth" as the gifted preacher abandons orthodoxy for prophecy.

Earlier we noted that Jeanette's ontological story, dedicated to God from birth by her mother, differentiates her from the other characters by depriving her of a conventional conversion story. "Joshua" and "Judges," however, represent Jeanette's own conversion story. The church's condemnation of Jeanette's sexual orientation, the attempted exorcism, and her eventual expulsion from the church induce the necessary stage of doubt and internal crisis that precipitates conversion. However, Jeanette's struggle does not duplicate the novel's other conversions which conclude with a turn toward the church; instead, her story mirrors them with an inverse image, reflecting her turn inward, away from the church. Furthermore, this inverted-conversion story is the axis upon which the other types of stories (ontological, fable, and hermeneutic) turn. A reading of the last three chapters will show that this turn directs all the energies of the novel toward the establishment of Jeanette's narrative voice as prophetic, which is by definition at once heretical and authoritative.

The church's attempt to exorcise the demon of "unnatural passions" forces Jeanette to confront her particular demon and choose a "difficult, different time" rather than sacrifice "what [she] found" (108-109). Thus, the attempt to drive out the "orange demon" only succeeds at driving it in. The physical deprivation and psychological brutality of the exorcism force Jeanette to choose between a known community and a self that she is only just coming to know. While awaiting a last meeting with her lover, Jeanette visits through a dream the city of Lost Chances. This episode expands the earlier link between sexuality and textuality, suggesting that her sexual identity and autonomy are inextricable from her need to write her own story.

In this Foucauldian nightmare Jeanette's fellow inmates are marked quite literally by signs that correspond to their place in the prison. Jeanette dreams of a long ascent:

> In the middle of the turret, an iron stairway spiralled up and up; I started to climb, along with many others, but each time we passed one of the nooks, its inmate tried to push us off. I was the only person left when the stairway stopped in front of a glass door. The letters on the door spelt BOOKSHOP: OPEN. I went inside, there was a woman at the counter, a number of buyers and browsers, and a team of young women translating *Beowulf.* (111)

Even this nightmare confirms a central message of all of Jeanette's ontological stories, that she is special, as she alone reaches the tower's peak. But her prize, the achievement of her destined place, threatens a fate worse than death. In this bookshop, also called the Room of the Final Disappointment, the only options are to buy, sell, or eternally translate an ancient canonical text. The fear of being destined to perpetuate *Beowulf* perhaps reflects an anxiety of authorship in the larger autobiographical narrative about her relationship to the canonical text by which she learned to read, the Bible. Foucault's explanation of the success of the panopticon reveals the particular dread driving this anxiety of authorship: "that the inmates should be caught up in a power situation of which they are themselves the bearers" (201). But if one must bear the words of the founding texts of culture because they are integral to all our subjectivities, how can one bear them differently to alter their significations and thus their cultural functions?

This question is not unrelated to this novel's fascination with ontologies. On a metalevel, Winterson rewrites the creative myth of purely masculine begetting by creating a dialogue between the Bible and gay and lesbian literary tradition. *Oranges* weaves its plot through a grid of references to literature by gay and lesbian authors. Vying for prizes in grade school, young Jeanette abandons "biblical themes" and reproduces Tennessee Williams's *A Streetcar Named Desire* in pipe cleaners (48). In another example, the self-righteous volume written by the fascistic prince in the fantastical episode in "Leviticus" no doubt misreads Oscar Wilde in its dedication "to the importance of being earnest" (62). Furthermore, the job Jeanette takes after she leaves home provides "at least" a "room of [her] own" (158). But it is really not surprising that Jeanette should understand her struggle for independence through Woolf's prose or her desire for "wild nights" (170) through Dickinson's poetry, since her church mentor, "Testifying Elsie," shared works like Rossetti's "Goblin Market" (30) with her even as her mother taught her to read by using Deuteronomy as a primer (15). As these few examples suggest, the existence of an alternative literary heritage aids Winterson in making a difference in the biblical word she bears. In short, the novel's intertextuality with a gay and lesbian literary heritage functions at the level of composition as yet another ontological story, claiming 'this too is where I come from, so this too is where I may go.'[16] This alternative ontology enables a writing beyond the heroine's traditional ending in death or marriage and a writing beyond the prison bookshop's stultifying model of literary production as translation.[17] In other words, Irigaray's "economy of the same" (74) implied in the patrilineal begetting in Numbers—"Father and Son. Father and Son" (89)—is implicitly countered by the alternative literary ontology embedded in the text.

Complications in the ontological story of the lesbian author, however, surface in an implicit response to a particularly influential textual precursor, Radclyffe Hall's *The Well of Loneliness*. Since its controversial appearance in 1928, Hall's novel has served as a cornerstone of the lesbian canon, even being described as "*the* lesbian novel" (Whitlock 558).

Though many readers resist as heterosexist the novel's description of homosexuality as "inversion," Hall strategically borrowed Havelock Ellis's ideas to promote the recognition and acceptance of homosexuality (Whitlock 557-559). The adoption in *The Well of Loneliness* of the patriarchal discourse of sexology to convey a representation of a lesbian subject offers a model for Winterson's appropriation of another patriarchal language, biblical discourse, as the ground against which to figure her representation of a lesbian subject. Indeed, Winterson's appropriation of the Bible seems to answer the concluding plea of Hall's novel to "'Acknowledge us, oh God, before the whole world. Give us also the right to our existence!'" (437).

In both novels, moreover, the emergence of a lesbian subject is aligned with a portrait of the artist's development. Readers are left with the sense in both cases that the story culminates in the transformation of protagonist into author.[18] Winterson's novel, though, reformulates the traditional *Künstlerroman* in postmodern fashion: endowing the heroine with the author's first name simultaneously underlines the function of this text as a portrait of the artist and destabilizes the implicit identification of author with protagonist. The dynamics of this representation suggest that Winterson's engagement of Hall's novel, like her engagement of the Bible, is inevitably a revision. Again, all of this revisionist energy focuses on the representation of a lesbian subject.

When Jeanette chooses what the orange demon calls "a difficult, different time" (109) she claims a lesbian identity; however, it is the novel's reformulation of both the precursors of the Bible and *The Well of Loneliness* that locate Jeanette's turning away from her church as no mere escape but as a liberating conversion of perspective. Despite dubious means of economic and emotional support, Jeanette characterizes her departure from the church as "not judgement day, but another morning" (137). This promise of hope suggests that Jeanette's rejection of the church in "Joshua" and "Judges" is simultaneously a rejection of lesbian plots which depict homosexual identity as divine damnation, for which Catherine Stimpson offers *The Well of Loneliness* as a prototype (98). Winterson answers and revises this traditional tragic plot by refiguring one of its key tropes, the representation of lesbian sexuality as monstrous or demonic.

The final, desperate plea for acknowledgement from God uttered by Hall's heroine, Stephen, echos the plea made to her by her own demons. Evoking Mark 5:9, Stephen's demons announce that they will not be cast out because "our name is legion–you dare not disown us!" (437). While Jeanette's irreverent orange demon gives her pretty much the same advice, Winterson's story converts the traditional narrative of damnation into one of salvation by two means. First, by the novel's close Jeanette stands not as supplicant of recognition, and thus of significance, but as recognizer of significance through her claiming of a prophetic role. Jeanette casts this partially as an act of will, reflecting that she could have been chosen to be a "priest instead of a prophet," reciting the "old," "known," words that "comfort and discipline." But she forsakes the "book with the words set out" for a self-made song of her own demons (161). Second, her assumption of this authoritative position is fostered by the conclusion that what is conventionally regarded as outside, despised, or cast out from the authorizing text is actually inseparable from it. In other words, while the church may expel her, she finds her demons, that complex package of her identity, sexuality, and creativity, always already inside the church's founding text, though often in buried ways.

The church council's insistence on reading Jeanette's lesbianism as a symptom of the diseased practice of granting women power in the church offers a final hermeneutical lesson that implicitly unlocks for her both the Bible and her own sense of authorial agency. For once, her community forgoes a literal interpretation and reads "the real problem" as contradicting "the teachings of St. Paul and allowing women power in the church" (134). The extremity of the church leaders' misogyny following a gruelling exorcism would seem to support Hillary Hind's argument that Winterson wins mainstream sympathy for her lesbian character at the expense of the conservative Christians. For some readers, lesbianism in the course of the novel may indeed become "an otherness preferable to the unacceptable otherness of fundamentalism" (Hinds 164). In this novel that is so much about reading, however, I would say that what becomes unacceptable is any totalizing interpretive rubric.[19]

The central event of this final chapter, Jeanette's Christmas visit to her mother, indeed extends "ruth"–compassion and tenderness–to the character most closely allied with fundamentalism in the novel. The warmth of the closing image of the mother, in fact, may jar some readers. Even recognizing the pull of closure towards a comforting ending, the final image of the mother seems at odds with the portrayal of her in the body of the novel as Jeanette's betrayer and maintainer of the phallocratic order.[20] Gone "electronic" with her new wireless (163), she searches for a larger church community in the concluding words of the novel: "This is Kindly Light calling Manchester, come in Manchester, this is Kindly Light" (176). The humor in the choice of a gentle, almost beatific radio alias for this violently dogmatic woman is consistent with the novel's lampooning of her throughout. However, it is very curious that she receives the last word of the novel when her radio mission includes her continuing efforts to combat demons such as those that plague her daughter (174). Perhaps this oddness or disjunction in the narrative's final presentation of the mother is related to a disjunction in the final retelling of the ontological story in this chapter.

The fable of Winnet Stonejar at once offers a frame for the whole novel by retelling the creation story of Winterson's "Genesis" and recapping the major developments of the autobiographic story. A Merlin-like sorcerer's capture of Winnet parallels the mother's denial of Jeanette's adoption and her insistence on a fleshless creation: Winnet eventually "forgot how she came there" and believed she had always been his daughter. He told her "she had no mother, but had been specially trusted to his care by a power-ful spirit" (145). Despite these strong parallels, this retelling of the onto-logical story differs significantly from the original version in genre and gender.

The switch in genre, the same plot delineated within the context of Arthurian legend rather than biblical story, serves to underscore the com-monality in these ancient myths. This narrative strategy simply performs the postmodern commandment of "Deuteronomy," to play with and remake stories. The switch in gender, however, is less easily explained. On one level, it makes sense for the sorcerer to be male because the mother, as we noted earlier, is appropriating a traditionally masculine script in her fantasy of fleshless, sole creation. However, the change in the gender of the parent parallels a strange change in the gender of the lover (146-7). Although this fable recounts in miniature the forbidden love, rebellion, expulsion, and escape of the larger narrative, Winnet takes a male lover.[21] Thus, in this miniature mirror of the novel, a heterosexual triangle of key characters (father, male lover, Winnet) displaces the homosexual triangle (mother, female lovers, Jeanette).

This odd substitution may reflect the paucity of examples of lesbian lovers in fairy tales; or, it may relate to the theme of male homosociality/homosexuality in the Arthurian fables which also interrupt the later chap-ters. Regardless of the reason for the substitution, the appearance of a heterosexual paradigm may have the effect for some readers of containing, or safely circumscribing, the homosexual plot of the primary narrative.[22] This effect only highlights the way that the *Bildungsroman* plot structure can be used to depoliticize as it universalizes the struggle of the heroine.[23]

Complicating this hypothesis about the effect of the heterosexual fable is the fact that it also functions to return Jeanette to her mother, and thus to the issues and the scene of the primary plot. The umbilical-like thread that her sorcerer-father secures to Winnet's button becomes the thread Jea-nette's mother may "tug" when she pleases to bring her home (148, 176).

The ability of the figure of the sorcerer-father to represent the mother's role in the narrative may point to another function of the heterosexual fable paradigm. While it may contain or recontextualize the lesbian plot, it also recontains the phallocratic order within masculine boundaries. More plainly, by making the "bad guy" male, the narrative retreats from the problem it foregrounded earlier of how women become bearers of the narratives that imprison them.

What this suggests to me is a strong need to split the crucial character of the mother into two halves: the crafty but limiting sorcerer-father and a crazed but "Kindly Light" of a mother. This need, I would argue, both explains the disjunction in the mother's portrayal that awards her the final words of the novel and points to a larger need of women writers for another "kindly light," a feminine-identified Logos that would offer a model of authority. The closing gap in the presentation of the mother, along with this novel's obsessive turning and re-turning of ontological stories of solely masculine fleshless creation, represents an attempt to rewrite what Margaret Homans has called "the story of language" (11). Whether in contemporary psychoanalytic theory or ancient biblical myth, this story predicates representation itself on the erasure of feminine body, be it preoedipal mother or goddess.

In this search for a "kindly light," the figure of the mother seems to metonymically stand in for the Bible; as Jeanette explains in the first chapter, "my mother was Old Testament all the way." Thus, the return to the mother in Winterson's "Ruth" underlines the potential of the Book of Ruth as a precursor text for this novel and its representation of a lesbian subjectivity. While Ruth and Naomi's relationship has been interpreted historically by other lights, the text certainly is available for a lesbian reading.[24] As Jean Kennard points out, the reader's sexual identification inevitably shapes her engagement and interpretation of texts (77). Furthermore, evoking the Book of Ruth as the presiding genius (or demon) of her final chapter reappropriates for a lesbian audience the heterosexual appropriation of Ruth and Naomi's love. Although her pastor casts Jeanette's sin as loving her friend with "the love reserved for man and wife" (105), Ruth's pledge to Naomi has become part of the conventional text of heterosexual wedding vows: "whither thou goest, I will go . . . thy people shall be my people, and thy God my God" (Ruth 1:16).

To borrow Margaret Homan's term, the abstract and ancient figure of Ruth and Naomi's love is "literalized" by the palpable lesbian subject presented here in the concluding figure of a mature Jeanette who reconfirms her lesbian identity even as she accepts her mother's continuing homophobia.[25] In the resignification of the Book of Ruth as a vehicle for the presentation of lesbian identity, the revisionist energies of the ontological and hermeneutic narratives climax in another inverted conversion. What this culmination of ontological and hermeneutical stories reveals is not only the discursive formation of the subject, but the fact which Judith Butler has stressed: "To be constituted by language is to be produced within a given network of power / discourse which is open to resignification, redeployment, subversive citation *from within*" (135, emphasis added). Thus, the final conversion of the novel, the turning back toward the mother, is another inverted conversion: a turning toward a newly articulated identity that is also a turning inside out of the more familiar grounds of identity. The implicit resignification of the Book of Ruth as a potentially lesbian text summarizes the novel's larger engagement of the Bible in two ways: it marks textual traditions as sources of identity and complicates the traditionally assumed distinction between biblical precursor texts and a lesbian and gay literary heritage.

NOTES

The author would like to thank Alicia Ostriker, Martine Brownley, Julie Abraham, and Karen Brown-Wheeler for readings of this essay at various stages in its development.

1. See Bollinger's article for a reading of Winterson's use of The Book of Ruth as an alternative model of female development to familiar psychoanalytic paradigms. Although Jeanette's relationship to her mother is more central to Bollinger's argument than her lesbianism, she does recognize a potentially lesbian subtext in Ruth that "represents a radical revaluing of connection between women" (368-369).

2. The King James Version of the Bible is the translation I favor for intertextual readings with *Oranges* precisely because of this metafictional dimension of the novel. Since The King James Version, in addition to its own status as a canonical work of literature, has been the most influential translation of the Bible in the western literary tradition, it seems to be the most likely version of the scriptures to which a writer concerned with literary history would turn.

3. On breaking the ideological "sentence" of gender conventions in narrative, see Rachel DuPlessis (34).

4. For further discussion of characteristics of literary appropriations of the Bible by women writers, see Alicia Ostriker.

5. The exception here is the brief chapter "Deuteronomy" which contains no fables; I discount it in this claim because it also contains none of the autobiographic narrative.

6. A narrating voice remarkably similar to the closing voice of *Oranges* remarks in Winterson's *Boating for Beginners* that "the Bible is probably the most anti-linear text we possess, which is why it's such a joy" (65). See Robert

Alter on the remarkable amount of intertextual "debate" and "play" within the Hebrew Bible (12-14).

7. See Bonnie Zimmerman on the importance of myths of origin in lesbian literature (27).

8. I suspect this layering or overlapping of narrative types within sequences explains what Winterson rather cryptically calls the "spiral" structure in her introduction to the 1991 Vintage edition.

9. See Laurel Bollinger's discussion of the themes of the biblical Book of Ruth as "paradigmatic" to the novel (376).

10. See J. P. Fokkelman's reading of the significance of the toledot genre (36-55).

11. See Jean Kennard's discussion of identification in textual interpretation in relation to the sexual orientation of the reader (77).

12. Since one of the Bible's most explicit injunctions against homosexuality appears in this book's long list of taboo sexual relations (see Lev. 18:22 and 20:13), perhaps a validation of the lesbian subject is a subtext of the meditation on perfection in Winterson's "Leviticus."

13. See DuPlessis's general argument.

14. Incidentally, pairing this novel with *Jane Eyre* works well in the classroom, provoking exploration of everything from techniques of storytelling to continuities and divergences of women's stories from the nineteenth to the twentieth century.

15. Later, Jeanette again links these issues when she compares the "uncertainty" provoked by her sexual feelings for Melanie to the uncertainty spawned by "The Awful Occasion" when her birth mother's attempted visit finally gives the lie to her mother's account of her origins (100).

16. For other examples of this novel's intertextuality with the lesbian literary tradition, see Paulina Palmer's reading of the roots of *Oranges* in the tradition of the lesbian comic novel (94).

17. Even the bookshop scene offers a nod at lesbian literary history since the choice of *Beowulf* as the canonical text being transcribed may playfully evoke Bryher, H. D.'s companion who wrote *Beowulf, A Novel* (New York: Pantheon, 1956). See DuPlessis for other strategies of circumventing traditional plots.

18. In this line of thought, I am indebted to Julie Abraham's readings of the author/protagonist in lesbian literary tradition in *Are Girls Necessary: Lesbian Writers and Modern Histories,* forthcoming from Routledge.

19. After all, the concern of the church elders in Winterson's "Judges" for denying women's power stands in contrast to the representations of powerful women in the biblical book. Sometimes promoting Israel, as Deborah and Jael do, and sometimes subverting it, as Delilah does, Judges offers some interesting reading for a girl with a prophetic, murderous, or seductive bent.

20. This novel's intertextuality with *Jane Eyre* may also be relevant here. I am grateful to Karen Brown Wheeler's reading of this study in manuscript for the suggestion that the oddly orthodox language at the end of *Jane Eyre* may shape the phenomenon I describe at the end of *Oranges.*

21. After escaping her sorcerer father, Winnet is cared for by a kind wise-woman, but their relationship is not presented as explicitly romantic or sexual.

22. Palmer, however, is undisturbed by this gender switch and reads it as a denial of "biologistic assumptions" (102).

23. See Hillary Hind's article on the tendency of the mainstream press to depoliticize the novel and the BBC production of it.

24. While Jack Sasson mentions that the story of Ruth and Naomi has been read as representing traces of Canaanite or Greek goddess worship, he notes that a more common reading emphasizes the role of Ruth and Boaz's child as part of the Davidic line (320). The recent collection *Reading Ruth* offers many diverse contemporary meditations on the significance of Ruth and Naomi's relationship, including a lesbian reading by Rebecca Alpert (Kates and Reimer 91-96).

25. For Homans, literalization is not an inferior representation or crutch for understanding, but a strategy of some nineteenth-century women writers for transforming the significance of their position in the symbolic order (26).

WORKS CITED

Alter, Robert. Introduction. *The Literary Guide to the Bible.* Ed. Robert Alter and Frank Kermode. Cambridge: Harvard UP, 1987. 11-35.

Bollinger, Laurel. "Models for Female Loyalty: The Biblical Ruth in Jeanette Winterson's *Oranges Are Not the Only Fruit." Tulsa Studies in Women's Literature* 13.2 (1994): 363-380.

Butler, Judith. "For a Careful Reading." *Feminist Contentions: A Philosophical Exchange.* Ed. Linda Nicholson. New York: Routledge, 1995. 127-143.

DuPlessis, Rachel. *Writing Beyond the Ending: Narrative Strategies of Twentieth-Century Women Writers.* Bloomington: Indiana UP, 1985.

Fokkelman, J. P. "Genesis." *The Literary Guide to the Bible.* Ed. Robert Alter and Frank Kermode. Cambridge: Harvard UP, 1987. 36-55.

Foucault, Michel. *Discipline and Punish: The Birth of the Prison.* Trans. Alan Sheridan. New York: Vintage, 1977.

Hall, Radclyffe. *The Well of Loneliness.* New York: Doubleday, 1928.

Hinds, Hillary. "*Oranges Are Not the Only Fruit*: Reaching Audiences that Other Lesbian Texts Cannot Reach." *New Lesbian Criticism.* New York: Columbia UP, 1992. 153-172.

Homans, Margaret. *Bearing the Word: Language and Female Experience in Nineteenth-Century Women's Writing.* Chicago: University of Chicago Press, 1986.

Irigaray, Luce. *The Sex Which Is Not One.* Trans. Catherine Porter and Carolyn Burke. Ithaca: Cornell UP, 1985.

Kates, Judith, and Gail Twersky Reimer, eds. *Reading Ruth: Contemporary Women Reclaim a Sacred Story.* New York: Ballantine Books, 1994.

Kennard, Jean E. "Ourself Behind Ourself: A Theory for Lesbian Readers." *Gender and Reading: Essays on Readers, Texts, and Contexts.* Ed. Elizabeth Flynn and Patrocino Schweickart. Baltimore: Johns Hopkins UP, 1986. 63-80.

Ostriker, Alicia. *Feminist Revision and the Bible.* Cambridge: Blackwell, 1993.

Palmer, Paulina. *Contemporary Lesbian Writing: Dreams, Difference, and Desire.* Philadelphia: Open UP, 1993.

Sasson, Jack M. "Ruth." *The Literary Guide to the Bible.* Ed. Robert Alter and Frank Kermode. Cambridge: Harvard UP, 1987. 320-328.

Stimpson, Catherine. *Where the Meanings Are: Feminism and Cultural Spaces.* New York: Meuthen, 1988.

Winterson, Jeanette. *Oranges Are Not the Only Fruit.* 1985; New York: Atlantic Monthly P, 1987.

_____. *Boating for Beginners.* London: Minerva, 1987.

Whitlock, Gillian. " 'Everything Is Out of Place': Radclyffe Hall and the Lesbian Literary Tradition." *Feminist Studies* 13.3 (1987): 555-582.

Zimmerman, Bonnie. *The Safe Sea of Women: Lesbian Fiction 1969-1989.* Boston: Beacon P, 1990.

Index for Biblical References

Acts, 172,204*n*14
  6, 172
  6-7, 193
  8, 172
  9:1-19, 219
  9:3-4, 219
  9:11, 222
1 Corinthians
  6:9, 143
  13, 141-43
  13:1, 140
  13:10, 143
  13:11-2, 142
Deuteronomy, 235,242,244
Ecclesiastes
  1:9, 195
  12:8, 195
Esther, 203*n*5
  1:6-7, 114
  3:6, 115
  3:8, 115
Galatians
  4, 170
  6:2, 192
Genesis, 112,214-15,218,229,
     236,238
  2:19-20, 228
  9, 202
  13:10, 200
  16:12, 192
  28:12, 225
  33:25-31, 223
Hebrews
  13:14, 192
Isaiah
  21:8-12, 16
  40:3, 190
  53:3, 168

Jeremiah
  17:5-6, 197
  23:11, 200
Job
  10:8, 181*n*4,204*n*13
John
  1:14, 131
  2:16, 132
  4, 196
  6:54, 132
  11:15, 211
  11:32, 210
  11:35, 213
  11:38, 211
  20:27, 132
Judges, 49,250*n*19
  19, 64
Kings
  1:11-39, 102
Leviticus, 240-41
  18, 179
  18:22, 250*n*12
  20:13, 250*n*12
Luke, 174,204*n*14
  8, 173,182*n*11
  8:30, 173
  11:7, 194
  11:11-13, 174
  24:39, 132
Mark, 213
  4, 182*n*11
  4:9, 183*n*11
  4:13, 182*n*11
  5:9, 245
  13:35, 177
  14:50-2, 66*n*11

   253

General Index

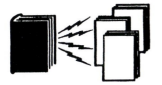

Haworth
DOCUMENT DELIVERY
SERVICE

This valuable service provides a single-article order form for any article from a Haworth journal.

- *Time Saving:* No running around from library to library to find a specific article.
- *Cost Effective:* All costs are kept down to a minimum.
- *Fast Delivery:* Choose from several options, including same-day FAX.
- *No Copyright Hassles:* You will be supplied by the original publisher.
- *Easy Payment:* Choose from several easy payment methods.

Open Accounts Welcome for . . .
- Library Interlibrary Loan Departments
- Library Network/Consortia Wishing to Provide Single-Article Services
- Indexing/Abstracting Services with Single Article Provision Services
- Document Provision Brokers and Freelance Information Service Providers

---

MAIL or *FAX* THIS ENTIRE ORDER FORM TO:

Haworth Document Delivery Service
The Haworth Press, Inc.
10 Alice Street
Binghamton, NY 13904-1580

or FAX: 1-800-895-0582
or CALL: 1-800-342-9678
9am-5pm EST

PLEASE SEND ME PHOTOCOPIES OF THE FOLLOWING SINGLE ARTICLES:

1) Journal Title: _____
   Vol/Issue/Year: _____ Starting & Ending Pages: _____
   Article Title: _____
   _____

2) Journal Title: _____
   Vol/Issue/Year: _____ Starting & Ending Pages: _____
   Article Title: _____
   _____

3) Journal Title: _____
   Vol/Issue/Year: _____ Starting & Ending Pages: _____
   Article Title: _____
   _____

4) Journal Title: _____
   Vol/Issue/Year: _____ Starting & Ending Pages: _____
   Article Title: _____
   _____

(See other side for Costs and Payment Information)

COSTS: Please figure your cost to order quality copies of an article.

  1. Set-up charge per article: $8.00

              ($8.00 × number of separate articles) _____

  2. Photocopying charge for each article:

              1-10 pages: $1.00 _____

              11-19 pages: $3.00 _____

              20-29 pages: $5.00 _____

              30+ pages: $2.00/10 pages _____

  3. Flexicover (optional): $2.00/article _____

  4. Postage & Handling: US: $1.00 for the first article/

                  $.50 each additional article _____

             Federal Express: $25.00 _____

             Outside US: $2.00 for first article/

                  $.50 each additional article _____

  5. Same-day FAX service: $.35 per page _____

                    GRAND TOTAL: _____

METHOD OF PAYMENT: (please check one)

❑ Check enclosed   ❑ Please ship and bill. PO # _____

             (sorry we can ship and bill to bookstores only! All others must pre-pay)

❑ Charge to my credit card: ❑ Visa; ❑ MasterCard; ❑ Discover;

                  ❑ American Express;

Account Number: _____ Expiration date: _____

Signature: ✗ _____

Name: _____ Institution: _____

Address: _____

_____

City: _____ State: _____ Zip: _____

Phone Number: _____ FAX Number: _____

MAIL or *FAX* THIS ENTIRE ORDER FORM TO:

Haworth Document Delivery Service	**or FAX:** 1-800-895-0582
The Haworth Press, Inc.	**or CALL:** 1-800-342-9678
10 Alice Street	9am-5pm EST)
Binghamton, NY 13904-1580	

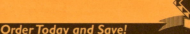